Voice
and
Agency

Voice
and Agency

Empowering Women and Girls for Shared Prosperity

Jeni Klugman, Lucia Hanmer, Sarah Twigg,
Tazeen Hasan, Jennifer McCleary-Sills,
Julieth Santamaria

 **WORLD BANK GROUP**

ISBN (paper): 978-1-4648-0359-8
ISBN (electronic): 978-1-4648-0360-4
DOI: 10.1596/978-1-4648-0359-8

Design: Miki Fernández/ULTRAdesigns, Inc.
Cover design: Bill Pragluski, Critical Stages, LLC.
Cover photo: A woman raises her hand to speak at a community meeting in Aurangabad, India. © Simone D. McCourtie/ World Bank. Used with permission, further permission required for reuse.
Additional photos: Used with permission, further permission required for reuse.
Overview: High school students in La Ceja, Department of Antioquía, Colombia. © Charlotte Kesl/World Bank.
Chapter 1: A group of women play soccer; Vila Da Canoas in the Amazon region of Brazil, near Manaus. © Julio Pantoja/World Bank.
Chapter 2: Women's empowerment workshop, Nepal. © Mary Ellsberg.
Chapter 3: Many residents of Delmas 32, a neighborhood in Haiti, are beneficiaries of the PRODEPUR- Habitat project. The neighborhood now has electricity until 11 p.m. with new improvements to sidewalks and homes. © Dominic Chavez/World Bank.
Chapter 4: A young boy smiles at the camera as his mother holds him, Nepal. © Aisha Faquir/World Bank.
Chapter 5: Woman in doorway, India. © Curt Carnemark/World Bank.
Chapter 6: Women's group, Kenya. © Curt Carnemark/World Bank.
Chapter 7: Mumbai, India. © Simone D. McCourtie/World Bank.

Library of Congress Cataloging-in-Publication Data
Klugman, Jeni, 1964-
  Voice and agency : empowering women and girls for shared prosperity / Jeni Klugman, Lucia Hanmer, Sarah Twigg, Tazeen Hasan, Jennifer McCleary-Sills, Julieth Santamaria.
    pages cm
  Includes bibliographical references and index.
  ISBN 978-1-4648-0359-8 (alk. paper) — ISBN 978-1-4648-0360-4 (electronic : alk. paper)
  1. Women—Developing countries—Economic conditions. 2. Women--Developing countries—Social conditions. 3. Women's rights—Developing countries. 4. Economic development—Developing countries. I. World Bank. II. Title.
  HQ1870.9.K62 2014
  305.409172′4—dc23
                                                                                                    2014026059

Contents

CHAPTER 3

FREEDOM FROM VIOLENCE

CHAPTER 4

CONTROL OVER SEXUAL AND REPRODUCTIVE HEALTH AND RIGHTS

CHAPTER 5

CONTROL OVER LAND AND HOUSING

CHAPTER 6

AMPLIFYING VOICES

CHAPTER 7

CLOSING GAPS IN DATA AND EVIDENCE

BOXES

FIGURES

Our flagship *World Development Report 2012* demonstrated that gender equality and economic development are inextricably linked. It showed that equality not only guarantees basic rights but also plays a vital role in promoting the robust, shared growth needed to end extreme poverty in our increasingly competitive, globalized world. The persistent constraints and deprivations that prevent many of the world's women from achieving their potential have huge consequences for individuals, families, communities, and nations. The 2012 report recognized that expanding women's agency—their ability to make decisions and take advantage of opportunities—is key to improving their lives as well as the world we all share.

Voice and Agency: Empowering Women and Girls for Shared Prosperity represents a major advance in global knowledge on this critical front. The vast data and thousands of surveys distilled here cast important light on the nature of constraints women and girls continue to face globally.

As an anthropologist, I especially welcome the report's focus on social norms, which act as powerful prescriptions for how men and women should behave. Even where women can legally own property, they may not, because those who do become outcasts. Even where girls go to school and take an interest in math, teachers and parents may direct them away from certain studies and jobs for which social norms say boys are better suited. Women then enter a smaller range of jobs with lower barriers to entry, less stability, and lower wages, continuing a vicious circle of inequality. Overwhelmingly, girls and women also perform the unpaid work of caregiving, for which they are often penalized with poverty in old age.

Norms over time may become legalized discrimination, which imposes its own steep economic cost. As the 19th-century philosopher John Stuart Mill wrote, laws start "by recognizing the relations they find already existing.... Those who had already been compelled to obedience became in this manner legally bound to it." Rightly, he added, what "color, race, religion, or in the case of a conquered country, nationality, are to some men, sex is to all women," their subordinate status often codified by law. Today, in 128 countries, laws in fact treat men and women differently—making it impossible, for example, for a woman to obtain independently an ID card, own or use property, access credit, or get a job. These constraints are fundamentally unjust. They are also economically unwise.

The good news is that social norms can and do change. This report identifies promising opportunities and entry points for lasting transformation, such as interventions that reach across sectors and include life-skills training, sexual and reproductive health education, conditional cash transfers, and mentoring. It finds that addressing what the World Health Organization has identified as an epidemic of violence against women means sharply scaling up engagement with men and boys.

The report also underlines the vital role information and communication technologies can play in amplifying women's voices, expanding their economic and learning opportunities, and broadening their views and aspirations. As Pakistan's young activist Malala Yousafzai said of herself and her peers during our conversation at the World Bank Group in 2013, "We spoke, we wrote, we raised our voices" through the media. "We spoke and we achieved our goal. Girls are going back to school and are allowed to go to the market."

A bold new path toward equality, grounded in fundamental human rights and backed by evidence and data, is long overdue. The World Bank Group's twin goals of ending extreme poverty and boosting shared prosperity demand no less than the full and equal participation of women and men, girls and boys, around the world.

The World Bank Group is committed to accelerating and enhancing equality in everything we do and to shining a spotlight on inequality wherever we find it. This report does both. It should inform the global development agenda going forward and advance momentum toward a better future for all.

Jim Yong Kim
President, World Bank Group

Acknowledgments

Background analysis was undertaken by Sarah Haddock, Matthew Morton, Josefina Posadas, Emma Samman, and Sofia Trommlerova, with thanks to Alicia Hammond for technical and editorial contributions. Zuzana Boehmova, Anjali Fleury, Lisa Fry, Sveinung Kiplesund, Nazia Moqueet, Sarah Nedolast, Marie-Anne Nsengiyumva, Milad Pournik, and Shaha Riza provided various inputs.

We are grateful to Caroline Anstey for her support in initiating the work and to the government of Sweden and the Nordic Trust Fund for their financial support. The Umbrella Facility for Gender Equality will support dissemination efforts. TrustLaw Connect of the Thomson Reuters Foundation, and Serena Grant, in particular, are thanked for supporting several country studies.

The report draws on 14 thematic and country papers, listed in the appendix. It is informed by more than a dozen consultations since December 2012 in venues ranging from Managua, Nicaragua, to Kathmandu, Nepal, and benefited greatly from the collective wisdom and research of our Technical Advisory Group: Gary Barker, Promundo; Lourdes Beneria, Cornell University; Cheryl Doss, Yale University; Mary Ellsberg, George Washington University; Naila Kabeer, London School of Economics; Sunita Kishor, Demographic and Health Surveys; Stephan Klassen, University of Göttingen; Kathleen Kuehnast, U.S. Institute of Peace; Susan Markham, National Democratic Institute; Lori Michau, Raising Voices; Eppu Mikkonen-Jeanneret, HelpAge International; Andrew Morrison, Inter-American Development Bank; Kathleen Newland, Migration Policy Institute; Agnes Quisumbing, International Food Policy Research Institute; Charlotte Watts, London School of Hygiene and Tropical Medicine; Alicia Yamin, Harvard University; and Lawrence Yanovitch, GSMA Foundation; as well as Sabina Alkire of the Oxford Poverty and Human Development Initiative and Alison Evans.

The team would also like to acknowledge the advice and support of World Bank Group colleagues, particularly Ana Revenga, Senior Director of the Poverty Global Practice; Luis Benveniste, Louise Cord, Luis-Felipe López-Calva, and Vijayendra Rao, who acted as peer reviewers; Sarah Iqbal and the Women, Business, and the Law team for collaboration; and the World Bank Group's Gender and Development Board members and others for valuable comments and inputs.

Led by Sarah Jackson-Han, Malcolm Ehrenpreis, Amy Adkins Harris, and Maura Leary provided communications support. Administrative support was provided by Dawn Ballantyne, Maureen Itepu, Ngozi Kalu-Mba, and Mame Niasse.

Lucia Hanmer is a lead economist in gender and development at the World Bank Group. In this capacity since 2013, she works to identify and pursue frontier research areas and develop new knowledge products aimed at filling key data gaps and operationalizing gender equality throughout the World Bank Group portfolio. She worked previously as senior economic adviser for the Economic Empowerment Section at UN Women and senior economic adviser in the chief economist's office at the U.K. Department for International Development, after serving as country representative for the World Bank Group in Guyana. Before moving into development policy, she was a researcher at the Overseas Development Institute in the United Kingdom and taught economics at the Institute of Social Studies in The Hague. She has worked on growth diagnostics, poverty reduction strategies and the Poverty Reduction Strategy Paper (PRSP) approach, and inequality and attainment of the antipoverty Millennium Development Goals, as well as on gender and development. Much of her work has been in Sub-Saharan Africa. She holds a PhD in economics from the University of Cambridge.

Tazeen Hasan is a senior gender specialist at the World Bank Group. She served as a legal specialist for the *World Development Report 2012: Gender Equality and Development* and the World Bank Group report *Opening Doors: Gender Equality in the Middle East and North Africa,* and she is a coauthor of *Empowering Women: Legal Rights and Economic Opportunities in Africa* (2013). She worked with the World Bank Group's Women, Business, and the Law program on a multiregional study analyzing legal rights and their impact on women's economic empowerment over the past 50 years. She previously practiced as a barrister in the United Kingdom specializing in civil and commercial law and subsequently worked in Kenya as a legal adviser to nongovernmental organizations. She holds a master's degree in international law from the London School of Economics and a BA in law from the University of Oxford.

Jeni Klugman is a senior adviser at the World Bank Group and fellow at the Kennedy School of Government's Women and Public Policy Program at Harvard University. She was director of Gender and Development at the World Bank Group until July 2014, where she acted as lead spokesperson on gender equality issues and developed strategic directions to promote the institution's gender agenda. She serves on the World Economic Forum's Advisory Board on Sustainability and Competitiveness and other advisory boards, including those related to the Council on Foreign Relations, Plan International, the International Civil Society Network, the Global

Forum on Women in Parliaments, and a European Union research program on GDP and beyond. She previously served as director and lead author of three global Human Development Reports published by the United Nations Development Programme (UNDP): *Overcoming Barriers: Human Mobility and Development* (2009), *The Real Wealth of Nations: Pathways to Human Development* (2010), and *Sustainability and Equity: A Better Future for All* (2011). She has published widely on topics ranging from poverty reduction strategies and labor markets to conflict, health reform, education, and decentralization. She holds a PhD in economics from the Australian National University as well as postgraduate degrees in both law and development economics from the University of Oxford, where she was a Rhodes Scholar.

Jennifer McCleary-Sills is a gender-based violence specialist at the World Bank Group. Her research interests include violence against women, sexual and reproductive health, and the translation of data and evaluations into effective programming. She has published on these topics in *Reproductive Health Matters, The Journal of International Women's Studies, The Journal of the American Medical Women's Association*, and *The Journal of Immigrant Health*. Prior to joining the Bank, she was a senior social and behavioral scientist with the International Center for Research on Women (ICRW), where she led the design and implementation of participatory research projects with adolescents and survivors of violence and those living in postconflict communities. She holds honors degrees from Yale University (BA) and the Boston University School of Public Health

(MPH) and a PhD from the Johns Hopkins Bloomberg School of Public Health.

Julieth Santamaria is a research consultant at the Inter-American Development Bank (IDB), where she works on issues related to cost-benefit analyses of early childhood development programs. She worked previously as a consultant at the World Bank Group, where she analyzed gender data for this report. She has also worked at the IDB Integration and Trade division as a research fellow, focusing her research on global value chains. Before moving to the United States, she worked at Universidad del Rosario in Colombia as a research assistant on issues related to competition in the health sector. She holds an MSc in economics from Universidad del Rosario.

Sarah Twigg is a gender and development consultant with the World Bank Group, where she has coordinated new knowledge products and led research on emerging gender and development issues. She worked previously as a gender and climate change specialist at UN Women, where she provided support to government representatives during international climate change negotiations. She served as a research and policy consultant for two UNDP Human Development Reports: *The Real Wealth of Nations: Pathways to Human Development* (2010) and *Sustainability and Equity: A Better Future for All* (2011). She has practiced corporate law with leading international firms in New York and New Zealand. She holds a master's degree in international politics and business from New York University and bachelor's degrees in law and international politics from the University of Otago, New Zealand.

CCT	conditional cash transfer
CEDAW	Convention on the Elimination of All Forms of Discrimination against Women
DHS	Demographic and Health Surveys
EDGE	Evidence on Data and Gender Equality (initiative)
GBV	gender-based violence
HIV/AIDS	human immunodeficiency virus/acquired immune deficiency syndrome
ICPD	International Conference on Population and Development
ICT	information and communication technology
IMAGES	International Men and Gender Equality Survey
IPV	intimate partner violence
LSMS–ISA	Living Standards Measurement Study–Integrated Surveys on Agriculture
RCT	randomized controlled trial
STI	sexually transmitted infection
TUP	Targeting the Ultra Poor (program)
UNSD	United Nations Statistics Division
UN Women	United Nations Entity for Gender Equality and the Empowerment of Women
VAW	violence against women

Overview

Why voice and agency?

By ratifying the Convention on the Elimination of All Forms of Discrimination against Women (CEDAW), 188 states have committed to advancing gender equality by confronting "any distinction, exclusion, or restriction made on the basis of sex which [impairs] the enjoyment or exercise by women ... of human rights and fundamental freedoms." Alongside CEDAW, which came into force in 1979, the 1995 Beijing Platform of Action and various United Nations Security Council resolutions buttress key universally accepted benchmarks. These benchmarks include recognition of women's right to sexual and reproductive health, the right to be free from gender-based violence, and equal rights for women and men to access and control land—rights that establish a clear framework for our global book on voice and agency. At the same time, accumulating evidence and experience have made clear that tackling poverty and

boosting shared prosperity demand that *all* people—women and men, girls and boys— have the opportunity to realize their potential and participate fully in all aspects of life.

At the individual level, this requires *agency*—meaning the capacity to make decisions about one's own life and act on them to achieve a desired outcome, free of violence, retribution, or fear. *Agency* is sometimes defined as "empowerment." As an Ecuadorean woman said in a focus group conducted as part of a World Bank Group study, "I have free space to decide for myself, no longer dependent on others. For me, this is a source of pride, my husband asking [my advice]. Now there isn't this machismo. There is mutual respect. Together we decide" (Narayan et al. 2000, 132). Similarly, one man in Vietnam commented that "happiness and equality are related. If the husband understands that and is supporting and helping his wife ... the happiness of the family will be reinforced"

(Muñoz Boudet, Petesch, and Turk 2013). Full and equal participation also requires that all people have *voice*—meaning the capacity to speak up and be heard, from homes to houses of parliament, and to shape and share in discussions, discourse, and decisions that affect them.

Increasing women's *voice* and *agency* are valuable ends in themselves. And both *voice* and *agency* have instrumental, practical value too. Amplifying the voices of women and increasing their agency can yield broad development dividends for them and for their families, communities, and societies. Conversely, constraining women's agency by limiting what jobs they can perform or subjecting them to violence, for example, can create huge losses to productivity and income with broader adverse repercussions for development. We argue that overcoming these deprivations and constraints is central to efforts to end extreme poverty and boost shared prosperity.

Nor is this a zero-sum game. Increasing women's agency need not curtail men's agency, and men and boys stand to gain from gender equality that improves the economic and psychological well-being of all household members, as many men have come to recognize. "The woman helps the man manage the household," one urban man in Niger said during discussions undertaken to inform this book. "It's a partnership. We want it that way. Here, in town, a man does better when his wife contributes" (World Bank 2014).

Context

There has been unprecedented progress in important aspects of the lives of girls and women over recent decades. Yet even

where gender gaps are narrowed, systematic differences in outcomes often persist, including widespread gender-based violence and lack of voice. These deprivations and constraints sometimes reflect persistent violations of the most basic human rights. And in many instances, constraints are magnified and multiplied by poverty and lack of education.

This book shines a spotlight on the value of voice and agency, the patterns of constraints that limit their realization, and the associated costs, not only to individual women but also to their families, communities, and societies. It highlights promising policies and interventions, and it identifies priority areas where further research and more and better data and evidence are needed. Underlining that agency has both intrinsic and instrumental, concrete value, we put advancing women's voice and agency squarely on the international development agenda.

Removing constraints and unleashing women's full productive potential can yield enormous dividends that help make whole societies more resilient and more prosperous. For example:

- Delays in marriage are associated with greater educational achievement and lower fertility. And lower fertility can increase women's life expectancy and has benefits for children's health and education.

- When more women are elected to office, policy making increasingly reflects the priorities of families and women.

- Property ownership can enhance women's agency by increasing their social status, amplifying their voice, and increasing their bargaining power within the household.

Recognizing agency constraints in development project design can also improve effectiveness. Use of reproductive health services by adolescents, for example, is better where projects address mobility constraints and train providers to address possible issues of stigma. This fact underlines the broader significance of understanding how agency constraints operate and how policies and public action can lift those constraints and enhance agency.

The good news is that promising directions for enhancing agency are emerging. Moreover, the global momentum to tackle this agenda is growing. This trend is perhaps most vivid in the case of ending gender-based violence, a major focus of this book. The number of countries recognizing domestic violence as a crime has risen from close to zero to 76 in just 37 years. In countries with legislation against domestic violence, women's acceptance of wife beating is lower. This finding suggests the value of enacting legislation that criminalizes violence. At the same time, laws are clearly not a panacea, and awareness of the law and effective implementation and enforcement are critical.

Where do we stand?

Expanding agency is a universal challenge. Agency constraints and deprivations affect women and girls in all countries, whatever their income level. The basic facts are sobering:

- **Gender-based violence is a global epidemic, affecting women across all regions of the world.** In most of the world, no place is less safe for a woman than her own home, with more than 700 million women globally subject to physical or sexual violence or both at the hands of their husbands, boyfriends, or partners. As shown in map O.1, regional rates of such violence range from 21 percent in North America to 43 percent in South Asia. Across 33 low- and middle-income countries, almost one-third of women say that they cannot refuse sex with their partners.

- **Many girls have limited control over their sexual and reproductive rights.** If present trends continue, more than 142 million girls will be married before the age of 18 in the next decade. And each year, almost one in five girls in developing countries become pregnant before age 18. The lifetime opportunity costs of teen pregnancy have been estimated to range from 1 percent of annual gross domestic product in China to as much as 30 percent in Uganda, measured solely by lost income. In developing countries, pregnancy-related causes are the largest contributor to the mortality of girls ages 15 to 19—nearly 70,000 deaths annually.

- **Fewer women than men own land and housing.** In some cases, this differential is wide. In Burkina Faso, for example, more than twice as many men as women (65 percent and 31 percent, respectively) report owning a house. In many countries, women can access land only through male relatives.

- **In too much of the world, women are grossly underrepresented in formal politics and positions of power.** Worldwide, women account for fewer than 22 percent of parliamentarians and fewer than 5 percent of mayors. Rates vary across countries and regions. In Nordic countries,

MAP O.1   Share of ever-partnered women who have experienced physical or sexual violence or both by an intimate partner

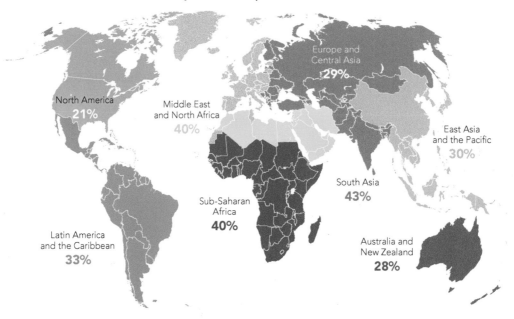

North America
21%

Europe and
Central Asia
29%

Middle East
and North Africa
40%

East Asia
and the Pacific
30%

South Asia
43%

Sub-Saharan
Africa
40%

Latin America
and the Caribbean
33%

Australia and
New Zealand
28%

Source: Preliminary analysis of the World Health Organization global prevalence database (2013) in World Bank Group regions.

Note: Data for the areas shaded in gray were not available.

for example, women hold 42 percent of parliamentary seats, and in Rwanda, the share is close to two-thirds.

Agency has multiple dimensions and is inevitably context specific. To enable global coverage and add value, this book limits its focus to four central domains of women's agency: freedom from violence, control over sexual and reproductive health, ownership and control over land and housing, and voice and collective action. At the same time, it recognizes that these are just a few areas of women's lives that are important for promoting women's agency and gender equality.

Determinants and drivers

This book focuses on key drivers and determinants of voice and agency. What we see in practice is a series of compounding constraints. Some arise from women's and girl's limited endowments (health, education, and assets) and economic opportunities. Even where endowments and economic opportunities are better, social norms about gender roles are limiting. This problem is evident, for example, in gender roles surrounding child care and housework. Even when women are taking on more work outside of the home, they typically remain largely responsible for housework and child care.

Social norms can limit women's mobility and ability to network, restrict their representation in politics and government, and be enshrined in discriminatory laws and practices. Unequal power relationships within households and in society as a whole have broad-based effects. Gender-based violence, for example, is associated with social norms and expectations that reinforce inequality and place the choices of women and girls outside their realm of control.

Legal discrimination is pervasive. In 2013, 128 countries had at least one legal difference between men and women, ranging from barriers to women obtaining official identification cards to restrictions on owning or using property, establishing creditworthiness, and getting a job. Twenty-eight countries—mainly in the Middle East and North Africa and South Asia—had 10 or more differences. In 26 countries, statutory inheritance laws differentiate between women and men. In 15 countries, women still require their husbands' consent to work. Other laws limit women's agency in marriages and family life. Laws and legal institutions also play a central role in prohibiting gender-based violence and in enabling women to realize their reproductive health rights.

Laws and social norms interact. Women's land ownership, for example, is determined by a complex interaction between some-times contradictory sets of statutory laws, customs, and norms. Social norms, customary practices, the inaccessibility and weak capacity of institutions, and, in many cases, women's lack of awareness pose important barriers to the full realization of women's land rights.

Overlapping disadvantages and agency deprivations

Constraints on agency do not occur in a vacuum and differ in nature across and within countries. A banker in Beijing may be struggling to balance elder care with work while also facing glass ceilings in her career. These challenges clearly differ in nature and scope from those faced by adolescent girls hoping to attend school in a low-income developing country. Here we explore overlapping disadvantages—that is, the systematic exclusion that many people experience as a result of multiple inequalities that limit their life chances. For example:

- Poverty increases the likelihood of agency deprivations. Girls living in poor households are almost twice as likely to marry before the age of 18 as those in higher-income households, as are girls from rural areas versus their urban counterparts. From other studies, we know that intimate partner violence is more frequent and severe in poorer groups across such diverse settings as India, Nicaragua, and the United States.

- Ethnic minority status can further magnify disadvantage. Nearly three-quarters of girls out of school globally belong to ethnic minority groups in their countries.

New analysis of Demographic and Health Surveys from 54 countries reveals that women often experience deprivations and constraints across multiple domains of agency at the same time. We find most women (four in five) lack control over household resources, believe wife beating is justified under certain circumstances, or were married before they turned 18. Just as striking, almost half of all women report being deprived in more than one of these areas, and almost one in eight experience all three (figure 0.1). However these averages mask vast differences across countries. In Niger, for example, almost all women experience at least one constraint (figure 0.2).

Agency deprivations and constraints are linked to other disadvantages—particularly access to education. Figure 0.3 shows that about 90 percent of women with a primary education or less experience at least one of the deprivations shown in figure 0.1, compared with 65 percent of women with secondary education and higher. Nearly 1 in 5 women with no more than primary education experience all three deprivations compared to 1 in 20 with a secondary education or higher. Almost 1 in 5 rural women with a primary education experience all three deprivations compared with 1 in 100 urban women with a higher education.

Overarching policies and measuring progress

The book identifies promising entry points for public actions to promote women's agency. These entry points include policies that change social norms and the law, alongside programs to promote economic opportunities, social protection, and education, where well-designed interventions and new approaches to implementation are demonstrating significant benefits for women's agency. The evidence on effectiveness of interventions designed to combat violence against women and other agency deprivations is also investigated in depth.

Addressing social norms is critical because adverse norms underpin and reinforce the multiple deprivations that many women and girls experience. Although there is no silver bullet for promoting changes in norms, evidence suggests a need for public actions that both enhance women's and girls' aspirations and change behaviors of women and men, boys and girls, so that social norms become gender equitable. Promising ways to promote such changes include working with men, boys, households, and communities, as in Australia, where the Male Champions of Change initiative works with male chief executive officers and leaders throughout business and the federal government to push for significant and sustainable increases in the representation of women in leadership. Similarly, promoting awareness of progressive laws can help stimulate changes in norms and behavior. Evidence across eight countries, for example, found that men who were aware of laws addressing violence against women were nearly 50 percent more likely to prevent a stranger's act of violence.

Progressive constitutions and legal reforms can support the transformation of social norms surrounding agency. We focus on three core areas: ensuring that all sources of law adhere to principles of gender equality; supporting effective implementation and enforcement of laws; and expanding access to justice for all women, including through customary processes.

Expanding women's economic opportunities can have wide-ranging benefits, including benefits for women's agency. Research on norms and agency drawing on conversations with women and men in 20 countries in all regions, for example, concluded that "women's ability to work for pay ... may be one of the most visible and game-changing events in the life of modern households and

FIGURE O.1 Share of women experiencing overlapping agency deprivations in three domains (percent)

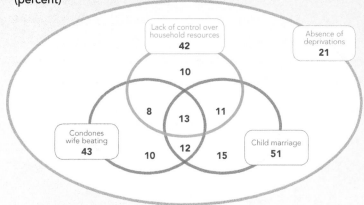

Source: Estimates based on Demographic and Health Surveys for 54 countries using the latest data available, 2001–12.
Note: Figure 1.3 lists the countries in this analysis.

FIGURE O.2 Share of women experiencing overlapping agency deprivations in three domains in Niger (percent)

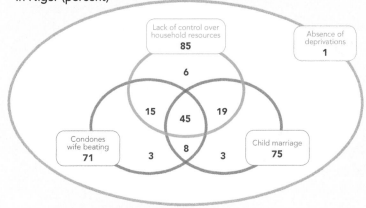

Source: Estimates based on 2006 Demographic and Health Survey for Niger.

FIGURE O.3 Correlation between education levels and deprivations in control over resources, child marriage, and condoning of wife beating

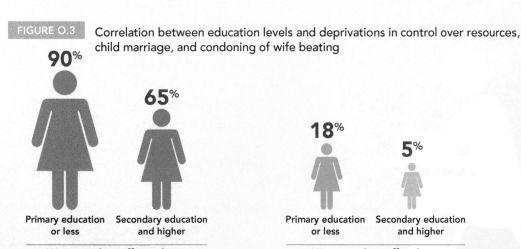

Source: Estimates based on Demographic and Health Surveys for 54 countries using the latest data available, 2001–12.

all communities" (Muñoz Boudet, Petesch, and Turk 2013, 190). But not all work is equally empowering—working conditions matter, as does the type of work that women do. Among the promising new approaches are programs that tackle norms and provide young women and girls with new information and opportunities; Uganda's Empowerment and Livelihoods for Adolescents program provides girls with life-skills training and local market–informed vocational training. In addition to the economic benefits, participating girls have demonstrated much greater control over their sexual and reproductive health.

Social protection can be transformative. Programs that go beyond protection per se and include elements to tackle regressive gender norms have had promising results. Such elements have included addressing child care responsibilities; increasing access to finance and assets; increasing skills, self-confidence, and aspirations; incentivizing girls' schooling; and providing information and building awareness about gender issues and rights.

Education has major significance in this story, with a focus beyond achieving basic levels to quality and content. Around the world, we see that better educated women are often better able to make and implement decisions and choices, even where gender norms are restrictive. In South Asia and the Middle East and North Africa, women with more education are less likely to have to ask their husband's or family's permission to seek medical care. In all regions, women with more education also tend to marry later and have fewer children. Enhanced agency is a key reason that children of better educated women are less likely to have stunted growth: educated mothers have more power to act for their children's benefit at all levels, including basic nutrition and health.

Promising interventions targeting agency deprivations

Promising interventions to tackle violence, enhance sexual and reproductive health, increase access to assets, and enable voice typically have multiple components and engage at different levels. They address norms and involve the wider community—engaging men, boys, women, and girls. And they reflect commitment over time—one-off or short-term interventions are less likely to be effective. As already indicated, a common factor of successful approaches across all of the domains explored in the book is an acknowledgment of the powerful role of gender norms. Effectively engaging men, boys, communities, and traditional authorities to change norms around violence, marriage, reproduction, household gender roles, and the roles of women and men in public life have helped to promote women's agency in countries as diverse as Australia and Senegal.

Several types of interventions have been shown to expand women's and girls' sexual autonomy and control over reproductive decisions. They include programs that promote more gender-equitable communication and decision making and improvements in access to and quality of information and health services. Interventions to expand life opportunities for women and girls offer promise when they include provision for safe spaces, life skills, and job skills. Women's sexual and reproductive agency can also be supported through more equitable laws related to marriage and property, among others, provided such legislation is coupled with strong implementation and enforcement.

Reform of discriminatory laws, particularly in the realm of family, inheritance, and property law, is an important first step for advancing women's access to land and housing. But legal reform must be coupled with actions to improve implementation and enforcement, gender-sensitive land administration, collection of richer sex-disaggregated data, and monitoring of results.

Women's collective action and autonomous women's movements play a pivotal role in building the momentum for progressive policy and legal reform. Development agencies and partners can help to enable change, including through knowledge exchange, support for innovative and locally driven pilot programs to shift behaviors, and help in capturing and sharing good practices. Such support should embody large elements of local problem solving and learning by doing.

At the same time, new information and communication technologies (ICTs) are opening up new spaces for collective action and women's participation in public life. Along with the media, ICTs are shaping the aspirations and hopes of current and future generations of women and girls. These wider horizons can be especially valuable for women and girls whose mobility and opportunities are most restricted.

Data gaps and the way ahead

The data challenges are large. We can establish profiles of women's voice and agency by using proxies to measures specific aspects, such as exposure to violence, levels of unmet need for contraception, prevalence of female land ownership, and representation of women in politics. But to better capture progress toward gender equality, greater investments are needed. We need to develop new measures and invest in higher-quality data that more accurately reflect constraints on and expressions of agency, hold governments and development agencies such as the World Bank Group to account, and incorporate these findings into our everyday work and decisions.

* * *

This book distills an array of data, studies, and evidence to shine a spotlight on the pervasive deprivations and constraints that women and girls worldwide face—from epidemic gender-based violence to laws and norms that prevent women from owning property, working, making decisions about their own lives, and having influence in society. It identifies some promising programs and interventions to address these deprivations and constraints.

Policy makers and stakeholders need to tackle this agenda, drawing on evidence about what works and systematically tracking progress in the field. This must start with reforming discriminatory laws and following through with concerted policies and public actions, including multisectoral approaches that engage men and boys and challenge adverse social norms. There is much to gain. Increasing women's voice and agency is a valuable end in its own right. And it underpins achievement of the World Bank Group's twin goals of eliminating extreme poverty and boosting shared prosperity for girls and boys, women and men, around the world.

References

Narayan, Deepa, Robert Chambers, Meera K. Shah, and Patti Petesch. 2000. *Voices of the Poor: Crying Out for Change.* Washington, DC: World Bank.

Muñoz Boudet, Ana Maria, Patti Petesch, and Carolyn Turk. 2013. *On Norms and Agency: Conversations about Gender Equality with Women and Men in 20 Countries.* Washington, DC: World Bank.

World Bank. 2014. "Voices of Men and Women Regarding Social Norms in Niger." PREM 4, Africa Region, Report 83296-NE, World Bank, Washington, DC.

CHAPTER 1

Framing the Challenge: Norms, Constraints, and Deprivations

Introduction

Women's voice and agency matter. They matter for the shared prosperity of people alive today and for the prospects of a better life for future generations.

Enormous development progress has occurred in the past two decades—many people are living longer and healthier lives, becoming better educated, and having more access to goods and services (Kenny 2011; UNDP 2010). Yet in the world today 1.2 billion people live in extreme poverty, 774 million adults are illiterate, 783 million people have no access to clean water, and 2.5 billion lack adequate sanitation (UNESCO 2014; UN Water 2013; World Bank 2013a).

Often, the same people face all of those deprivations simultaneously, and the markers of disadvantage typically include being a woman, being poor, and lacking education.

Less often discussed is that far too many women and girls also are unable to own basic assets such as land, have no voice in their communities and governments, have limited control over their sexual and reproductive rights, and lack freedom from violence, even in their own homes. One of the most alarming facts is that more than 800 million women alive today have experienced either physical or sexual partner violence or nonpartner sexual violence during their lifetimes (WHO 2013). Freedom from these kinds of deprivations is a fundamental aspect of well-being that is too often denied.

Tackling these gaps matters—and expanding voice and agency is central—for reducing extreme poverty and boosting shared prosperity. Moreover, the expansion of agency is a universal challenge. Gaps exist in all countries, regardless of their level of income.

This chapter starts by elaborating the case for strengthening agency and closing gaps. Next, we present a framework for understanding how agency is affected by drivers of other gender equality outcomes. We go on to investigate agency, looking at how deprivations of women's agency in certain domains overlap with other disadvantages that women experience, and we reveal new findings on the different ways in which women experience such deprivations and how they overlap. Finally, we examine two drivers—social norms and laws and legal institutions—in greater depth.

Why agency?

World Development Report 2012: Gender Equality and Development highlighted wide-ranging and unprecedented progress in important aspects of the lives of girls and women over recent decades (World Bank 2011). More countries than ever guarantee women and men equal rights under the law in such areas as property ownership, inheritance, and marriage (World Bank and IFC 2013). Gender gaps in primary schooling have narrowed in many countries. Globally, more women than men attend university, and women are now living longer than men in every region of the world.[1] In all but a handful of countries, women have the right to vote and stand for election.

At the same time, *World Development Report 2012* and the broader literature—including Esther Duflo's (2012) article "Women Empowerment and Economic Development" and a body of work by Naila Kabeer that includes *Paid Work, Women's Empowerment, and Inclusive Growth* (Kabeer 2013)—establish that even where such gaps are narrowed, systematic differences in outcomes often persist. These include differences in economic opportunities, where there has been too little progress in closing key gaps, as the recent global report "Gender at Work" documented (World Bank 2014a).

This book focuses on what we see as a key driver of persistent gaps: limited agency. Agency is about the ability to make effective choices and to transform those choices into desired outcomes (box 1.1). Women are often at a systematic disadvantage in their ability to make effective choices in a range of spheres, from making decisions at home, to deciding what kind of work to do, to choosing whether or when to get married and how many children to have, to becoming politically active. Agency is an outcome that matters in its own right. It is an important driver of other aspects of gender equality, and it also has value as a process, as we will show.

The reality of making choices and exercising agency is complex and varies enormously, even within the same country. Valuable insights can be drawn from qualitative approaches to capture that diversity. One valuable and recent source is *On Norms and Agency*, which draws on discussions with more than 4,000 women and men in 20 economies[2] and explores the nature and effects of gender differences and inequalities in their lives to uncover the part played by gender norms and roles (Muñoz Boudet, Petesch, and Turk 2013). We commissioned additional work in Chad (Alkire, Pratley, and Vaz forthcoming) and Niger (World Bank 2014b), which provides further insights.

The gender equality agenda requires much greater progress in expanding agency. This book advances the agenda by examining and helping to understand the facts, while systematically documenting what we

Box 1.1   What is agency?

Agency is the ability to make decisions about one's own life and act on them to achieve a desired outcome, free of violence, retribution, or fear. The ability to make those choices is often called *empowerment*.

Agency is critical at the individual level, as demonstrated by women worldwide who have spoken of having agency and of being empowered in many different ways:

> *My opportunity is that I have free space to decide for myself, no longer dependent on others. For me, this is a source of pride, my husband asking me [my advice]; now there isn't this machismo … there is mutual respect … together we decide.* —Woman from Ecuador (Narayan et al. 2000)

> *What is an empowered woman? A woman who is able to work and able to fulfil the needs that she has identified for herself. As long as she has the strength to work, she can solve all her problems. Empowered women can manage their own lives, no matter what the circumstances.* —Egypt Pathways fieldwork (Kabeer 2013)

> *An empowered woman is one who can help herself and others, who has a job, knows about herself and her environment and her community. You cannot stay in the house and be empowered. If you join societies, organizations, communities, and other social things, even spiritually, you will be empowered. If you are enlightened, empowerment will follow.* —Woman from Ghana (Darkwah and Tskiata 2011)

> *I am free and I have some power; my partner has the same: sovereign decisions are freedom and power.* —Urban man, Olsztyn, Poland (Muñoz Boudet, Petesch, and Turk 2012)

Agency is also about group and collective action, as we examine in chapter 6:

> *Men used to shut us up and say we shouldn't speak. Women learned to speak up in a sangathan [group]. Earlier, we couldn't speak up even at home. Now, we can be more assertive and also go out. I am able to help other women gain confidence as well.* —Woman leader of savings group, Gujarat, India (Agarwal 2010)

don't know, and by presenting new evidence that allows us to compare across communities, countries, and regions of the world. We deepen the evidence base in ways that foster a better understanding of constraints and possible ways forward. Just as importantly, we examine how change can come about, identify policies and programs that have worked to increase agency, and highlight promising future options. At the same time, we underline that this is a sphere where generalizations are especially risky and that country-specific diagnostic work and dialogue are essential to move ahead at the national level.

Agency is difficult to capture in its entirety. Agency can be expressed in many ways: through personal relationships; through autonomy in decision making and ability to amass endowments (such as land or property, education, or good health); through participation in politics; and through freedom of movement. Given its complexity, agency is inherently difficult to measure. Chapter 7 discusses some of the commonly used techniques and the agenda for closing data gaps.

One way to measure agency is to use information about what people say they do in different domains of life. Such actions are called *expressions of agency*. This approach has the advantage that it is more comparable and more objective than data on personal perceptions of agency (how much freedom and choice people say they have) in the abstract—which can be distorted by social norms and may not be comparable across individuals, let alone countries.

Building on *World Development Report 2012*, we investigate several specific expressions of agency:

- Freedom from violence
- Control over sexual and reproductive health and rights
- Ability to own and control land and housing
- Voice and collective action

Each of these topics is explored in the chapters that follow. This mirrors the approach laid out in *World Development Report 2012*, although we do not devote a separate chapter to freedom of mobility.[3] Mobility is critical and is a recurring theme in different parts of this book, with highlights presented in box 1.2.

Why does agency matter for development?

Agency has intrinsic value: the ability to exercise choice and to take action is important in its own right. Amartya Sen powerfully argued this value in *Development as Freedom*, published in 1999, and the intrinsic value of process freedoms is now an accepted element of mainstream development thinking. More than a decade ago, *World Development Report 2000/2001: Attacking Poverty* included voicelessness as a social dimension of poverty. That report found that poverty meant lack of freedom of choice and action and lack of power to control one's life: "Poverty is like living in jail, living in bondage, waiting to be free," the report stated, quoting a young Jamaican woman (World Bank 2001, 16).

Agency also has instrumental value— that is, expanding agency is likely to bring broader gains for development and to advance the agenda of eliminating poverty and sharing prosperity. We show in chapter 3 that the estimated costs of intimate partner violence for a range of countries run from 1.2 percent to 3.7 percent of gross domestic product (GDP), equivalent to what many governments spend on primary education (see figure 3.5). And if girls are educated but their work choices are restricted, then the forgone costs in productivity and income can be huge. The lifetime opportunity costs of adolescent pregnancy range as high as 12 percent of annual GDP in India and 30 percent in Uganda.[4]

Agency has intergenerational benefits too. A large body of evidence shows that women have greater agency when they are educated, and that, in turn, benefits their children.

Box 1.2   Women's mobility: Evidence on freedom of movement

Mobility includes an individual's physical capacity to move freely beyond the household, as well as the ability to move across social and economic spheres. It helps women and men build and maintain social and professional networks and enables participation in the economy and civic life.

Physical mobility influences social and economic mobility, and it significantly affects women's and girls' opportunities and choices. In Bangladesh, for example, women working outside the home, in both formal and informal employment, are more likely to vote and to do so according to their own decisions compared with women who work from home or do not work for pay (Kabeer 2013). Yet widespread restrictions on women's mobility arise from social norms. Women who leave the house too often may be branded "bad girls" or "bad wives" (Muñoz Boudet, Petesch, and Turk 2013).

> *Only a good-for-nothing, a "girl of the wind," can ride a taxi motorbike.*
> —Women's focus group, Communauté Urbaine de Zinder, Niger (World Bank 2014b)

Our analysis from 52 developing countries found that one in three women agree that wife beating is justified if a woman goes out without permission; the same number of women report having no say over visits to family or friends. Women's mobility can change with age; for example, only 20 percent of respondents ages 45 to 49 have no say over visits to family and friends, compared with 60 percent of those ages 15 to 19. On average, women report greater freedom of movement if they are educated, identify themselves as head of the household, or belong to a richer household. For example, 43 percent of women without an education have no say in decisions about visits to friends and family, compared with 17 percent of those with a higher education.

A woman's mobility can be restricted by laws that dictate the need for her husband's consent to work outside the home or that restrict the types of jobs or industries in which she may work. A number of countries in Eastern Europe and Central Asia, for example, have lengthy lists of jobs that are prohibited for women; in Russia, the list includes 456 jobs, ranging from woodworker to truck driver in agriculture. Such restrictions originated from a desire to protect women, but in practice, they limit women's earnings potential and opportunities outside the home (World Bank and IFC 2013).

Lack of appropriate transportation is often a constraint, and unsafe public spaces where women risk sexual harassment and other forms of gender-based violence make it difficult or impossible for them to move about freely. In the Republic of Yemen, for example, lack of mobility is cited as a major restriction on girls' ability to go to school, and one-third of women deliver babies without medical care because appropriate transportation is lacking (Middle East and North Africa Region Transport and Energy Unit 2011). In central Afghanistan, constrained mobility limits women's ability to find work, socialize, and build networks (Echavez 2012).

Lack of social mobility can limit women's success as entrepreneurs, as in Sierra Leone, where limited access to networks is a key factor in restricting women's ability to scale up microenterprises (Cherie Blair Foundation for Women 2014).

For example, a mother's education improves child nutrition, even after taking into account other factors linked to better nutrition, such as household wealth, mother's height, breast-feeding practices, water, and sanitation (UNESCO 2014):

- In Ethiopia, one-year-olds whose mothers had a primary school education along with access to prenatal care were 39 percent less likely to have stunted growth.

- In Vietnam, infants whose mothers had attained a lower-secondary education were 67 percent less likely to have stunted growth.

Lack of agency can prevent women and girls from accessing a range of services—from health care, to secondary education (see chapters 2, 3, and 4), to new information technologies and services (see chapter 6).

Women's lack of agency can compromise the effectiveness of development projects, effectively lowering the return on investments. Explicit attention to project design in a whole range of sectors—from service provision to the expansion of economic opportunities—can address this risk. For example, in Peru, incorporating components to increase the aspirations of female beneficiaries of a social protection program doubled the effect of the intervention (Perova and Vakis 2013). Similarly, a recent study in Pakistan shows that—despite the efforts to improve maternal health—the use of health services has been far from universal; the average uptake of prenatal care and postnatal care is 50 percent and 21 percent, respectively. But the uptake of those services increases by up to 10 percent when women's decision-making power increases by 1 percent, after taking into account the effect of other factors,

such as poverty and education (Hou and Ma 2013). In other words, a range of public programs can produce substantially stronger results when the women those programs are designed to serve understand their choices and are empowered to exercise them.

Women's limited voice in society and the economy is reflected in their underrepresentation in politics and in government, as well as in the corporate world. Women make up fewer than 22 percent of parliamentarians, and their number has been increasing by only half a percent per year since 1996.[5] Important exceptions exist. In Rwanda almost two-thirds of parliamentarians are women (IPU 2014). Yet despite such high representation, the country still has the second-largest share of women experiencing intimate partner violence (56 percent), reminding us that representation on its own is unlikely to be sufficient (National Institute of Statistics of Rwanda, Rwanda Ministry of Health, and ICF International 2012). In the corporate world, women hold just under one-quarter of senior management positions and fewer than one-fifth (19 percent) of board seats (Serafin 2013).

These constraints are not confined to the public arena. In most of the world, no place is less safe for a woman than her own home, a shocking fact that we investigate in chapter 3. The gravity of this challenge is increasingly well recognized, as evidenced by proposals to include commitments to end violence against women and girls in the global development framework beyond 2015.[6]

Our conceptual framework

This book adopts the framework of *World Development Report 2012*, in which the functioning of households, markets, and institutions and their interactions shape gender outcomes. Gender outcomes are multidimensional and are considered in relation to economic opportunities (for example, jobs and entrepreneurship); endowments (for example, investments in education and health and asset ownership); and agency, the focus of this book.

In figure 1.1, agency, economic opportunities, and endowments are connected and often (but not always) mutually reinforcing gender equality outcomes. The left side of the chart shows sets of determinants, the importance of which varies by context. A particular focus of this book is on laws (statutory and customary and religious), as well as on social norms. The latter are also being explored in the upcoming

World Development Report 2015: Mind and Culture.

But the causality is not only one-way—gender equality outcomes also affect how markets and institutions work and how households allocate resources and make decisions. For example, more educated women may go to court to use the law to establish their right to inherit property, as in Ethiopia (Ashenafi and Tadesse 2005), demonstrating practices that influence norms and that change how formal institutions function. Similarly, greater economic opportunities for women can change social norms about girls' education and the status of female children. Such a change is evident in Bangladesh, where a 2012 survey found that, compared with data from 1979, most women interviewed wanted fewer children

FIGURE 1.1   Agency, endowments, economic opportunities, and drivers of change

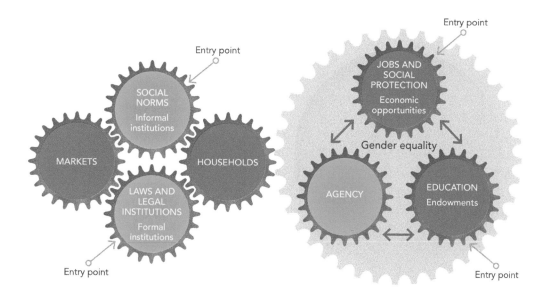

Source: Adapted from World Bank 2011.

Note: The orange cogs represent the main focus of analysis of the drivers of change in this book.

and no longer cared much whether they had boys or girls. Indeed, some expressed a preference for daughters (Kabeer 2012).

In practice, women's agency is often limited by a series of compounding constraints. These constraints can arise from limited endowments and economic opportunities. For example, across 18 of the 20 countries with the highest prevalence of child marriage, girls with no education were up to six times more likely to marry than girls who had received a secondary education (ICRW 2006). And as we show in the next section, constraints on agency are typically worse for women and girls who also experience other sources of disadvantage, in particular poverty, ethnicity minority status, and lack of education, among others. For example, girls living in poorer households are almost twice as likely to marry before the age of 18, compared with girls in higher-income households.

Even where endowments and economic opportunities are closer to gender parity, social norms about gender roles impose limitations. Limitations can be seen in gender roles surrounding child care and housework. When women work outside the home, they also continue to bear most of the responsibility for housework and child care. Differences in the amount of time spent on housework range from 50 percent more time by women than men in Cambodia and Sweden to about three times more in Italy and six times more in Iraq (Berniell and Sánchez-Páramo 2012). Social norms can limit women's mobility and their ability to network, restrict their political representation, and result in discriminatory legal rules and practices. They shape power relationships within households and in the society more broadly. Evidence from the United States, for example, shows that

despite comparable backgrounds, accomplished women are less likely than men to believe they meet the criteria to run for public office (Fox and Lawless 2011).

Equally important to gender equality and poverty reduction outcomes is *how* those outcomes are achieved: agency has normative value as a process. For policy, valuing agency as a process to help achieve development outcomes means paying attention to how women and men can engage with policy formulation and implementation—whether they are included in consultative processes and whether their views and needs are taken into account in project design. For example, roads may be planned and built by including consultations with communities that give women a voice and take into account gender-specific security concerns. Taking steps to ensure that those who are frequently excluded have access to information and services that increase their agency—for example, text messages can be a feasible method for sending information and service referrals, especially for youth—illustrates how valuing agency as a process has benefits for development outcomes.

Overlapping disadvantages and deprivations

It is obvious that constraints on agency do not come about in a vacuum and differ in nature across and within countries. A banker in Beijing may be struggling to balance elder care with work and facing glass ceilings in her career. Those challenges clearly differ in nature and scope from the struggles of adolescent Pakistani girls hoping to go to school, as we illustrate in chapter 6.

It is important to set the stage for the socioeconomic correlates of agency deprivation, as well as for how deprivations can accumulate. This section presents new results that draw on Demographic and Health Surveys (DHS) for 54 countries, which importantly inform the cross-cutting agenda for policies and public actions in the next chapter and the analysis of the specific expressions of agency that follow: freedom from violence, control over sexual and reproductive health and rights, control over land and housing, and voice and collective action.

Overlapping disadvantages

In almost every region of the world, certain groups of people face systematic social exclusion as the result of multiple inequalities that constrict their life chances.

—Naila Kabeer (2011, 1)

Sustainable paths toward ending extreme poverty and promoting shared prosperity involve creating an inclusive society not only in terms of economic welfare but also in relation to the voice and agency of all people and groups (World Bank 2013d). Worldwide, some people are more likely to be disadvantaged than others, and common markers of such disadvantage include being a woman, having a disability, being young or old, and being a member of a minority ethnic group (Kabeer 2011).

Those inequalities can intersect to produce a "multiplication of disadvantage.... For instance, the intersection of gender, age, ethnicity, and place of residence can have significantly more deleterious effects than the effects of gender alone" (World Bank

2013b, 74–75). Somali women refugees in East Africa, for example, face multiple exclusions that stem from their ethnicity, religion, and refugee status, which are compounded by being female. Those are among the themes explored in a recent report, *Inclusion Matters* (World Bank 2013b). Increasing women's agency requires addressing other markers of disadvantage as well—for example, poverty, ethnicity, or location.

Poverty often increases gender gaps, as illustrated in figure 1.2 for the case of schooling. In a recent study across 27 countries, boys from the poorest households were nine percentage points more likely to complete their primary education than girls, whereas boys and girls from rich households were equally likely to complete primary school. In India, the median boy and girl ages 15 to 19 in the richest quintile reaches grade 10 (with no gender gap), whereas the median boy in the poorest quintile reaches only grade 6 and the median girl only grade 1 (World Bank 2011). In contrast, in Cambodia, Tanzania, and Zambia, girls and boys from poor families are equally less likely than their better-off peers to complete higher grades. In sum, opportunities for girls compared with boys vary by country—but they are always worse for poor children.

Ethnic minority status can further magnify disadvantage. It has been estimated that nearly three-quarters of the girls out of school globally belong to ethnic minority groups (Lewis and Lockheed 2006). Here are some country examples from the Latin American region, where this challenge is being increasingly well recognized:

- In Guatemala, 60 percent of indigenous women are illiterate, compared with

FIGURE 1.2 Share of 15- to 19-year-olds completing school grades (current cohort), by wealth quintile and gender

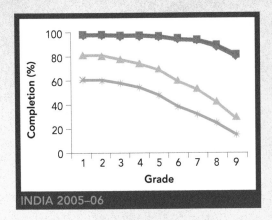

INDIA 2005–06

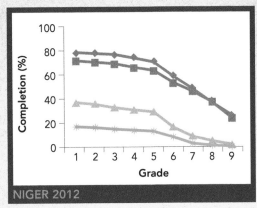

NIGER 2012

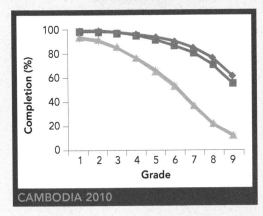

CAMBODIA 2010

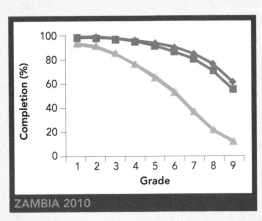

ZAMBIA 2010

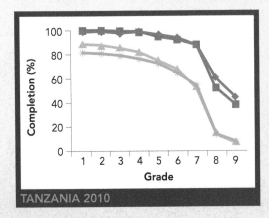

TANZANIA 2010

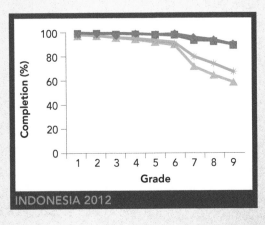

INDONESIA 2012

Richest 20% – Male   Richest 20% – Female
Poorest 40% – Male   Poorest 40% – Female

Source: Estimates based on World Bank Group data on educational attainment and enrollment at http://econ.worldbank.org/projects/edattain.

40 percent of indigenous men and 30 percent of nonindigenous women (Chioda, Garcia-Verdú, and Muñoz Boudet 2011, as cited in World Bank 2011).

- In Bolivia, the probability that a Quechua-speaking woman will complete secondary school is 28 percentage points lower than that for a Spanish-speaking man (World Bank 2013b).

- In Brazil, white men generally earn the highest wages for any level of education, whereas black women earn the least (Kabeer 2013).

Gender, youth, and ethnicity may work together to limit agency, as among adolescent Hmong girls in Vietnam (box 1.3).

Intimate partner violence (IPV) is more frequent and severe among poorer groups across such diverse countries as India, Nicaragua, and the United States—though not in others, such as South Africa (Jewkes 2002). Being a member of an ethnic minority

or lower caste can also worsen the threat of gender-based violence. Gender-based violence is explored further in chapter 3, but some striking examples are highlighted here:

- In India, Muslim women and women from scheduled castes are the most often exposed to IPV. A recent study found that 35 percent of Muslim women and 41 percent of women from scheduled castes were exposed to physical violence. Of those women, 15 percent and 18 percent, respectively, were exposed to emotional violence, and 11 percent of both groups were exposed to sexual violence (Dalal and Lindqvist 2012).

- In Australia, indigenous women are five times more likely to be subject to domestic violence, 38 times more likely to be hospitalized for assault, and 10 times more likely to die from assault than nonindigenous women (Burchfield and Braybook 2009).

Box 1.3 Multiple disadvantages among adolescent Hmong girls

Vietnam has achieved tremendous progress in development, but the gains have been unevenly enjoyed. In Ha Giang Province in northern Vietnam, Hmong children and adolescents, especially girls, face multiple disadvantages. Among the Hmong ethnic minority, poverty rates exceed 80 percent, compared with 20 percent for Vietnam as a whole.

Traditional preference for sons and filial piety mean that girls spend long hours on domestic chores—only 4 percent of Hmong girls are enrolled in secondary school, and as adults, their opportunities for paid work are negligible.

Rates of child marriage and total fertility for Hmong are double the rate for the Kinh majority ethnic group. Hmong girls also have inadequate access to sexual and reproductive health information and services. Recent fieldwork in Ta Lung commune found that girls often struggle to imagine future lives that differ from those of their mothers. Most Hmong girls reported very little say in family or community decisions, where they face discrimination on the grounds of both their gender and their age. That was reflected in one mother's plans for her children: "My daughter will finish grade 9 only, and then she will get married. My son won't go anywhere; he will live with me, so I let him reach the high grade."

Sources: Jones, Presler-Marshall, and Anh 2013; http://data.worldbank.org/country/vietnam.

Multiple deprivations

We now examine how women can experience multiple deprivations of agency at the same time. We look at three key areas where deprivations are widespread: control over household resources, attitudes that expose women to increased risk of gender-based violence, and whether women were married as children.

The evidence from 54 countries covered by the DHS immediately highlights several striking points (figure 1.3). First, most (four in five) women experience at least one of these three deprivations of agency. Second, almost half of all women report agency-related deprivations in more than one area of their lives. Third, nearly one in eight women experience agency-related deprivations in all three areas.

However, these averages mask vast differences across countries. In Niger, for example, almost all women experience at least one constraint, and almost half (45 percent) experience all three (figure 1.4).

Further analysis shows that agency deprivations are linked to other sources of disadvantage, especially lack of education. Figure 1.5 shows that about 90 percent of women with no more than a primary education experience at least one of the constraints shown in figure 1.3, compared with 65 percent of women with a secondary education and higher. Nearly 1 in 5 women with no more than a primary education experience all three deprivations, compared to 1 in 20 with secondary schooling and higher. Almost one in five (18 percent) of rural women with a primary education experience all three deprivations compared with 1 in 50 urban women with a higher education.

Figure 1.6 shows how agency deprivations in one area—lack of control over household resources—vary according to whether women work and the type of work women do. On average, women who work in wage employment have more control over household resources than do those who are paid in kind and those who do not work outside the home. For example, in Mozambique, fewer than 20 percent of women wage earners lack control over household resources, compared with 21 to 40 percent of women who worked but were paid in kind or who did not work in the past year.

Education levels are also highly correlated with a woman's degree of sexual autonomy—measured here by whether a woman says that she is able to refuse sex, to ask her partner to use a condom, or both (figure 1.7). Again, women with higher education have greater agency in all 10 countries shown in figure 1.7, and secondary education often has major benefits too. In Cameroon, Côte d'Ivoire, and Mozambique, for example, 61 to 80 percent of women with no education lack sexual autonomy, compared with fewer than 20 percent of women with higher education.

This analysis underlines that agency deprivations are not experienced in isolation; many women face multiple constraints and deprivations in different areas of their lives simultaneously. At the same time, women who experience other forms of disadvantage—especially poverty and lack of education—are more likely to face deprivations in their agency as well. This point has important implications for policy, which are explored further in chapter 2.

FIGURE 1.3 Share of women experiencing overlapping agency deprivations in three domains (percent)

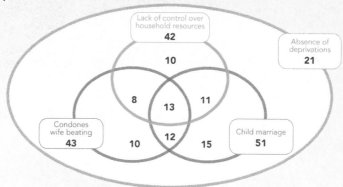

Source: Estimates based on Demographic and Health Surveys for 54 countries using the latest data available, 2001–12.
Note: East Asia and Pacific (Cambodia, Indonesia, the Philippines, Timor-Leste); Europe and Central Asia (Albania, Armenia, Azerbaijan, Moldova, Ukraine); Latin America and the Caribbean (Bolivia, Colombia, the Dominican Republic, Guyana, Haiti, Honduras, Nicaragua, Peru); Middle East and North Africa (Arab Republic of Egypt, Jordan, Morocco); South Asia (Bangladesh, India, Maldives, Nepal); Sub-Saharan Africa (Benin, Burkina Faso, Burundi, Cameroon, the Democratic Republic of Congo, the Republic of Congo, Côte d'Ivoire, Ethiopia, Gabon, Ghana, Guinea, Kenya, Lesotho, Liberia, Madagascar, Malawi, Mali, Mozambique, Namibia, Niger, Nigeria, Rwanda, São Tomé and Príncipe, Senegal, Sierra Leone, Swaziland, Tanzania, Uganda, Zambia, Zimbabwe).

FIGURE 1.4 Share of women experiencing overlapping agency deprivations in three domains in Niger (percent)

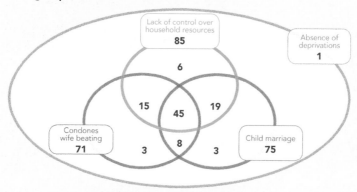

Source: Estimates based on 2006 Demographic and Health Survey for Niger.

FIGURE 1.5 Correlation between education levels and deprivations in control over resources, child marriage, and condoning of wife beating

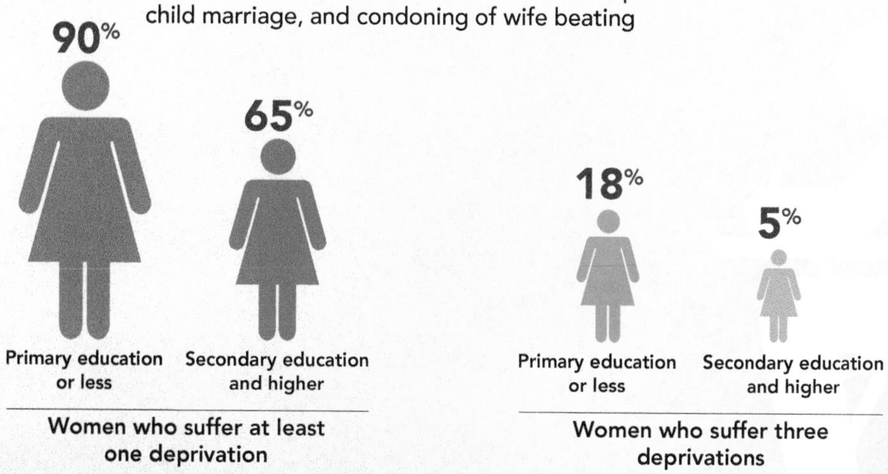

90%
Primary education or less

65%
Secondary education and higher

Women who suffer at least one deprivation

18%
Primary education or less

5%
Secondary education and higher

Women who suffer three deprivations

Source: Estimates based on Demographic and Health Surveys for 54 countries using the latest data available, 2001–12.

FIGURE 1.6   Correlation between women's work and lack of control over household resources

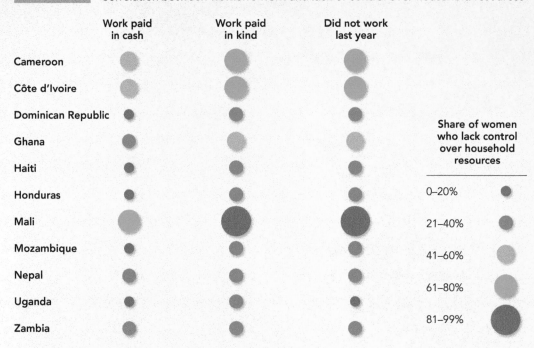

	Work paid in cash	Work paid in kind	Did not work last year
Cameroon			
Côte d'Ivoire			
Dominican Republic			
Ghana			
Haiti			
Honduras			
Mali			
Mozambique			
Nepal			
Uganda			
Zambia			

Share of women who lack control over household resources

0–20%
21–40%
41–60%
61–80%
81–99%

Source: Estimates based on Demographic and Health Surveys using the latest available data, 2006–12.

FIGURE 1.7   Correlation between women's level of education and lack of sexual autonomy

	No education	Primary	Secondary	Higher
Armenia				
Cambodia				
Cameroon				
Côte d'Ivoire				
Haiti				
Honduras				
Mozambique				
Nepal				
Uganda				
Zimbabwe				

Share of women who lack sexual autonomy

0–20%
21–40%
41–60%
61–80%
81–99%

Source: Estimates based on Demographic and Health Surveys using the latest available data, 2010–12.

Focus on key drivers: Social norms and the law

The expansion of agency encompasses an enormous agenda. We narrow our detailed investigation to selected drivers and determinants that are particularly relevant to policy and program decisions and to instances where recent evidence sheds light on promising directions—namely, social norms and the law. Markets and households are also critical, but they are not our focus here.[7]

Different types of norms shape agency. Here we focus on social norms and international legal norms that can be implemented at the national level through legislation.

Social norms

The idea that social norms affect development outcomes is not new; it was established in the early development literature. *Economic Development and Cultural Change*, a journal founded in 1952, focused on the microlevel and drew on sociology, economics, and analysis of tradition to advance the understanding of development and growth. Today, the importance of understanding microlevel behaviors for policy is reemerging with the convergence of ideas across economics, politics, philosophy, and behavioral psychology. The upcoming *World Development Report 2015: Mind and Culture* will examine how policy design that recognizes psychological and cultural factors can better achieve development goals.

Social norms are powerful prescriptions reflected in formal structures of society and in its informal rules, beliefs, and attitudes (Muñoz Boudet, Petesch, and Turk 2013). Such norms are reinforced by sanctions, which can be positive or negative, imposed by people belonging to the same reference group or by the state (Mackie and LeJeune 2009). Social norms define what is deemed appropriate behavior and desirable attributes for women, men, boys and girls, creating gender roles (Muñoz Boudet, Petesch, and Turk 2013). Across the 20 countries studied in *On Norms and Agency*, for example, men and women reported similar ideals for men's and women's roles: men are seen as providers, heads of households, and benevolent decision makers, whereas ideal women are depicted as obedient, caring, and good mates for their husbands and as being responsible for all of the housework and care of all members of the household (Muñoz Boudet, Petesch, and Turk 2013).

If an individual's behavior is seen as conforming to a social norm, status and community acceptance can be secured. Conversely, behaviors that stray from or conflict with prevailing norms may be subject to negative social sanctions. In Niger, notwithstanding a woman's right to inherit land under Qur'anic law, few women claim their right to inheritance: "Women cannot inherit land. They live with their husbands."[8] These constraints operate for men as well as for women (box 1.4). Transgression of social norms may reflect not just on the individual but also on family members, and in some cases also

Box 1.4 Norms about masculinity shape men's behavior

Men's and boys' actions and behaviors are subject to norms of masculinity just as women's and girls' are subject to norms of femininity. Norms about masculinity are often characterized as being aggressive, risk taking, virile, unemotional, and dominant over women. Even though men may often have more decision-making power and resulting agency than do women, they also may feel pressured to conform to societal expectations. For example, men may not agree to use contraception if it will reflect negatively on their virility. In the words of one Tanzanian woman:

You cannot tell men to use birth control; they want children. The more they have, the more manly they appear to be. —Young woman, Zabibu village, Tanzania (Muñoz Boudet, Petesch, and Turk 2013)

Men are also expected to be providers and protectors of their families. When they are unable to meet those roles, they may compensate by finding alternative ways to prove their masculinity. They may engage in risky behavior—becoming more sexually active, drinking excessively, or becoming more aggressive—to demonstrate their masculinity to peers. To maintain an appearance of invulnerability, men may be less inclined to use the health services that they need. Norms about masculinity can also result in aggression and violence toward women.

Harmful norms can be transmitted across generations; a boy who has witnessed his father beat his mother is much more likely to become a perpetrator of violence as an adult. As a result of

on the community (Dorais and Lajeunesse 2004).

Social norms affect both day-to-day and major decisions. The workings and interactions of formal and informal institutions, markets, and households are all affected by social norms in ways that are often inexplicit. Social norms affect decisions about who receives schooling, who in the household gets a job, and who does the majority of unpaid care and housework. Across six developed and developing countries, for example, women devote 1 to 3 more hours a day to housework than do men, 2 to 10 times the amount of time to child or elder care, and 1 to 4 hours less a day to market activities (World Bank 2011).

Social norms influence which occupations men and women work in and how markets work—who is trusted, who is hired, and how contracts are negotiated. They affect women's ability to participate in formal institutions, such as parliaments, and to hold leadership positions in businesses, legal institutions, and other associations. For example, in the countries of the Middle East and North Africa, women hold only 7 percent of seats in parliament, despite the expansion of women's participation in civil society and politics in the rest of the world (World Bank 2013c). Norms affect people's daily actions and act as an underlying and sometimes patriarchal power structures within society that give men power and status over women, men have little incentive to challenge those norms.

The good news, however, is that norms about masculinity can and do shift. A recent analysis of the International Men and Gender Equality Survey has shown that younger generations of men are more supportive of gender equality and more likely to engage in household tasks. Similarly, evidence from urban Niger suggests that both women and men are becoming more open to sharing economic responsibility for providing for the household:

> *The woman helps the man manage the household. It's a partnership. We want it that way. Here, in town, a man does better when his wife contributes.* —Men's focus group, Niamey, Niger (World Bank 2014b)

And men have much to gain from gender equality. Data show that men in more gender-equal relationships are more likely to be happy; men who participate actively as fathers are more likely to have better physical and mental health; and men who take on greater caregiving roles report benefits to their friendships and relationships with their children, as well as improved relationships with their spouses (Fleming et al. 2013). Studies from developed countries have found that men who are more actively involved in caregiving live longer and report lower rates of mental and physical health problems, including high blood pressure and cardiovascular disease (Brown et al. 2003; Holt-Lunstad et al. 2009).

Photo: The first day of study for children in Uzbekistan. © Matluba Mukhamedova/World Bank. Further permission required for reuse.

subconscious factor that affects processing information, making decisions, and taking actions. One obvious implication is that interventions that fail to address the underlying norms may have limited effects. For example, success in eliminating female genital mutilation/cutting started when interventions tackled community-level norms about the eligibility of young women for marriage, rather than focusing on the health risks alone (Mackie 2000).

The good news is social norms about gender roles do change and evolve over time. Girls' education is a recent example. Many people all over the world are now as likely to send their daughters to school and on to higher education as their sons. Over the past decade, the gender gap in school enrollment has closed in many countries; globally, the gap between the number of boys and girls enrolled in secondary school is narrowing, with 69 percent of girls and 72 percent of boys enrolled (UNESCO 2014). And norms about men's and women's roles are also changing in many places, as discussed in box 1.4. The role of men in fostering progressive norm change is explored further in chapters 2 and 3.

Social norms can shift in response to market incentives. Better earning prospects for women may encourage parents to invest in their girls' schooling. In Bangladesh, for example, the increasing value placed on women as economic earners explains why parents now educate their daughters as well as their sons. As Shanu, a 36-year-old married woman said, "Earlier, people used to educate their sons but not their daughters. Now girls get the same education, they have the same value, they get the same respect" (Kabeer, Mahmud, and Tasneem 2001, 36).

Even norms deeply embedded in cultural and religious beliefs can change. A notable recent example in some countries has been changing norms about homosexuality. Coupled with legal reform, those changes together now mean that partnerships other than marriages are recognized under the law and same-sex couples can marry. In the United States, public acceptance of gay and lesbian relationships has increased by 19 percentage points in the past 12 years, with 59 percent of Americans reporting in 2013 that they believe such relationships are morally acceptable (Newport and Himelfarb 2013). Similarly, over the past six years in Canada and the Republic of Korea, acceptance rose by at least 10 percentage points (Pew Research Global Attitudes Project 2013).

However, gender norms may even be perpetuated by those who are most adversely affected. As we explore in chapter 3, large numbers of women say they think husbands are justified in beating their wives.

Norms can also persist even when circumstances change (see World Bank 2011, 174, box 4.7). Such persistence may occur for various reasons:

■ *Cultural beliefs distort views.* Evidence from psychology and other sciences shows that the beliefs of individuals shape what they pay attention to and how they interpret it. People have cognitive biases that can lead them to misinterpret new information so that it reinforces their initial beliefs, and they therefore continue to act in the same way (World Bank 2011).

■ *Widespread practices reinforce views.* When nearly all people adhere to a social norm and when the consequences of departing from the norm are significant, voluntary compliance with the practice can be universal. For example, one reason that female genital mutilation/cutting continues to be practiced is that parents believe that they are acting in the best interests of their daughters, as young women who are not cut will not be able to marry in their communities (Mackie 2000).

■ *Elite groups suppress dissent.* When social norms benefit an elite group, that group is better able to suppress dissent and maintain the status quo. Laws, for example, can be deliberately shaped to ensure that men have greater control and economic advantage.

Norms and the law

More generally, norms can be enshrined in law. Different sources of law may reflect norms that may be at odds with each other. International legal rights—such as those reflected in the International Convention on Human Rights—reflect moral and social norms that are broadly held and prescribe international standards. At the national level, constitutions embody norms that are supposed to be universal for the nation. Seventy-five countries have constitutions that include the principle of nondiscrimination by gender, for example.

Here we briefly review the legal context, showing how international norms are generally supportive of equality, but how national laws often limit women's agency, including in their marriages and family life and in their ability to access and control property. We return to the role of the law in later chapters, including its role in prohibiting gender-based violence and in enabling women to realize their reproductive health rights and to own land.

International norms

The 1979 Convention on the Elimination of All Forms of Discrimination against Women (CEDAW), ratified by 188 states, provides a key foundation for fostering progressive gender norms to expand agency.[9] It covers such key areas as equality in marriage and family life, mobility, citizenship rights, and family formation, and it is a key reference document for this book. Articles 15 and 16 of CEDAW call for equal rights for spouses in marriage (for example, to choose where to live and work), as well as equal rights of women and men to acquire, own, manage, and dispose of property. CEDAW has been used effectively by women's groups to mobilize for reform of discriminatory laws (Htun and Weldon 2012). However, as documented by the CEDAW Committee, which undertakes regular reviews at the national level, implementation continues to be hampered by states' reservations about family and citizenship laws, by states' failure to fully integrate their treaty obligations into national laws, and by weak implementation of the laws that exist.[10] The Republic of Yemen, for example, ratified CEDAW in 1984, but then in 1999 introduced

a number of regressive laws, such as requiring spousal permission for women to work outside the home (World Bank 2013c).

National laws

Regressive laws and legal institutions can impede women's agency and perpetuate discriminatory norms in many ways. What do we mean by regressive? We mean laws that, for example, restrict women from working in certain jobs or restrict married women from being the head of household. Those are extensively documented in the World Bank Group's Women, Business, and the Law database and report (World Bank and IFC 2013). For example, in the Democratic Republic of Congo, a married woman needs her husband's permission to work and to register land or a business. In Egypt and Jordan, if a woman opts for a no-fault divorce (*khula*) to avoid having to establish grounds for the divorce, she must forgo all financial claims (World Bank 2013c). Custody laws that favor fathers, as in Iraq and Jordan, can act as an additional disincentive to divorce. In Nepal, married daughters are excluded from inheriting property from their parents.

Table 1.1 illustrates the ways in which laws can restrict married women's agency, including their mobility. Women's choices about where to live can be constrained by family laws and citizenship laws, for example, such as laws that restrict awarding citizenship to a nonnational husband or the children of their marriage.

Customary laws and plural legal systems

Plural legal systems are common; 58 of the 143 economies for which information is available formally recognize either

| TABLE 1.1 | Legal restrictions on married women's agency |

Restriction (total number of economies in brackets)	Economies in which married women are restricted compared to married men
Choose where to live (25)	Benin, Burkina Faso, Cameroon, Chad, Democratic Republic of Congo, Republic of Congo, Gabon, Guinea, Haiti, Islamic Republic of Iran, Jordan, Kuwait, Malaysia, Mali, Nicaragua, Niger, Oman, Rwanda, Saudi Arabia, Senegal, Sudan, Syrian Arab Republic, United Arab Emirates, West Bank and Gaza, and Republic of Yemen
Confer citizenship on her children (16)	Guinea, Islamic Republic of Iran, Jordan, Kuwait, Lebanon, Madagascar, Malaysia, Mali, Mauritania, Nepal, Oman, Saudi Arabia, Sudan, Syrian Arab Republic, United Arab Emirates, and West Bank and Gaza
Get a job without permission (15)	Bolivia, Cameroon, Chad, Democratic Republic of Congo, Gabon, Guinea, Islamic Republic of Iran, Jordan, Kuwait, Mauritania, Niger, Sudan, Syrian Arab Republic, United Arab Emirates, and West Bank and Gaza
Travel outside the home (9)	Islamic Republic of Iran, Jordan, Kuwait, Malaysia, Oman, Sudan, Syrian Arab Republic, West Bank and Gaza, and Republic of Yemen
Travel outside the country (4)	Oman, Saudi Arabia, Sudan, and Syrian Arab Republic

Source: World Bank and IFC 2013.

customary or religious law, or both, alongside national statutes (World Bank and IFC 2013). The effect of customary laws on women's agency varies across countries and depends on the area of law—for example, in some matrilineal and matrilocal traditions, women have clear and independent land rights, although such rights tend to be the exception rather than the rule. In some cases, customary laws may be grounded in discriminatory traditional practices (Chopra and Isser 2012), as in Kenya, where customs dictate that a married women's control over property can be exercised only with her husband's consent (Kameri-Mbote 2005).

Out of the 31 countries that recognize customary law, 11 exempt such laws from the constitution.[11] And even where customary and religious laws are subject to constitutional principles, in practice, constitutional oversight is often lacking. In Nigeria, customary law is supposed to be subject to constitutional principles of equality. Yet in 2004, the Supreme Court overruled a case in which a lower court had found the custom that only male children could inherit their father's property to be unconstitutional, on the basis that customary law could not be undermined merely because it did not recognize a role for women.[12]

* * *

This chapter has set the stage for the more detailed investigations that follow. We have seen that expanding women's agency is critical for individual and collective well-being and for the promotion of shared prosperity and elimination of poverty.

Yet many women—especially those who are poor and lacking education—experience agency deprivations across a range of domains, and they often face multiple constraints simultaneously. These empirical patterns illuminate the need to consider policy and programming design options as part of a comprehensive approach to advancing agency and gender equality.

We have explored the importance of social norms and laws and legal institutions as drivers of gender equality outcomes and have made the case for increased policy attention in those areas, which is the focus of the next chapter.

Notes

1. Since 1980, women have been living longer than men in all world regions. Before 1980, men lived longer than women in South Asia (World Bank 2011).

2. The study covered Afghanistan, Bhutan, Burkina Faso, the Dominican Republic, Fiji, India, Indonesia, Liberia, Moldova, Papua New Guinea, Peru, Poland, Serbia, South Africa, Sudan, Tanzania, Togo, Vietnam, the West Bank and Gaza, and the Republic of Yemen.

3. The topic of mobility is being explored under the Global Knowledge Partnership on Migration and Development (KNOMAD). For more information on KNOMAD, see its website at http://www.knomad.org/. See also Temin et al. (2013).

4. Opportunity cost is measured by the young mother's forgone annual income over her lifetime (Chaaban and Cunningham 2011).

5. These figures are computed on the basis of data in the World Bank Group's World Development Indicators database. The data, which are from Inter-Parliamentary Union, are for 1990 and yearly from 1997 through 2012 and show the representation of women in the single or lower house of parliament.

6. A report of the High-Level Panel of Eminent Persons on the Post-2015 Development Agenda (2013, 17) stated, "Barriers [to women's opportunity] can only be removed when there is zero tolerance of violence towards women and girls and when they have full and equal rights in political economics and public spheres."

7. For more on economic opportunities, see World Bank (2014a).

8. Quotation is from a men's focus group, Morey, Département of Keita, Région of Tahoua, as reported in World Bank (2014b).

9. There are 99 signatories and 188 parties to CEDAW. See the United Nations Treaty Collection website at https://treaties.un.org/Pages/ViewDetails.aspx?src=TREATY&mtdsg_no=IV-8&chapter=4&lang=en.

10. For more information, see the overview on the CEDAW website at http://www.un.org/womenwatch/daw/cedaw/.

11. Those countries are Botswana, Chad, Fiji, Ghana, India, Lesotho, Malaysia, Mauritius, Sierra Leone, Sri Lanka, and Zambia.

12. The case, *Mojekwu v. Mojekwu*, is cited in Hallward-Driemeier and Hasan (2013).

References

Agarwal, Bina. 2010. *Gender and Green Governance: The Political Economy of Women's Presence within and beyond Community Forestry*. New York: Oxford University Press.

Alkire, Sabina, Pierre Pratley, and Ana Vaz. Forthcoming. "Women's Autonomy in Chad: Measurement and Distinctiveness." Women's Voice, Agency, and Participation Research Paper Series, World Bank, Washington, DC.

Ashenafi, Meaza, and Zenebeworke Tadesse. 2005. *Women, HIV/AIDS, Property, and Inheritance Rights: The Case of Ethiopia*. New York: United Nations Development Programme.

Berniell, María Inés, and Carolina Sánchez-Páramo. 2012. "Overview of Time Use Data Used for the Analysis of Gender Differences in Time Use Patterns." Background paper for *World Development Report 2012: Gender Equality and Development*, World Bank, Washington, DC.

Brown, Stephanie L., Randolph M. Nesse, Amiram D. Vinokur, and Dylan M. Smith. 2003. "Providing Social Support May Be More Beneficial Than Receiving It: Results from a Prospective Study of Mortality." *Psychological Science* 14 (4): 320–27.

Burchfield, Shelley, and Antoinette Braybrook. 2009. "Improving Law and Justice Outcomes for Indigenous Women and Children." *Indigenous Law Bulletin* 7 (12): 6–9.

Chaaban, Jad, and Wendy Cunningham. 2011. "Measuring the Economic Gain of Investing in Girls: The Girl Effect Dividend." Policy Research Working Paper 5753, World Bank, Washington, DC.

Cherie Blair Foundation for Women. 2014. "Sierra Leone Women Entrepreneurs." Cherie Blair Foundation for Women, London. http://www.cherieblairfoundation.org/sierraleone-women-entrepreneurs/.

Chioda, Laura, Rodrigo Garcia-Verdú, and Ana María Muñoz Boudet. 2011. *Work and Family: Latin American Women in Search of a New Balance*. Washington, DC: World Bank.

Chopra, Tanja, and Deborah Isser. 2012. "Access to Justice and Legal Pluralism in Fragile States: The Case of Women's Rights." *Hague Journal on the Rule of Law* 4 (2): 337–58.

Dalal, Koustuv, and Kent Lindqvist. 2012. "A National Study of the Prevalence and Correlates of Domestic Violence among Women in India." *Asia-Pacific Journal of Public Health* 24 (2): 265–77.

Darkwah, Akosua, and Dzodzi Tsikata. 2011. "Does It Matter What Work You Do? An Empirical Investigation of Waged and Self-Employment as Pathways to Women's Empowerment in Ghana." Centre for Gender Studies and Advocacy, University of Ghana, Accra.

Dorais, Michel, and Simon L. Lajeunesse. 2004. *Dead Boys Can't Dance: Sexual Orientation, Masculinity, and Suicide*. Montreal: McGill-Queen's University Press.

Duflo, Esther. 2012. "Women Empowerment and Economic Development." *Journal of Economic Literature* 50 (4): 1051–79.

Echavez, Chona R. 2012. "Gender and Economic Choice: What's Old and What's New for Women in Afghanistan." Afghanistan Research and Evaluation Unit, Kabul.

Fleming, Paul J., Gary Barker, Jennifer McCleary-Sills, and Matthew Morton. 2013. "Engaging Men and Boys in Advancing Women's Agency: Where We Stand and New Directions." Women's Voice, Agency, and Participation Research Paper 1, World Bank, Washington, DC.

Fox, Richard L., and Jennifer L. Lawless. 2011. "Gendered Perceptions and Political Candidacies: A Central Barrier to Women's Equality in Electoral Politics." *American Journal of Political Science* 55 (1): 55–73.

Hallward-Driemeier, Mary, and Tazeen Hasan. 2013. *Empowering Women: Legal Rights and Economic Opportunities in Africa.* Washington, DC: World Bank.

High-Level Panel of Eminent Persons on the Post-2015 Development Agenda. 2013. "A New Global Partnership: Eradicate Poverty and Transform Economies through Sustainable Development." United Nations, New York.

Holt-Lunstad, Julianne, Wendy Birmingham, Adam M. Howard, and Dustin Thoman. 2009. "Married with Children: The Influence of Parental Status and Gender on Ambulatory Blood Pressure." *Annals of Behavioral Medicine* 38 (3): 170–79.

Hou, Xiaohui, and Ning Ma. 2013. "The Effect of Women's Decision-Making Power on Maternal Health Services Uptake: Evidence from Pakistan." *Health Policy and Planning* 28 (2): 176–84.

Htun, Mala, and S. Laurel Weldon. 2012. "The Civic Origins of Progressive Policy Change: Combating Violence against Women in Global Perspective, 1975–2005." *American Political Science Review* 106 (3): 548–69.

ICRW (International Center for Research on Women). 2006. "Child Marriage and Education." ICRW, Washington, DC. http://www.icrw.org/files/images/Child-Marriage-Fact-Sheet-Education.pdf.

IPU (Inter-Parliamentary Union). 2014. "Women in National Parliaments." IPU, Geneva. http://www.ipu.org/wmn-e/world.htm.

Jewkes, Rachel. 2002. "Intimate Partner Violence: Causes and Prevention." *The Lancet* 359 (9315): 1423–29.

Jones, Nicola, Elizabeth Presler-Marshall, and Tran Thi Van Anh. 2013. "Gender Justice: Listening to the Aspirations and Priorities of Hmong Girls in Vietnam." Overseas Development Institute, London.

Kabeer, Naila. 2011. "MDGs, Social Justice, and the Challenge of Intersecting Inequalities." Policy Brief 3, Centre for Development Policy and Research, London.

———. 2012. "The Rise of the Daughter-in-Law: The Decline of Missing Women in Bangladesh." *Anokhi Magazine,* October. http://www.anokhimagazine.com/percolator-talk/rise-of-daughter-in-law.

———. 2013. *Paid Work, Women's Empowerment, and Inclusive Growth: Transforming the Structures of Constraint.* New York: UN Women.

Kabeer, Naila, Simeen Mahmud, and Sakiba Tasneem. 2011. "Does Paid Work Provide a Pathway to Women's Empowerment? Empirical Findings from Bangladesh." IDS Working Paper 375, Institute of Development Studies, London.

Kameri-Mbote, Patricia. 2005. "The Land Has Its Owners! Gender Issues in Land Tenure under Customary Law." Presented at the UNDP–International Land Coalition Workshop Land Rights for African Development: From Knowledge to Action, Nairobi, October 31–November 3.

Kenny, Charles. 2011. *Getting Better: Why Global Development Is Succeeding—And How We Can Improve the World Even More.* New York: Basic Books.

Lewis, Maureen A., and Marlaine E. Lockheed. 2006. *Inexcusable Absence: Why 60 Million Girls Aren't in School and What to Do about It.* Washington, DC: Center for Global Development.

Mackie, Gerry. 2000. "Female Genital Cutting: The Beginning of the End." In *Female Circumcision: Multidisciplinary Perspectives,* edited by Bettina Shell-Duncan and Ylva Hernlund, 245–82. Boulder, CO: Lynne Rienner.

Mackie, Gerry, and John LeJeune. 2009. "Social Dynamics of Abandonment of Harmful Practices." Innocenti Working Paper 2009-06, Innocenti Research Centre, United Nations Children's Fund, Florence, Italy.

Middle East and North Africa Region Transport and Energy Unit. 2011. "Gender and Transport in the Middle East and North Africa

Region: Case Studies from West Bank and Yemen." Report 54788-MNA, World Bank, Washington, DC.

Muñoz Boudet, Ana Maria, Patti Petesch, and Carolyn Turk. 2013. *On Norms and Agency: Conversations about Gender Equality with Women and Men in 20 Countries*. Washington, DC: World Bank.

Narayan, Deepa, Robert Chambers, Meera Kaul Shah, and Patti Petesch. 2000. *Voices of the Poor: Crying Out for Change*. Washington, DC: World Bank.

National Institute of Statistics of Rwanda, Rwanda Ministry of Health, and ICF International. 2012. *Rwanda Demographic and Health Survey 2010*. Calverton, MD: ICF International.

Newport, Frank, and Igor Himelfarb. 2013. "In U.S., Record-High Say Gay, Lesbian Relations Morally OK: Americans' Tolerance of a Number of Moral Issues up since 2001." *Gallup Politics*, May 20. http://www.gallup.com/poll/162689/record-high-say-gay-lesbian-relations-morally.aspx.

Perova, Elizaveta, and Renos Vakis. 2013. "Improving Gender and Development Outcomes through Agency: Policy Lessons from Three Peruvian Experiences." World Bank, Washington, DC. https://openknowledge.worldbank.org/bitstream/handle/10986/16259/797130WP0Impro0Box0377384B00PUBLIC0.pdf?sequence=1.

Pew Research Global Attitudes Project. 2013. "The Global Divide on Homosexuality: Greater Acceptance in More Secular and Affluent Countries." Pew Research Center, Washington, DC. http://www.pewglobal.org/2013/06/04/the-global-divide-on-homosexuality/.

Sen, Amartya K. 1999. *Development as Freedom*. Oxford, U.K.: Oxford University Press.

Serafin, Tatiana. 2013. "Women in Senior Management: Setting the Stage for Growth." Grant Thornton International, Chicago. http://www.gti.org/files/ibr2013_wib_report_final.pdf.

Temin, Miriam, Mark R. Montgomery, Sarah Engebretsen, and Kathyrn M. Barker. 2013. *Girls on the Move: Adolescent Girls and Migration in the Developing World*. Washington, DC: Population Council. http://www.popcouncil.org/uploads/pdfs/2013PGY_GirlsOnTheMove.pdf.

UNDP (United Nations Development Programme). 2010. *Human Development Report 2010: The Real Wealth of Nations—Pathways to Human Development* (New York: United Nations).

UNESCO (United Nations Educational, Scientific, and Cultural Organization). 2014. *Teaching and Learning: Achieving Quality for All*. Paris: UNESCO.

UN Water. 2013. "Facts and Figures." http://www.unwater.org/water-cooperation-2013/water-cooperation/facts-and-figures/en/.

WHO (World Health Organization). 2013. "Global and Regional Estimates of Violence against Women: Prevalence and Health Effects of Intimate Partner Violence and Non-Partner Sexual Violence." World Health Organization, Geneva.

World Bank. 2001. *World Development Report 2000/2001: Attacking Poverty*. Oxford, U.K.: Oxford University Press.

———. 2011. *World Development Report 2012: Gender Equality and Development*. Washington, DC: World Bank.

———. 2013a. "Annual Report 2013." World Bank, Washington, DC.

———. 2013b. *Inclusion Matters: The Foundation for Shared Prosperity*. Washington, DC: World Bank.

———. 2013c. *Opening Doors: Gender Equality and Development in the Middle East and North Africa*. Washington, DC: World Bank.

———. 2013d. "The World Bank Group Goals: End Extreme Poverty and Promote Shared Prosperity." World Bank, Washington, DC. http://www.worldbank.org/content/dam/Worldbank/document/WB-goals2013.pdf.

———. 2014a. "Gender at Work: A Companion to the World Development Report on Jobs." World Bank, Washington, DC. http://www.worldbank.org/content/dam/Worldbank/document/Gender/GenderAtWork_web.pdf.

———. 2014b. "Voices of Men and Women regarding Social Norms in Niger." Poverty Reduction and Economic Management Africa Region Report 83296-NE, World Bank, Washington, DC.

World Bank and IFC (International Finance Corporation). 2013. *Women, Business, and the Law 2014: Removing Restrictions to Enhance Gender Equality*. London: Bloomsbury.

CHAPTER 2

Enhancing Women's Agency: A Cross-Cutting Agenda

The role of cross-cutting public actions

This chapter lays out some key policy and programming responses to widespread deprivation of voice and agency. We are motivated by the fact that many women and girls face multiple and overlapping deprivations of their agency, which points to the importance of broad-based and systemic change. Of particular importance are changing regressive social norms, moving beyond legal reforms and amendments on paper to changes in practice, and addressing the multiple forms of disadvantage that women and girls often face at the same time. If these fronts can be successfully tackled, real and transformational changes could ensue.

We have seen encouraging elements of change in practice. In Turkey, for example, extending the compulsory education age by

three years changed parents' and girls' aspirations for the future—in just five years, the share of 15-year-old girls who were married fell by 50 percent and the probability of giving birth by age 17 fell by 43 percent (Kırdar, Dayıoğlu, and Koç 2012). In Rwanda, the implementation of changes to land titling rules designed to help women register land has improved access to land for married women (Ali, Deininger, and Goldstein 2011).

But clearly results such as these are not yet a generalized nor a global phenomenon. Our goal is to enable progress by outlining promising directions that can help bring about change. Our framework in figure 1.1 suggests several entry points for policy. Here, we focus on changing social norms and the law, which can have potentially cross-cutting significance, alongside programs around economic opportunities, social protection, and education, in which well-designed

The quality of education is likely to be central to the post-2015 global framework—it is estimated that 250 million children are currently unable to read, write, or do basic arithmetic, 130 million of whom are in school.

interventions and new approaches to implementation are proving to have significant benefits for women's agency. There is more general evidence suggesting that women's agency can be positively affected by interventions in other sectors—transport and infrastructure, for example—which is potentially important but not explored here.

To help set the scene, table 2.1 illustrates a selection of programs that have successfully enhanced agency at the same time as advancing other development outcomes. We have already seen in chapter 1 that education, especially at the secondary level and above, reduces the likelihood that women will experience agency deprivations. For example, a social protection program in Malawi provided a cash transfer that was conditional on keeping girls in school. The program had a number of agency-enhancing results: girls received more schooling, and early marriage was reduced along with teenage pregnancy and self-reported sexual activity of teenage girls. We discuss all the programs illustrated in table 2.1 in greater depth in this chapter and the chapters that follow.

It is important to underline that although there is promising evidence, the results are context specific. Clearly there is no one-size-fits-all solution, but rather a need to distill promising directions.

Changing social norms

Adverse social norms underpin and reinforce the multiple deprivations that many women and girls experience. So, what sorts of policies and public actions can affect these norms? No silver bullet exists, but evidence suggests that public actions are needed on two broad fronts: first, to enhance women's and girls' own sense of capacity and their aspirations to depart from existing limiting gender norms and their associated behaviors (Perova and Vakis 2013), and second, to change behaviors of women and men, boys and girls so that social norms become gender equal. As we will discuss in chapter 6, politics and collective action are important on both these fronts.

Changing norms by working with men and boys, households, and communities

Norms often subconsciously affect the decisions people make and the actions they take, or norms can operate partly outside of people's awareness. Norms often persist even when circumstances change.

Women's agency cannot increase in isolation from the wider community. Men, boys, community leaders, and family elders who support gender equality are key allies and stakeholders in changing gender norms.

Increasing women's agency is not a zero-sum game. Increasing women's agency need not curtail men's agency. And, as box 1.4 showed, men have plenty to gain from gender equality, which contributes to increased economic and psychological well-being of all household members.

TABLE 2.1   Selected illustrations of programs to enhance agency

	Selected outcomes			
Entry point	**Freedom from violence**	**Sexual and reproductive health and rights**	**Control over assets**	**Voice and collective action**
Work with men, boys, households, and communities	Promundo's Program P promotes men's roles as gender-equitable caregivers.	In Uzbekistan, men, religious leaders, and mothers-in law are trained on sexual and reproductive health.		In Australia, the Male Champions of Change initiative promotes women's leadership.
Legal reform	In Papua New Guinea, new legislation created specialized Family and Sexual Violence Units and survivor-centered training and strengthened prosecution.	Compulsory education laws in Turkey delayed age of marriage and early childbirth.	In Rwanda, mandatory joint titling increased married women's land ownership to over 80 percent.	In Burkina Faso, a quota law is tied to federal campaign funding and offers extra funding incentives to parties with at least 30 percent women.
Expansion of economic opportunities	In El Salvador, one-stop centers provide vocational training, access to microfinance, child care services, and crisis support for survivors of violence.	In Uganda, the BRAC Empowerment and Livelihoods for Adolescents program provided girls with life skills and vocational training.		The Haiti Adolescent Girls Initiative provides mentorship services to girls through local internships and nongovernmental organizations.
Social protection	In Peru, the Juntos conditional cash transfer program is associated with a 9 percent decrease in physical violence and 11 percent decrease in emotional violence.	In Malawi, a conditional cash transfer program kept girls in school longer and significantly reduced early marriage, teenage pregnancy, and self-reported sexual activity.	In West Bengal, the Targeting the Ultra Poor Program reduced food insecurity and increased access to assets.	In Nicaragua, an asset transfer program that included beneficiary contact with community leaders changed aspirations and goals.
Education	In India, the Gender Equality Movement in Schools program included discussions of violence, emotion management, and relationships.	The Forum of African Women Educationalists Centre of Excellence in 14 countries provides gender-responsive training for teachers and sexual education for girls.		In the Republic of Yemen, youth councils taught young women and men conflict prevention and mitigation skills, allowing them to work together to advocate and resolve community disputes.

A number of programs show promising new ways to challenge common norms about gender roles by engaging men proactively in change (Fleming et al. 2013). Two current examples include the following:

- In Brazil, Promundo supports the implementation of alcohol control policies to help limit health risks and self-destructive behavior and to reduce gender violence, alongside programs that help men to access associated health services (Fleming et al. 2013).

- Australia's Male Champions of Change initiative works with 21 male chief executive officers, department heads, and nonexecutive directors from across Australian businesses and the government to push for significant and sustainable increases in the representation of women in leadership roles as a business priority.[1]

Engaging men in challenging the acceptability of violence is essential, as the next chapter shows. Although gender-based violence is often framed as a "women's issue," many groups worldwide are working to extend prevention and advocacy efforts beyond a single-sex movement. For example, the United States–based organization Men Stopping Violence includes community activities and training to engage men, with programs specifically targeted toward fathers as community allies, in the fight to end violence against women and girls.[2] Promundo's Program P, developed as part of the global MenEngage campaign, aims to promote men's practices as gender-equitable caregivers, in the process preventing violence against women and children and transforming the social institutions that influence men's caregiving practices (Promundo, CulturaSalud/EME, and REDMAS 2013). In Burundi, men started

an awareness campaign by traveling to nearby villages to share personal experiences around their transition from violence to nonviolence (Wallacher 2012).

Interventions that engage with men and boys to change violent behaviors need to start early. We will see in the next chapter that men who witnessed their mothers being beaten by a partner were more than two and one-half times more likely to have ever perpetrated violence against their own partners. Recent research from East Asia and the Pacific shows that 58 percent of men who have perpetrated rape report having done so for the first time as adolescents (Jewkes et al. 2013).

Family planning programs that include men with their partners can spur greater buy-in and have a strong effect on the uptake and continuing use of contraception (Mwaikambo et al. 2011). This effect is in part because opposition from husbands constrains the use of maternal health care and contraceptives (see chapter 4). Understanding such opposition is important. Communication is often an influential predictor of family planning, with women who characterize communication with their husbands as difficult or infrequent reporting limited use of family planning (Biddlecom and Fapohunda 1998; Kim and Lee 1973; Storey et al. 1999). Conversely, open communication and joint decision making about family planning can promote contraceptive use and the achievement of fertility intentions (Amatya et al. 1994; Ezeh 1993; Kimuna and Adamchak 2001). New approaches to reproductive and sexual health have engaged men, senior household members, and community leaders, as well as women of reproductive age. In Uzbekistan, for example, a community-based approach trained men, religious leaders, and mothers-in-law in reproductive and sexual health education. These trainees then facilitated dialogue with other men and mothers-in-law in their communities to discuss reproductive health issues, existing gender roles, and gender stereotypes. The program led to a 74 percent increase in health promotion activities in the pilot regions and a 72 percent increase in knowledge and awareness of reproductive health issues among men and mothers-in-law who participated in community sessions (GIZ 2012).

Where social norms are deeply entrenched, as is often the case, it is critical to design interventions that include community leaders and those with the power to endorse change. Successful programs to reduce gender-based violence have enlisted community leaders and have sought endorsement from the broader community. Some examples include the following:

- In Senegal, community-based awareness campaigns enlisted the support of religious leaders to successfully reduce the accepted practice of female genital cutting (see box 2.1).

- In Afghanistan and Ethiopia, community awareness projects have successfully reduced the incidence of early marriage (Mackie 2000; Malhotra et al. 2011).

- In Morocco, the endorsement by religious authorities of the draft family code helped facilitate its passage into law (Hallward-Driemeier and Hasan 2013).

- In Jordan, the Religious Leaders Program built the capacities of male and female religious leaders to advocate for family health. Six months after the training, religious leaders identified several modern methods as acceptable under Islam and expressed more positive attitudes toward family planning.[3]

Using broadcast media

Low barriers to access mean that broadcast media—radio and television—can be a powerful tool for changing social norms and enhancing women's agency. In India, for example, the arrival of cable television was associated with significant increases in women's reported autonomy, decreases in the reported acceptability of wife beating, and decreases in reported son preference. Female school enrollment also increased, along with increased birth spacing. The impacts were stronger where women held more traditional attitudes—in places where women had formerly held high preferences for sons, the share preferring sons fell 20 percentage points with the arrival of cable television, compared with a 12 percent decline overall (Jensen and Oster 2009). Television was also identified as an important medium through which Afghan women learned about new laws on gender equality as well as about male and female relations in other societies (Kabeer 2011). In South Africa and Nicaragua, television shows encouraged dialogue about gender issues and challenged traditional social norms. In South Africa, exposure to a television series focused on domestic violence was linked to an increase in help-seeking and support-giving behaviors. A similar series in Nicaragua was associated with a 62 percent greater probability of having talked to someone about domestic violence, HIV, homosexuality, or the rights of youth (Heise 2011).

In rural areas, where television may be less accessible, radio programming can

Box 2.1 In Tostan's footsteps

Tostan, which means "breakthrough" in the Wolof language, is an international nonprofit organization working in eight African countries. It was founded in 1991 in Senegal and now operates in more than 450 communities in Djibouti, Guinea, Guinea-Bissau, The Gambia, Mali, Mauritania, Senegal, and Somalia. Tostan spreads awareness of human rights issues using social networks. Known primarily for its success in accelerating the abandonment of female genital cutting, Tostan has also achieved results in governance, health, economic growth, education, and the environment, as well as child protection, empowerment of women and girls, and early childhood development.

Tostan works through a community empowerment program. It assigns trained facilitators to live in participating villages for three years. The facilitator is fluent in the local language and is from the same ethnic group as the community. In each village, two classes of 25 to 30 participants are held, one for adults and one for adolescents. The classes draw on customary African oral traditions, such as theater, storytelling, dance, artwork, song, and debate in their teaching. Participants are taught basic management and literacy skills to help them implement small projects. In another program, villagers learn about human rights, including the right to health and the right to be free from all forms of violence, and discuss how new practices can help build a healthier community.

Participants follow up by speaking with friends and family and by traveling to other villages to raise awareness—an outreach system first used by Demba Diawara, a Senegalese imam. The imam recognized that just as tradition requires female genital cutting for a girl to marry, ending the practice requires an agreement between the groups whose children marry one another. The imam walked from village to village to raise awareness, and consequently, 13 neighboring villages pledged to abandon the practice of female genital cutting.

Tostan's work has led to changes in social norms. One reason is that other communities that are considering abandoning the custom can send delegates to the successful villages to see that an alternative is possible, collective abandonment works, daughters' reputations remain undamaged, the effort does not bring shame to the community. Another reason is that incorporating participatory human rights teaching into this approach ennobles the process of norm revision: individuals are not rejecting the bad but embracing the good.

Tostan's approach has encouraged 5,423 villages in Senegal to move away from female genital cutting, as well as child and forced marriage. The movement has spread to communities in other African countries, with hundreds of other villages joining the pledge. The government of Senegal has now adopted Tostan's development model and is working with the organization to end female genital cutting by 2015.

Sources: Dugger 2011; Mackie and LeJeune 2009; http://www.tostan.org/tostan-model.

Photo: Portrait of men and children, Mali. © World Bank. Further permission required for reuse.

support social norm change, empower women, and increase their access to information and their connection to social support networks. For example:

- In Mozambique, research suggests that around 95 percent of women listen to community radio and that the programs they listen to provide information on a broad range of topics such as HIV/AIDS and children's health (Macueve et al. 2009). The programs reduce the feeling of isolation for women in an often physically sparse environment and provide valuable information to them in their own language, empowering them to deal with issues within their family and community.

- In Nepal, the "Samajhdari" weekly radio show promotes productive dialogue about sex, teaching women how to speak unhesitatingly. It shows women how to think critically about their rights and choices and about the causes, consequences, and interconnectedness of HIV/AIDS and gender-based violence, and how to organize collective action to minimize those problems.[4]

- In postgenocide Rwanda, radio programming designed to challenge social norms of deference to authority had substantial impacts in terms of increasing willingness to express dissent and reducing the likelihood of listeners deferring to local officials when solving local problems (Paluk and Green 2009).

Through transmission of messages about culturally appropriate behavior, media can influence social and political norms, as individuals and collectives begin to discuss and adopt the messages across all facets of society.

In South Africa, exposure to a television series focused on domestic violence was linked to an increase in help-seeking and support-giving behaviors.

And yet the media can be a double-edged sword. The media can reflect and influence social norms and promote positive change, but can also reinforce gender stereotypes and perpetuate gender biases, especially among children (Browne 1998). Recent analysis of popular family films and television in the United States, for example, found that males outnumber females by a ratio of 3 to 1 in G-rated family films. This has not changed since 1946. More than 80 percent of all working characters in family films produced from 2006 to 2009 were male and no female characters were depicted in the field of medical science, law, or politics or as a business leader (Smith and Cook 2008). Evidence from other countries similarly suggests a varied impact of the media on women, depending on the content and format. In Bangladesh, watching television was associated far more positively with women's empowerment than in the Arab Republic of Egypt. Qualitative analysis in this case suggests that the positive impacts were a result of Bangladeshi women watching talk shows, which cover many contemporary issues (Kabeer 2011).

A progressive legal framework

National laws play an important role in sanctioning discrimination and violence, and reforms can help transform social norms surrounding women's agency. Here the focus is on how progressive constitutions and law reforms can support gender norm changes and how to promote their effective implementation.

Evolving constitutions and principles of equality

There are many examples of constitutions evolving to accommodate new norms about gender equality—from women's suffrage in the late 19th and early 20th centuries to South Africa's postapartheid constitution, the first in the world to outlaw discrimination based on sexual orientation. Several new constitutions during the past decade, including the Kosovo Constitution (2008), the Tunisian Constitution (2014), and the South African and Kenyan Constitutions (box 2.2), reflect widespread popular consultations and lobbying by women's networks and embody principles of nondiscrimination and gender equality.

Constitutions can provide the framework to ensure that laws are nondiscriminatory and comply with international treaties, including the Convention on the Elimination of All Forms of Discrimination against Women (CEDAW). In doing so, constitutions can promote affirmative protections for women and girls. For these protections to be effective, all laws, whether statutory, customary, or religious, must be subject to constitutional protections on nondiscrimination.

Constitutional oversight can be an effective tool to address discrimination. Nongovernmental organizations, women's networks, and other groups have used the constitution to challenge discriminatory statutory or customary laws in court, as in South Africa, where customary inheritance laws that favor

---

Box 2.2 New African constitutions reshaping gender norms: South Africa and Kenya

The purpose of the South African Constitution is the "creation of a nonracial and nonsexist egalitarian society underpinned by human dignity, the rule of law, a democratic ethos, and human rights" (Andrews 2005, 1163).

Women's movements—including the African National Congress Women's League; the Women's National Coalition of South Africa; and the lesbian, gay, bisexual, and transgender movement—played a critical role in the struggle against apartheid and the framing of the postapartheid constitution in South Africa. The 1996 constitution enshrines concepts of dignity, equality, and protection of vulnerable groups. Its bill of rights explicitly prohibits discrimination "directly or indirectly against anyone on one or more grounds including ... gender, sex, pregnancy, marital status...." South Africa's postapartheid constitution is the first in the world to outlaw discrimination based on sexual orientation.

male heirs were declared unconstitutional and invalid in 2005 (Hasan and Tanzer 2013). In Kuwait, the constitutional protection of equality under the law was used successfully in 2009 to challenge discriminatory laws that required a husband's signature on a wife's passport application (Marinero 2009).

It is, however, very difficult to address structural inequalities and discriminatory social norms using formal laws alone. In Rwanda, women can claim land equally under statutory law, but the discriminatory social norms, practices, and power relations that underlie the customary application of land rights continue (IDLO 2013). Reforms designed to overcome discriminatory customary practices need to be accompanied by processes that address underlying norms, for example, by working with traditional leaders to incorporate human rights values into tribunals or other customary decision-making bodies and by including women as judges and decision makers. For example, in Uganda, 30 percent of judges in local council customary courts must legally be women, and operational guidelines have been developed to incorporate human rights and gender sensitization training of court staff (Hallward-Driemeier and Hasan 2013).

Supporting effective implementation and enforcement

For progressive laws to make a difference in practice, people must be aware of their rights, and all citizens must have equal access to justice. Yet, as we saw in the previous chapter and will see in our discussions of gender-based violence and land and property

The constitution affirms the role of customary law within the country's legal framework and makes all laws subject to the principles of nondiscrimination.

The new constitution catalyzed new legislation and case law, which reshaped the definition of family, the relations between family members, and the meaning of marriage (Sloth-Nielsen and Van Heerden 2003). The 1998 Domestic Violence Act, for example, covers "persons who are or were married to each other according to any law, custom, or religion and persons of the same or opposite sex who live or have lived together in a relationship in the nature of a marriage."

In Kenya, Article 60 of the 2010 constitution specifically calls for "the elimination of gender discrimination in law, customs, and practices related to land and property." It also establishes constitutional oversight of customary law, and international treaties automatically become part of the national legal framework upon ratification. Under Article 27(6), the new constitution requires the government to take legislative and other measures to redress any disadvantage suffered by individuals or groups because of past discrimination.

These reforms have already influenced how disputes are decided in courts. In 2011, in the case of *Kiogora Rukunga v. Zipporah Gaiti Rukunga*, a judge declared that a divorced daughter was allowed to inherit her parents' estate because the constitution eliminated all gender discrimination related to land. But in 2014, the new Matrimonial Property Act stripped women of their rights to family property unless they could prove financial contribution.

Photo: Theresa is the only female Marine pilot and tug master in South Africa. © Trevor Samson/World Bank. Used with permission. Further permission required for reuse.

ownership in the chapters that follow, this equality is often not the case: rural women and men often have limited awareness and limited access to legal aid and appeal mechanisms, which prevents them from exercising their rights. Women often face multiple barriers to the full enjoyment of their legal rights. And the individuals and institutions responsible for implementation often lack full knowledge or understanding of what the law provides or do not have the resources and capacity to implement and enforce the law. Public officials posted to remote rural areas, for example, may be unaware of new laws. On both sides, norms that reinforce the status quo are a constraint.

At best, statutory courts will almost always be the last resort, especially in developing countries and for the poor. Scarcity and geographic remoteness of courts, weak capacity of legal personnel and legal services, and a lack of legitimacy and accountability of legal institutions—particularly in fragile and conflict-affected states—may make the formal justice system inaccessible for most. Measures such as lowering court fees; providing legal aid, paralegal services, and mobile court services; and providing training and institutional capacity building for police, lawyers, paralegals, court staff, and judges can all help expand the access and reach of the formal justice system. In Jordan, the World Bank Group is helping to provide low-cost legal services for women (Prettitore 2012), and in Indonesia, paralegal services are helping women bring claims to court and to access basic identification documents, such as birth and marriage certificates (Summer and Zurstrassen 2011). The ability to access this type of documentation can improve women's ability to access other services, including land titles, as reviewed in chapter 5.

Partnerships can help overcome barriers to access to justice and help implementation. For example, service providers and advocates working on women's economic empowerment or protection from violence can forge effective partnerships with legal services. Such partnerships can encompass legal aid providers teaming up with domestic violence counselors in women's shelters or bundling the delivery of legal aid with services women already access, such as midwifery services or microcredit schemes (IDLO 2013). The Philippine Judicial Academy and the Ateneo Human Rights Centre worked together to create an interactive guide on gender-based violence, which was used to track legal cases, provide technical guidance for judges, and train court personnel (UN Women 2011).

Awareness of laws makes a difference. For example, in eight countries, men who reported awareness of laws addressing violence against women were nearly 50 percent more likely to prevent a stranger's act of violence.[5] Dissemination of information about laws and legal rights can be effective to raise awareness. The Huairou Commission's *Tools for Change*, a manual on human rights law, seeks to raise awareness of land rights and HIV/AIDS in Cameroon, Uganda, and Zambia.[6] Legal empowerment strategies, through legal literacy programs, legal aid, or alternative dispute resolution mechanisms, can also help ensure that principles of equality and nondiscrimination are translated into practice (IDLO 2013). Kosovo's Law on Reproductive Health, for example, guarantees the right of information and education on sexual and reproductive health for every person and charges the Ministry of Health to provide information, education, and advice on reproductive health.[7]

People's awareness of laws makes a difference. In eight countries, men who reported awareness of laws addressing violence against women were nearly 50 percent more likely to prevent a stranger's act of violence.

Collective action, including by women's groups, often plays an important role in transmitting information and raising awareness about legal and other rights. Information and communication technologies are offering new ways to share information quickly and providing effective ways to communicate with peer groups and to reach out to groups that may otherwise be excluded (see chapter 6).

Expanding access to justice through customary processes

At least 58 countries formally recognize either customary or personal law (World Bank and IFC 2013), and customary, religious, or community-based redress mechanisms may be the most readily available dispute resolution instruments for most people, especially the poor or those living in rural areas. The U.K. Department for International Development has estimated that in some countries as many as four out of five people turn to informal justice systems to resolve disputes (DFID 2003). For example, in Tanzania, where 44 percent of women experienced spousal abuse in 2010[8] and where reporting of such incidents to the police is very low, community-level redress mechanisms may provide an effective viable alternative to statutory mechanisms (IRIN 2013).

Understanding the interface between informal and formal justice and how women negotiate their way through plural systems is therefore critical. The same barriers can affect their uptake of services in both settings, including limited resources, cultural biases among those responsible for upholding the law, and adverse gender norms. Statutory reforms undertaken to improve women's access to informal mechanisms have, so far, had minimal success,[9] although there are some promising directions. In Namibia, the involvement of more women leaders and the integration of gender equality provisions into the customary system enhanced the perceived fairness and equity of traditional rule and the customary dispute resolution process for women (IDLO 2013). Similarly in Bougainville, Papua New Guinea, women mediators were much more effective at reaching equitable solutions in cases of domestic violence, including threatening perpetrators with action in the state court if the violence did not stop and simultaneously informing the victim of her right to refer the case to the court and providing information on how to do so (IDLO 2013).

Increasing women's agency through sectoral policies and programs

We turn now to entry points through selected sectoral programs—namely, expanding economic opportunities and training, designing gender-responsive social protection, and increasing access to quality education. Well-designed policies and new approaches to program implementation in these sectors are proving to have significant positive benefits for women's agency, as well as often improving results and overall effectiveness.

Expanding economic opportunities and training

One important conclusion emerging from a wide range of work on agency is the potential for promoting agency through expanding economic opportunities. Research on norms and agency that drew on data from women and men in 20 countries in all world regions concluded that "women's ability to work for pay, which most women in the study aspired to, may be one of the most visible and game-changing events in the life of modern households and all communities" (Muñoz Boudet, Petesch, and Turk 2013, 145). The study found that women's agency increased not only from the direct effects of economic participation but also as women gained a greater sense of self-efficacy, broadened their aspirations, and forged new ways to reconcile their identities as workers with their identities as mothers. But not all work is equally empowering—working conditions matter, as does the type of work that women do. Naila Kabeer concludes from an analysis of Bangladesh, Egypt, and Ghana that "formal and semi-formal employment is found to be most likely to contribute to women's ability to decide on the use of their income, to make decisions about their own health, to gain respect within the community, to participate in politics, and to express support for a more equitable distribution of unpaid workloads and, in cultures characterized by son preference, less discriminatory attitudes toward their daughters" (Kabeer 2013, 80).

Expanding economic opportunities is a major policy challenge. Opportunities for women to work are opening up slowly at best in most regions—globally, women's labor force participation has actually fallen slightly since 1990, from 57 percent to 55 percent (World Bank 2014a). As the World Bank Group's (2014a) report "Gender at Work" shows, compared to men, a wide range of measures indicates that women are at a disadvantage at work. The measures include gender wage gaps, labor market participation, ability to get work in the most profitable sectors and enterprises, and the balance between paid and unpaid work. Labor market and growth policies for job creation need to include measures to address the gender-specific constraints that prevent women from accessing productive jobs, such as child care responsibilities, lack of skills and training, and gender-biased attitudes and expectations about women's abilities. Further, while jobs can create agency, women's lack of agency limits their ability to get good jobs and benefit from them. "Gender at Work" identifies policy actions to address women's agency constraints across the lifecycle and shows how the private sector—the main creator of jobs—can lead and innovate for gender equality.

Multisectoral policy interventions that address agency as part of efforts to promote economic opportunities can do better on both fronts. Indeed, failure to do so can stymie efforts to promote economic opportunities (World Bank 2014a). Promising interventions combine training in vocational business or trade-related skills with programmatic elements to increase aspirations and confidence, social networks, freedom from violence, and healthy gender dynamics in the household.

Evidence is emerging that economic empowerment programs can reduce women's exposure to violence when components geared toward building women's collective voice and fostering more gender-equitable relationships are included. For example, this evidence was found for microcredit interventions in South Africa (Pronyk et al. 2006). One-stop shops that support economic empowerment as well

Women's agency cannot increase in isolation from the wider community. Men, boys, community leaders, and family elders who support gender equality are key allies and stakeholders in changing gender norms.

as broader agency-related objectives are also showing promise. For example, in El Salvador, Ciudad Mujer establishes community-based one-stop centers for women that provide vocational training, access to microfinance, child care services, crisis support for victims of violence, and community education about gender norms and women's health.[10]

Training programs have a mixed record of success and need to be well grounded in the needs of the labor market as well as the needs and constraints of participants (World Bank 2012). Combining work and training increases the success rates of training programs, and programs that aim to increase women's job opportunities need to be designed to equip women and girls with the skills needed by employers and enterprises (World Bank 2012). That approach has yielded examples of promising programs with positive impacts for women and girls. To be successful, programs need to incorporate specific design features. Box 2.3 shows how the World Bank Group's Adolescent Girls Initiative has deliberately sought to tackle gender biases.

Programs that tackle gender norms and provide young women and girls with new information can open up new opportunities. The following are some examples:

- Life-skills training and provision of safe spaces for girls to discuss their future, along with the development of support

networks, have reduced the risk of early marriage in Ethiopia.[11]

- In Uganda, the BRAC Empowerment and Livelihoods for Adolescent program targets girls and women ages 14 to 20 and consists of a social space where girls and women receive life-skills training and local market–informed vocational training. So far, the program has significantly improved adolescent girls' ability to make choices, with a 26 percent reduction in rates of early childbearing and a 58 percent reduction in rates of marriage and cohabitation. A 50 percent increase in condom use among the sexually active was also reported. The share of girls reporting sex against their will dropped from 14 percent to 7 percent (Bandiera et al. 2014).

- A study of graduates of a yearlong information and communication technology course in Mumbai found that women's self-confidence was boosted. Female and male respondents highlighted different reasons for encouraging others to learn to use computers, including a greater number of girls (56 percent) than boys (40 percent) who noted job-related benefits (Khan and Ghadially 2009).

- Similarly, the Intel Learn program, which has provided skills training with a focus on technology literacy, problem solving, critical thinking, and teamwork to 875,000 girls and young women from 16 countries, has been found to increase participants' self-confidence and sense of power (Broadband Commission Working Group on Broadband and Gender 2013).

Jobs strategies that pay attention to gender equality issues, diagnosing the main constraints that women face in accessing jobs and identifying and addressing

Box 2.3 How the Adolescent Girls Initiative is helping to overcome agency constraints

In 2008, the World Bank Group launched the Adolescent Girls Initiative (AGI) to generate evidence on how to promote young women's transition to productive work. Interventions are being implemented and rigorously evaluated in eight countries: Afghanistan, Haiti, Jordan, the Lao People's Democratic Republic, Liberia, Nepal, Rwanda, and the Republic of South Sudan.[a] Table B2.3.1 outlines some important lessons on program design, implementation, and monitoring and evaluation to help improve programming decisions.

TABLE B2.3.1 The Adolescent Girls Initiative: Lessons Learned

Constraint	Design and Responses
Skills	› Several AGI interventions use rapid market assessments to identify labor demands and train young women in relevant skills. › In Haiti, Liberia, and Nepal, the AGI trains young women to enter more lucrative nontraditional fields. › In Liberia, the AGI provides literacy training, which is important for post-conflict settings.
Norms	› AGI interventions help to build self-confidence and "soft skills" through life-skills training. › In the Republic of South Sudan, the AGI created safe-space community clubs, and the project goes door-to-door to recruit harder-to-reach younger girls. › In Afghanistan, the program recruits participants through the community *Shura* (elders).
Chores	› In Liberia, classes are held at different times so participants can balance training with other activities. › Several AGI interventions provide participants with stipends to offset costs of attendance, which can be prohibitive for poor young women. › AGI interventions in Liberia, Nepal, and South Sudan offer child care services to young mothers.
Networks	› In Liberia, coaches support and mentor trainees. Service providers are responsible for placement. › In Haiti, the AGI offers mentorship services to participants through internships and local nongovernmental organizations. › In Nepal, the AGI provides financial incentives to training providers who train and place vulnerable young women.

a. Rigorous impact evaluations are being conducted in six of the eight pilots (excluding Lao PDR and Rwanda). For more information about the AGI, see http://www.worldbank.org/gender/agi.

gender-based disparities in access to skills, training, and credit, are an important entry point for increasing women's agency. Standards for work are important if work is to contribute to people's agency and well-being. The International Labour Organization's Decent Work Agenda gives guidance for actions that can improve the quality of work and target gender inequalities and provides important benchmarks to ensure that creating jobs goes hand in hand with increased agency (World Bank 2014a).[12]

Designing gender-responsive social protection

Social protection can be transformative. Programs that go beyond protection per se and include elements to tackle regressive gender norms by increasing women's voice and participation, building their aspirations, and opening up new economic opportunities have had promising results (Jones and Shahrokh 2013). Such elements have included addressing child care responsibilities; increasing access to finance and assets and tackling other constraints that limit work options; increasing skills, self-confidence, and aspirations; incentivizing girls' schooling; and providing information and building awareness about social issues and rights.

The BRAC Challenging the Frontiers of Poverty Reduction–Targeting the Ultra Poor (TUP) program channels skills training and assets to ultra-poor women in Bangladesh and is proving transformational. A randomized controlled trial (RCT) finds that participants spend more time in self-employment and less time in wage labor. Moreover, they increase their labor market participation, which leads to a 36 percent increase in annual income on average. Benefits spill over to other poor women as wages increase at the village level (Das and Shams 2011). An RCT of a TUP program in rural West Bengal, India, found increases in per capita household consumption exceeded 25 percent, along with reduced food insecurity, increased assets, and improved emotional well-being (Banerjee et al. 2011). Early findings from pilot programs modeled on TUP in Haiti, Honduras, India, and Pakistan suggest these results can be replicated (de Montesquiou and Hashemi 2012).

> *"Through experience one learns and opens up towards the future. By talking to others one understands and learns."*
>
> —Female program participant in Atención a Crisis, Nicaragua (Macours and Vakis 2009, 8–9)

> *"It was the first time we three had stepped out of this village on our own. How could our husbands stop us from joining Bandhan? They had no financial strength to do so."*
>
> —Female participant in the Targeting the Ultra Poor pilot, West Bengal, India (Sengupta 2013, 21)

Worldwide, women report a valued sense of security, self-esteem, and enhanced psychological well-being because of cash or asset transfers, including in Bangladesh, Mexico, Nicaragua, Peru, Uganda, and the West Bank and Gaza (Bukuluki and Watson 2012; Jones and Stavropoulou 2013; ODI and DFID 2013; Perova and Vakis 2013). These benefits can spill over to women's agency in other areas of their lives. Here are some examples:

- Enrollment in Peru's Juntos conditional cash transfer (CCT) program has been associated with a 9 percent decrease in physical violence and an 11 percent decrease in emotional violence (Perova and Vakis 2013).

- Early findings from RCTs of TUP programs in Haiti, Honduras, India, and Pakistan found that mental health, happiness, and hope rose among participants. In one of the India TUP programs, women reported that abuse had stopped since their economic conditions had stabilized, because men had less "idle" time on their hands, thereby reducing alcoholism and subsequently domestic violence (Sengupta 2013).

At the same time, however, there are cases in which CCTs have reinforced traditional gender roles and worsened time constraints by making mothers primarily responsible for various obligations linked to childrearing. This problem was found in Bolivia, Ecuador, and Peru, indicating that context is important (Molineux and Thomson 2011). Violence against women is not always reduced, as is the case in Mexico and Ecuador, where there is evidence of increased emotional violence triggered by women's receipt of CCTs (Perova and Vakis 2013).

Including elements that increase participants' contact with leaders from the community into the design of a social protection program is a promising new approach. A recent experimental study found that social interactions with nearby female leaders substantially increased the program's impact on human capital investments and income diversification, as well as improved attitudes toward the future. Nine months after the program, incomes of beneficiaries who interacted with leaders increased almost twice as much as those of individuals in the control groups. The effect is attributed to the role that increased social interaction plays in raising aspirations and changing attitudes (Macours and Vakis 2009).

In some countries, pensions for women have been shown to increase investments in girls. In South Africa, the effect was to significantly increase the educational enrollment of granddaughters of women with pensions and to improve health outcomes for girls. These effects did not pertain to boys, and neither boys nor girls were affected when men were the beneficiaries (Case and Menendez 2007; Duflo 2003). Similarly, in Brazil, a monthly old-age pension of R$100 (about US$43.50 in 2013) increased girls' school enrollment rates by 10 percent. Again, no such effects were found for boys, and impacts on girls were mostly attributable to female rather than male beneficiaries (Filho 2012).

Increasing incentives for girls' schooling through CCTs can be an effective way to tackle regressive gender norms. This approach has been successful in Bangladesh, Pakistan, and Turkey, for example (Fiszbein, Schady, and Ferreira 2009). A recent systematic review found that CCTs tend to have larger effects on enrollment, especially girls' enrollment, than unconditional cash transfers, particularly when explicit schooling conditions for payments are monitored and enforced (Woolcock et al. 2013). Benefits to girls of staying in school can extend beyond the value of educational attainment, enhancing their agency in other ways as well. For example, in Malawi, a CCT targeting 13- to 22-year-old girls and women led to recipients staying in school longer and to significant declines in early marriage, teenage pregnancy, and self-reported sexual activity (Baird et al. 2010).

Increasing gender equality in education

Education's importance for development and gender equality is widely recognized: education increases skills and capabilities and allows people to live longer, healthier, and more productive lives. It can also help shift gender norms that restrict women's voice and choice. For example, we saw in figure 1.5 that women with more education experienced fewer constraints to their agency and that more educated women have greater sexual autonomy (figure 1.7). The impact that education has on women's agency is illustrated by an example from rural Bangladesh, where, when girls were asked how education had made their lives different from their mothers', they typically replied that it had helped them "find a voice," allowed them to "have a say," to "speak," and to "be listened to" (World Bank 2008, 40).

Increasing school enrollment and achieving gender equality in enrollment are long-standing development goals. Ensuring school enrollment through upper-secondary levels for girls is even more critical. Equally important is the quality of education that girls and boys receive in school. Studies also show that girls are subject to educational streaming and stereotyping that restricts their learning and, in turn, contributes to gender sorting in the labor market (World Bank 2014a). Improving the quality of education is likely to be more central to the post-2015 global framework

> *"Education is a girl's best weapon to face the world."*
>
> —Girl from Rafah, Gaza
> (Muñoz Boudet, Petesch, and Turk 2013, 77)

than access alone. It is estimated that 250 million children are currently unable to read, write, or do basic arithmetic, 130 million of whom are in school (UNESCO 2014).

Education increases women's agency, and more educated women are often more able to make decisions and have choices, even where gender norms are restrictive. In South Asia and the Middle East and North Africa, women with more education are less likely to have to ask for their husbands' or families' permission to seek medical care; women with more education also tend to marry later and have fewer children, as discussed further in chapter 4 (Muñoz Boudet, Petesch, and Turk 2013). Among some Roma in Bulgaria, more educated women are renegotiating gender roles in communities, challenging traditional gender roles, and demanding that men play a more active role in child care and household chores (World Bank 2014b).

Enhanced agency is a key reason children of more educated women are less likely to have stunted growth: educated mothers have greater autonomy in making decisions and more power to act for their children's benefit (UNESCO 2014). Educated mothers are more likely to take preventive actions, such as purifying water and vaccinating their children; to recognize common illnesses and to treat them; to seek help at the right time; and to use health care services effectively.

Policies that get more girls and boys into school are critical, but equally important is what happens when they get there. We must ensure that both girls and boys leave school literate and numerate and that the values of the school system promote gender equality and protect children from abuse. This requires building allegiances between parents and teachers and boys and girls to provide safe and supportive school environments that are free from gender-based violence and bullying (box 2.4) and to provide textbooks and curricula that are free from stereotypes and discrimination (box 2.5). It also entails training teachers to embody equitable attitudes and practices and to pay specific attention to understanding gender relations and building competencies beyond educational basics.

Addressing violence in schools requires a comprehensive, multilevel approach. Establishing school policies and committees to address violence and putting in place appropriate disciplinary measures can help to support and monitor student and teacher behavior. Working with teachers and school staff members is essential, as is engaging parents and the wider community and working directly with students. For example:

- In Tanzania, female teachers were trained as guardians for female students, with the result that girls felt there was someone to turn to for advice about school-based violence and the wider community began to confront sexual violence more openly (Mgalla, Schapink, and Boerma 1998).

Box 2.4 Promoting gender equality in school and improving the learning environment

Girls', and sometimes boys', ability to acquire an education is tragically disrupted by gender-based violence. In schools where sexual violence against girls is the norm, the education system itself may increase a girl's chances of dropping out, of having her studies interrupted, of experiencing an unintended pregnancy, or of becoming infected with HIV. Addressing harassment and violence in schools is important to promote gender equality in education.

South Africa's Girls' Education Movement is a civil society organization seeking to promote gender equality and to address the very high levels of violence experienced in schools through student-led clubs and community workshops. It has created a network for improving girls' education, knowledge, and self-esteem, with boys and adults as allies. The clubs equip children to address issues of education, clean and safe school environments, and good communication among peers, as well as other things. The program gives children the opportunity to work together to find solutions to the problems affecting their school lives.

The program has seen some progress in reducing aggressive behavior and conflict and in changing attitudes of the students and program leaders who received training. But the results varied significantly by context, and impacts on the broader school environment were not significant. Findings suggest that changes in underlying norms around the acceptability of violence and the unequal treatment of girls are needed to realize the full impact of the program.

Source: Wilson 2009.

Box 2.5   Curriculum reform to promote gender equality through education

Although global progress has been made in increasing girls' school enrollment, gender equality in education encompasses much more than access. Social norms influence textbooks, curricular choices, the sex distribution of teachers and administrators, teacher attitudes and behavior, classroom and discipline practices, and the presence of violence—all of which shape opportunities for boys and girls. National curricula can reinforce existing social and gender inequalities by implicitly upholding traditional gender stereotypes or by disregarding the diversity of learning needs and learning styles among girls and boys. At the same time, schools have enormous potential to effect social change and to transform gender relations by expanding the range of possibilities for both boys and girls.

One avenue for transformation is the gender sensitization of school curriculum, including revising textbooks. Research suggests that the treatment of girls and women in school textbooks is broadly similar across countries. There are fewer images of women and girls compared to men and boys, men and women are generally portrayed in stereotypical roles and professions, men and women are described as having specific gendered attributes, and contributions of important women are ignored or given less consideration than those of important men. An increasing number of countries are taking action to address these biases. For example, in Thailand, policies have been instituted directing textbooks to be revised and all gender stereotypes to be removed. In Vietnam, in 2009, the Ministry of Education, supported by 12 United Nations agencies, conducted a national textbook review and developed teacher-training modules to promote gender equality, and in Indonesia, teachers are being trained in gender-sensitive methodologies to engage boys and girls. Similarly, the Australian National Curriculum directs teachers to address certain issues within their classes—for example, the year 7 English curriculum recommends teaching how languages and images create character by identifying and challenging gender stereotypes in girls' and women's magazines and popular television programming.

Mainstreaming gender into curricula goes beyond revising textbooks and requires incorporating gender equality across the range of studies. Evidence suggests that intensive and long-term attention to gender as part of school coursework has an impact on improving children's attitudes and behaviors related to gender equality. In Mumbai, India, for example, the Gender Equity Movement in Schools, which includes sessions taught over two years, focused on understanding gender roles, power dynamics, violence, and physical and emotional changes related to adolescence. Participating children reported more gender-equitable attitudes. In Tanzania, the national syllabi for secondary schools contain topics related to gender as part of civics education and national examinations.

Sources: Achyut et al. 2011; Connell 2010; Levtov 2014; http://www.australiancurriculum.edu.au.

■ The Gender Equity Movement in Schools program in Indian middle schools included discussions of violence in the context of relationships between boys and girls. Participating students reported less tolerance of violence and greater likelihood of taking positive action in response to peer violence compared to students who did not participate (Achyut et al. 2011).

Promising evidence is emerging on the effectiveness of programs that incorporate elements such as the reform of textbooks and curricula and the provision of safe spaces for girls and boys. Some examples include the following:

- The Child Friendly Schools model, implemented in multiple countries by the United Nations Children's Fund (UNICEF), is designed to improve the quality of public primary schools and to create gender-sensitive, healthy, safe, and inclusive learning environments. A 2009 evaluation across six countries found that the approach created school environments where female students feel included, safe, supported, and challenged (UNICEF 2009).

- The Forum of African Women Educationalists Centre of Excellence model has transformed ordinary schools in 14 African countries into gender-responsive schools that focus on the physical, academic, and social dimensions of both girls' and boys' education. Elements include gender-responsive training for teachers; an emphasis on science, mathematics, and technology for girls; empowerment training for students; a sexual maturation management program for girls; gender-responsive school infrastructure; and community involvement in school management (Lloyd 2012).

***

Constraints to agency stem from many sources. Often, deeply rooted social norms are an unrecognized driving factor behind the actions taken by men and women, boys and girls, sometimes entrenched by laws on paper and in practice.

The good news outlined in this chapter is that there is a range of policies that can work to promote change across a broad spectrum. We also saw how such programs are working to couple development results related to income and access to services together with increases in women's agency. Indeed, we saw that improvements in women's agency are sometimes necessary for other desired development results to be achieved.

This is an important stage to set for the examination of major agency deprivations—freedom from violence, control over sexual and reproductive health, land and housing ownership, and participation in politics and collective action—and the more targeted policy and program responses in the chapters that follow.

Notes

1. More information about the Male Champions of Change initiative is available on the website of the Australian Human Rights Commission at http://www.humanrights.gov.au/male-champions-change.

2. For more information about Men Stopping Violence, see the organization's website at http://www.menstoppingviolence.org/educating-and-advocating-for-change.

3. More information about the program is available on the website of the Center for Communication Programs at http://www.jhuccp.org/whatwedo/projects/jordan-health-communication-partnership-jhcp.

4. The "Samajhdari" radio program can be downloaded at http://www.equalaccess .org.np/samajhdari.

5. The eight countries are Bosnia, Brazil, Chile, Croatia, the Democratic Republic of Congo, India, Mexico, and Rwanda. For more information, see Fleming et al.

6. For more information, see the commission's website at http://huairou.org/land-housing.

7. Text of the law is available at http:// www.gazetazyrtare.com/e-gov/index .php?option=com_content&task=view&id =128&Itemid=28&lang=en.

8. This figure represents the share of women reporting ever having experienced physical or sexual partner violence in the 2010 Demographic and Health Surveys (NBS and ICF Macro 2011).

9. For a more comprehensive discussion of the challenges and promising approaches associated with women's access to formal and informal legal systems, see IDLO (2013, 11–25).

10. For more information about Ciudad Mujer, see the entity's website at http://www .ciudadmujer.gob.sv.

11. For more information about this initiative, known as the End Child Marriage Programme, see http://www.qedgroupllc.com/project /end-child-marriage-programme.

12. The International Labour Organization describes the Decent Work Agenda on its website at http://www.ilo.org/global/about -the-ilo/decent-work-agenda/lang--en/.

References

Achyut, Pranita, Nandita Bhatla, Sujata Khandekar, Shubhada Maitra, and Ravi Kumar Verma. 2011. "Building Support for Gender Equality among Young Adolescents in School: Findings from Mumbai, India." International Center for Research on Women, New Delhi.

Ali, Daniel Ayalew, Klaus Deininger, and Markus Goldstein. 2011. "Environmental and Gender Impacts of Land Tenure Regularization in Africa: Pilot Evidence from Rwanda." Policy Research Working Paper 5765, World Bank, Washington, DC.

Amatya, Ramesh, Halida Akhter, James McMahan, Nancy Williamson, Deborah Gates, and Yasmin Ahmed. 1994. "The Effect of Husband Counseling on NORPLANT Contraceptive Acceptability in Bangladesh." Contraception 50 (3): 263–73.

Andrews, Penelope E. 2005. "Perspectives on Brown: The South African Experience." New York Law School Review 49: 1155–72.

Baird, Sarah, Ephraim Chirwa, Craig McIntosh, and Berk Özler. 2010. "The Short-Term Impacts of a Schooling Conditional Cash Transfer Program on the Sexual Behavior of Young Women." Health Economics 19 (suppl. 1): 55–68.

Bandiera, O., N. Buehren, R. Burgess, M. Goldstein, S. Gulesci, I. Rasul, and M. Sulaiman. 2014. "Women's Empowerment in Action: Evidence from a Randomized Control Trial in Africa." Working Paper, The International Growth Center, London School of Economics. http://www.theigc.org/sites/default/files /Bandiera%20et%20al%202014.pdf.

Banerjee, Abhijit, Esther Duflo, Raghabendra Chattopadhyay, and Jeremy Shapiro. 2011. "Targeting the Hard-Core Poor: An Impact Assessment." Abdul Latif Jameel Poverty Action Lab, Cambridge, MA. http://www .povertyactionlab.org/publication/targeting -hard-core-poor-impact-assessment.

Biddlecom, Ann E., and Bolaji M. Fapohunda. 1998. "Covert Contraceptive Use: Prevalence, Motivations, and Consequences." Studies in Family Planning 29 (4): 360–72.

Broadband Commission Working Group on Broadband and Gender. 2013. "Doubling Digital Opportunities: Enhancing the Inclusion of Women and Girls in the Information Society." International Telecommunications Union and United Nations Educational Scientific and Cultural Organization, Geneva.

Browne, Beverly A. 1998. "Gender Stereotypes in Advertising on Children's Television in the 1990s: A Cross-National Analysis." *Journal of Advertising* 27 (1): 83–96.

Bukuluki, Paul, and Carol Watson. 2012. *Transforming Cash Transfers: Beneficiary and Community Perspectives on the Senior Citizen Grant (SCG) in Uganda.* London: Overseas Development Institute.

Case, Anne, and Alicia Menendez. 2007. "Does Money Empower the Elderly? Evidence from the Agincourt Demographic Surveillance Site, South Africa." *Scandinavian Journal of Public Health* 35 (suppl. 69): 157–64.

Connell, Raewyn. 2010. *Education, Change, and Society.* Victoria: Oxford University Press Australia & New Zealand.

Das, Narayan C., and Raniya Shams. 2011. "Asset Transfer Programme for the Ultra Poor: A Randomized Control Evaluation." Challenging the Frontiers of Poverty Reduction Working Paper 22, BRAC, Dhaka.

de Montesquiou, Aude, and Syed M. Hashemi. 2012. "Creating Pathways for the Poorest: Graduation Model Shows Early Promise." Consultative Group to Assist the Poor, Washington, DC. http://www.cgap.org /blog/creating-pathways-poorest -graduation-model-shows-early-promise.

DFID (U.K. Department for International Development). 2003. "The Policy Statement on Safety, Security and Accessible Justice." DFID, London.

Duflo, Esther. 2003. "Grandmothers and Granddaughters: Old-Age Pensions and Intrahousehold Allocation in South Africa." *World Bank Economic Review* 17 (1): 1–25.

Dugger, Celia W. 2011. "Senegal Curbs a Bloody Rite for Girls and Women." *New York Times,* October 15.

Ezeh, Alex Chika. 1993. "The Influence of Spouses over Each Other's Contraceptive Attitudes in Ghana." *Studies in Family Planning* 24 (3): 163–74.

Filho, Irineu Evangelista de Carvalho. 2012. "Household Income as a Determinant of Child Labor and School Enrollment in Brazil: Evidence from a Social Security Reform." *Economic Development and Cultural Change* 60 (2): 399–435.

Fiszbein, Ariel, Norbert Rüdiger Schady, and Francisco H. G. Ferreira. 2009. *Conditional Cash Transfers: Reducing Present and Future Poverty.* Washington, DC: World Bank.

Fleming, Paul J., Gary Barker, Jennifer McCleary-Sills, and Matthew Morton. 2013. "Engaging Men and Boys in Advancing Women's Agency: Where We Stand and New Directions." Women's Voice, Agency, and Participation Research Paper 1, World Bank, Washington, DC.

GIZ (German Society for International Cooperation). 2012. "Mahallas, Men, and Mothers-in-Law: Community-Based Approaches on Awareness-Raising in Reproductive Health." Regional Programme Health in Central Asia, GIZ, Tashkent.

Hallward-Driemeier, Mary, and Tazeen Hasan. 2013. *Empowering Women: Legal Rights and Economic Opportunities in Africa.* Washington, DC: World Bank.

Hasan, Tazeen, and Ziona Tanzer. 2013. "Women's Movements, Plural Legal Systems, and the Botswana Constitution: How Reform Happens." Policy Research Working Paper 6690, World Bank, Washington, DC.

Heise, Lori. 2011. *What Works to Prevent Partner Violence? An Evidence Overview.* London: STRIVE Research Consortium.

IDLO (International Development Law Organization). 2013. "Accessing Justice: Models, Strategies, and Best Practices on Women's Empowerment." IDLO, Rome.

IRIN (Integrated Regional Information Networks). 2013. "Justice without Jail for Tanzanian Wife-Beaters." *IRIN News,* November 1. http://www.irinnews.org /report/99049/justice-without-jail-for -tanzanian-wife-beaters.

Jensen, Robert, and Emily Oster. 2009. "The Power of TV: Cable Television and Women's Status in India." *Quarterly Journal of Economics* 124 (3): 1057–94.

Jewkes, Rachel, Emma Fulu, Tim Roselli, and Claudia Garcia-Moreno. 2013. "Prevalence of and Factors Associated with Non-partner Rape Perpetration: Findings from the UN Multi-Country Cross-Sectional Study on Men and Violence in Asia and the Pacific." *The Lancet Global Health* 1 (4): e208–18.

Jones, Nicola, and Thea Shahrokh. 2013. "Social Protection Pathways: Shaping Social Justice Outcomes for the Most Marginalized, Now and Post-2015." Background Note, Overseas Development Institute, London.

Jones, Nicola, and Maria Stavropoulou. 2013. "Resilience for All? Towards Gender-Responsive Social Protection in South-East Asia." Bangkok: UN Women.

Kabeer, Naila. 2011. "Contextualising the Economic Pathways of Women's Empowerment: Findings from a Multi-country Research Program." Pathways Policy Paper, Pathways of Women's Empowerment RPC, Brighton, U.K.

———. 2013. *Paid Work, Women's Empowerment, and Inclusive Growth: Transforming the Structures of Constraint.* New York: UN Women.

Khan, Farida, and Rehana Ghadially. 2009. "Gender-Differentiated Impact on Minority Youth of Basic Computer Education in Mumbai City." *Gender Technology and Development* 13 (2): 245–69.

Kim, C. H., and S. J. Lee. 1973. "The Role of Husbands in Family Planning Behavior." *Psychological Studies in Population/Family Planning* 1 (5): 1–23.

Kimuna, Sitawa R., and Donald J. Adamchak. 2001. "Gender Relations: Husband–Wife Fertility and Family Planning Decisions in Kenya." *Journal of Biosocial Science* 33 (1): 13–23.

Kırdar, Murat G, Meltem Dayıoğlu, and İsmet Koç. 2012. "The Effect of Compulsory Schooling Laws on Teenage Marriage and Births in Turkey." Munich Personal RePEc Archive Paper 38735, Munich University. http://mpra.ub.uni-muenchen.de/38735/1/MPRA_paper_38735.pdf.

Levtov, Ruti. 2014. "Addressing Gender Inequalities in Curriculum and Education: Review of Literature and Promising Practices to Inform Education Reform Initiatives in Thailand." Women's Voice and Agency Research Paper 9, World Bank, Washington, DC. http://www.worldbank.org/content/dam/Worldbank/document/Gender/Levtov%202014.%20Addressing%20gender%20inequalities%20in%20education.pdf.

Lloyd, Cynthia B. 2012. "Priorities for Adolescent Girls' Education." Population Council, New York.

Mackie, Gerry. 2000. "Female Genital Cutting: The Beginning of the End." In *Female Circumcision: Multidisciplinary Perspectives*, edited by Bettina Shell-Duncan and Ylva Hernlund, 245–82. Boulder, CO: Lynne Rienner.

Mackie, Gerry, and John LeJeune. 2009. "Social Dynamics of Abandonment of Harmful Practices." Innocenti Working Paper 2009-06, Innocenti Research Centre, United Nations Children's Fund, Florence, Italy.

Macours, Karen, and Renos Vakis. 2009. "Changing Households' Investments and Aspirations through Social Interactions." Policy Research Working Paper 5137, World Bank, Washington, DC.

Macueve, Gertrudes, Judite Mandlate, Lucia Ginger, Polly Gaster, and Esselina Macome. 2009. "Women's Use of Information and Communication Technologies in Mozambique: A Tool for Empowerment?" In *African Women and ICTs: Investigating Technology, Gender and Empowerment*, edited by Ineke Buskens and Anne Webb, 21–32. London: Zed Books.

Malhotra, Anju, Ann Warner, Allison McGonagle, and Susan Lee-Rife. 2011. "Solutions to End Child Marriage: What the Evidence Shows." International Center for Research on Women, Washington, DC.

Marinero, Ximena. 2009. "Kuwait Constitutional Court Rules Women Do Not Need Permission to Get Passport." *Jurist Legal News and Research*, October 22. http://jurist.org /paperchase/2009/10/kuwait-constitutional -court-rules-women.php.

Mgalla, Zaida, Dick Schapink, and J. Ties Boerma. 1998. "Protecting School Girls against Sexual Exploitation: A Guardian Programme in Mwanza, Tanzania." *Reproductive Health Matters* 6 (12): 19–30.

Molineux, Maxine, and Marilyn Thomson. 2011. "Cash Transfers, Gender Equity, and Women's Empowerment in Peru, Ecuador, and Bolivia." *Gender and Development* 19 (2): 195–212.

Muñoz Boudet, Ana Maria, Patti Petesch, and Carolyn Turk. 2013. *On Norms and Agency: Conversations about Gender Equality with Women and Men in 20 Countries*. Washington, DC: World Bank.

Mwaikambo, Lisa, Ilene Speizer, Anne Schurmann, Gwen Morgan, and Fariyal Fikree. 2011. "What Works in Family Planning Interventions: A Systematic Review." *Studies in Family Planning* 42 (2): 67–82.

NBS (Tanzania National Bureau of Statistics) and ICF Macro. 2011. *Tanzania Demographic and Health Survey 2010*. Dar es Salaam: NBS and ICF Macro.

ODI (Overseas Development Institute) and DFID (U.K. Department for International Development). 2013. "Beneficiary and Community Perspectives on the Palestinian National Cash Transfer Programme." ODI, London.

Paluk, Elizabeth Levy, and Donald P. Green. 2009. "Deference, Dissent, and Dispute Resolution: An Experimental Intervention Using Mass Media to Change Norms and Behavior in Rwanda." *American Political Science Review* 103 (4): 622–44.

Perova, Elizaveta, and Renos Vakis. 2013. "Improving Gender and Development Outcomes through Agency: Policy Lessons from Three Peruvian Experiences." World Bank, Washington, DC. https:// openknowledge.worldbank.org/bitstream /handle/10986/16259/797130WP0Impro0 Box0377384B00PUBLIC0.pdf?sequence=1.

Prettitore, Paul. 2012. "Who Needs Legal Aid Services? Addressing Demand in Jordan." MENA Knowledge and Learning Quick Note 62, World Bank, Washington, DC.

Promundo, CulturaSalud/EME, and REDMAS (Network of Men for Gender Equality). 2013. *Program P: A Manual for Engaging Men in Fatherhood, Caregiving, and Maternal and Child Health*. Rio de Janeiro: Promundo.

Pronyk, Paul M., James R. Hargreaves, Julia C. Kim, Linda A. Morison, Godfrey Phetla, Charlotte Watts, Joanna Busza, and John D. H. Porter. 2006. "Effect of a Structural Intervention for the Prevention of Intimate-Partner Violence and HIV in Rural South Africa: A Cluster Randomised Trial." *The Lancet* 368 (9551): 1973–83.

Sengupta, Anasuya. 2013. "Bandhan's Targeting the Hard Core Poor: A Qualitative Study on Participants' Ascent Out of Extreme Poverty." BRAC Development Institute, Dhaka.

Sloth-Nielsen, Julia, and Belinda Van Heerden. 2003. "The Constitutional Family: Developments in South African Family Law Jurisprudence under the 1996 Constitution." *International Journal of Law, Policy, and the Family* 17 (2): 121–46.

Smith, Stacy L., and Crystal Allene Cook. 2008. "Gender Stereotypes: An Analysis of Popular Films and TV." Geena Davis Institute on Gender in Media, Emmitsburg, MD. http://www.thegeenadavisinstitute.org /downloads/GDIGM_Gender_Stereotypes.pdf.

Storey, J. Douglas, Marc Boulay, Yagya Karki, Karen Heckert, and Dibya Man Karmacha. 1999. "Impact of the Integrated Radio Communication Project in Nepal, 1994–1997." *Journal of Health Communication* 4 (4): 271–94.

Summer, Cate, and Matthew Zurstrassen. 2011. "Increasing Access to Justice for Women, the Poor, and Those Living in Remote Areas: An Indonesian Case Study." *Justice for the Poor* 6 (2): 1–8.

UNESCO (United Nations Educational, Scientific, and Cultural Organization). 2014. *Teaching and Learning: Achieving Quality for All.* Paris: UNESCO.

UNICEF (United Nations Children's Fund). 2009. *Child Friendly Schools Programming: Global Evaluation Report.* New York: UNICEF.

UN Women (United Nations Entity for Gender Equality and the Empowerment of Women). 2011. *Progress of the World's Women: In Pursuit of Justice, 2011–2012.* New York: UN Women.

Wallacher, Hilde. 2012. "Engaging Men: The Abatangamuco and Women's Empowerment in Burundi." Policy Brief 5, Peace Research Institute Oslo, Oslo.

Wilson, Felicia Renee. 2009. "Girls' Education Movement (GEM): Study of Program Implementation and Partnerships for Education Development in Cape Town, South Africa." PhD dissertation, Pennsylvania State University, State College, PA.

Woolcock, Michael, Berk Özler, Sarah Baird, Francisco H. G. Ferreira. 2013. "Relative Effectiveness of Conditional and Unconditional Cash Transfers for Schooling Outcomes in Developing Countries: A Systematic Review." *Campbell Systematic Review* 9 (8): 1–24.

World Bank. 2008. *Whispers to Voices: Gender and Social Transformation in Bangladesh.* Washington, DC: World Bank.

———. 2012. *World Development Report 2013: Jobs.* Washington, DC: World Bank.

———. 2014a. "Gender at Work: A Companion to the World Development Report on Jobs." World Bank, Washington, DC. http://www.worldbank.org/content /dam/Worldbank/document/Gender /GenderAtWork_web.pdf.

———. 2014b. *Gender Dimensions of Roma Inclusion: Perspectives from Four Roma Communities in Bulgaria.* Washington, DC: World Bank.

World Bank and IFC (International Finance Corporation). 2013. *Women, Business, and the Law 2014: Removing Restrictions to Enhance Gender Equality.* London: Bloomsbury.

Chapter 3 Key messages

> Violence is a major theme of this book because it is among the most egregious and commonly experienced abuses of women's rights.

> The media often present violence as a tragic event or a side effect of war or armed conflict. But around the world, no place is less safe for a woman than her own home—almost one-third (30 percent) of women have experienced physical or sexual violence or both by an intimate partner.

> Gender-based violence stems from social norms and expectations that reinforce inequality and place women's and girls' choices outside of their realm of control. Major individual risk factors are family history, early marriage, and husband's alcohol use, while education emerges as the most significant protective factor.

> The effects of intimate partner violence (IPV) are felt at the individual, family, and economy levels.

> The development costs are substantial. Estimated costs of IPV are close to the average that governments in developing countries spend on primary education.

> Preventing violence relies in part on changing norms and attitudes that perpetuate gender inequalities and sanction gender-based violence.

> Treatment and support for survivors are critical—but across the globe, the majority of women (6 in 10) who experience violence never seek help or report the violence to anyone.

> Economic empowerment interventions can expand women's agency by adding strategic design features to address IPV—"economic empowerment plus" interventions.

> Promising interventions have multiple components, intervene at different levels, address norms, involve the wider community, engage both men and women, and span long periods.

CHAPTER 3

Freedom from Violence

Gender-based violence as a development challenge

In 2013, tragic episodes of gender-based violence (GBV) generated a firestorm in the global media. At center stage were brutal gang rapes in India and the United States and cases of celebrity women being physically assaulted or even murdered by their husbands and boyfriends (Brown and Surdin 2009; Pepin 2013; Singh 2013; *Washington Post* 2013). There was also renewed attention to the horrors of sexual violence in conflict-affected countries. But gender-based violence goes far beyond those high-profile cases, isolated incidents, and specific cultures or countries. A recent global study revealed that over 35 percent of women worldwide have experienced physical or sexual partner violence or nonpartner sexual violence (WHO 2013). That is 818 million women—almost the total population of Sub-Saharan Africa.[1] The most common form is abuse by an intimate partner, which has profound consequences on the health and well-being of women and their families, as well as effects on wider communities and development outcomes (WHO 2013).

Gender-based violence is a violation of basic human rights and a pervasive challenge all around the world. GBV is an "umbrella term for any harmful act that is perpetrated against a person's will and that is based on socially ascribed (gender) differences between males and females" (IASC 2005, 7). Men and women across all socioeconomic groups and development contexts are at risk of GBV. However, women are much more affected because violence both reflects and reinforces underlying gender-based inequalities (UNFPA 2007). Freedom from violence is an essential domain of agency for both its intrinsic value in asserting fundamental human rights and its instrumental value in promoting gender equality in a wide range of outcomes at the individual, family, and society levels.

Because it is more pervasive, our focus is on violence against women, which the United Nations (UN) defines as "any act of gender-based violence that results in, or is likely to result in, physical, sexual, or psychological harm or suffering to women, including threats of such acts, coercion, or arbitrary deprivation of liberty, whether occurring in public or in private life" (United Nations 1993). As the report of the High-Level Panel of Eminent Persons on the Post-2015 Development Agenda (2013) notes, such violence takes many forms, including acts of physical, sexual, and economic abuse. It takes place in the home, on the streets, in schools, in the workplace, in farm fields, in refugee camps, in times of peace as well as during armed conflicts and crises (Coomaraswamy 1999). Part of the spectrum of violence that women suffer is described in box 3.1.

Social norms and institutions—both formal and informal—perpetuate such violence through norms and expectations that reinforce inequality and place women's and girls'

decision making about their bodies outside their realm of control (McCleary-Sills et al. 2011; Underwood et al. 2011). But within and across countries, there is no universal agreement about what constitutes *violence*. Definitions of the forms of violence along the continuum are culturally derived. For example, women in Tanzania define *forced sex* as sexual assault by an acquaintance or boyfriend, *coercion* as the use of guilt and emotional manipulation, and *rape* as sexual assault by a stranger (McCleary-Sills, Douglas, et al. 2013). Although such rape is viewed as unacceptable, physical, emotional, and even sexual violence against a wife or partner is frequently viewed as normal (McCleary-Sills, Namy, et al. 2013).

> *Yes, it's normal, being beaten, yelled at. If you tell [anyone], your peers will ask you, is this your first time to be beaten? Some of us are used to it, just like the way we are used to eating ugali.*
>
> —Female focus group participant, Mbeya, Tanzania (McCleary-Sills, Namy, et al. 2013, 19)

Box 3.1 What is gender-based violence? Stories from survivors in Tonga

The Women and Children Crisis Centre in Tonga provides care and support to survivors of violence. The organization collected stories from survivors describing the range of violence they had suffered at the hands of the men in their lives—husbands, fathers, and fathers-in-law.

Women described being pushed and punched. They had their hair pulled and cut. Men cut their bodies with knives and hit them with heavy objects, such as tire jacks and hammers. Men stood and stepped on their faces and beat their backs, burned their bodies with scalding objects, and spat and urinated on them. Women reported being kicked, including being kicked while pregnant. Women and children were forced to have sex. Very young girls were forced to perform fellatio on their fathers. They were raped by their fathers and by their fathers-in-law, some every night. Yet the abuse is not limited to young women by any means. Grandsons attacked their grandmothers, verbally terrorized them, and hit them in the face. Crisis centers around the world record countless similar testimonies every day. And myriad similar stories are never told at all.

Source: Guttenbeil-Likiliki 2014.

While the acceptance of wife beating as part of marital life is commonplace (Rani and Bonu 2009; Rani, Bonu, and Diop-Sidibé 2004), recent evidence suggests that rejection of violence globally has risen rapidly in the past decade (Pierotti 2013). As shown in figure 3.1, in a number of repeat Demographic and Health Surveys (DHS), acceptance of spousal violence dropped or leveled out near zero. At the same time, our analysis of DHS data from 55 countries for the most recent year shows that 4 in 10 women still agree with at least one justification for a husband beating his wife.[2]

The good news is that the momentum to end GBV is growing, and evidence about what works is accumulating. The number of countries recognizing domestic violence as a crime has risen from close to zero to 76 in just 37 years.[3] Combating violence has emerged as a key priority for the post-2015 agenda, and in March 2013, more than 100 UN member states pledged to end violence against women and girls (Commission on the Status of Women 2013). And since 2000, several UN Security Council resolutions have addressed sexual violence and the effect of armed conflict on women and girls.[4]

In this chapter, we focus on physical and sexual intimate partner violence (IPV). We do not tackle other forms of violence

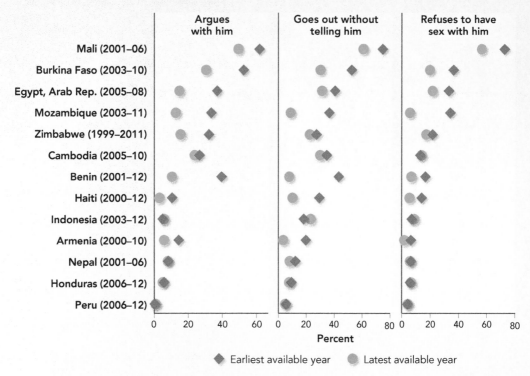

FIGURE 3.1 Change in the percentage of women who agree that wife beating can be justified, by situation and country

Source: Estimates based on Demographic and Health Surveys for 13 countries for which data over time are available.

against women, although child marriage is addressed in the next chapter. The next section reviews the prevalence of IPV and the barriers to reporting. We then highlight the costs of IPV at the individual, family, and economywide levels and the key risk and protective factors. The final section of this chapter lays out promising directions gleaned from evidence about prevention and response efforts.

How large is the challenge?

Around the world, no place is less safe for a woman than her own home. Domestic violence is especially pernicious "because it occurs in a space that is also central to the development of human capabilities—the family" (Agarwal and Panda 2007, 362). Since the 1990s, numerous studies have shown that women are more likely to be physically or sexually assaulted or murdered by someone they know—often a family member or intimate partner (Heise, Ellsberg, and Gottemoeller 1999). A recent systematic review using data from 66 countries found that the share of homicides by an intimate partner was six times higher for female victims compared with male victims (39 percent versus 6 percent, respectively) (Stöckl et al. 2013).

A solid global evidence base about the prevalence and patterns of IPV, the most common form of gender-based violence, is now emerging. This path was forged by the landmark 2005 World Health Organization (WHO) *Multi-country Study on Women's Health and Domestic Violence against Women*, which systematically documented multiple forms of violence using a standardized questionnaire, training, and methodology (García-Moreno et al. 2005). The study

revealed the high prevalence of IPV and underscored the repercussions for women's health and well-being on a global scale. It should be noted, however, that because of the sensitive nature of collecting such information, all survey estimates are subject to some degree of underreporting (box 3.2). The need to develop tools and methodologies to more accurately estimate prevalence and incidence of violence is discussed in chapter 7.

Prevalence of intimate partner violence

IPV is the focus of this chapter, largely because it is both the most pervasive form of gender-based violence and one that too few governments even recognize as a crime. IPV includes "all acts of physical, sexual, psychological, or economic violence that occur within the family or domestic unit or between former or current spouses or partners, whether or not the perpetrator shares or has shared the same residence with the victim."[5] The 2005 WHO study documented wide variation in rates of violence (García-Moreno et al. 2005). Among 24,000 women interviewed in 10 countries, between 15 percent and 71 percent reported having experienced physical or sexual IPV or both in their lifetime. Up to 75 percent had experienced emotionally abusive and controlling behavior in the preceding year. A preliminary analysis of the 2013 WHO global prevalence data set (by World Bank regions) illustrates the regional variation, as shown in map 3.1. Among women who had ever been in a relationship (ever-partnered women), the average prevalence across developing regions is 30 percent, ranging from 29 percent in Europe and Central Asia to a high of 43 percent in South Asia.

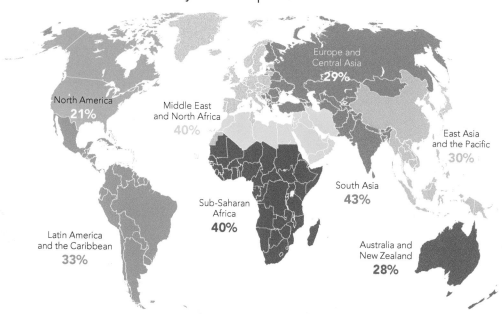

MAP 3.1 Share of ever-partnered women who have experienced physical or sexual violence or both by an intimate partner

Source: Preliminary analysis of the World Health Organization global and regional estimates of violence against women, global prevalence database (2013) using World Bank regions.

Note: Data for the areas shaded in gray were not available.

These regional averages can mask considerable variation across and within countries but provide a useful overall snapshot. Our analysis of DHS data shows the prevalence of violence across ethnic groups in five countries (figure 3.2). Although differences exist among the groups in each country, the data also show that no ethnic group is immune to violence.

The types of partner violence range from minor to severe and include physical, emotional, economic, and sexual abuse. Demographic and Health Surveys categorize the severity of physical violence as follows:

- Less severe: pushing, shaking, slapping, punching, and kicking

- Severe: trying to strangle or burn, threatening with a weapon, and attacking with a weapon

DHS data from 31 countries show that about 3 in 10 women (31 percent) report having experienced "less severe violence" and about 1 in 10 (11 percent) report having experienced "severe" violence. One in 10 (10 percent) report having experienced sexual violence, and one-fifth of women report having experienced emotional violence, including threats of harm and humiliation in front of others. Box 3.2 provides an overview of the domestic violence module in the DHS.

Yet of course—as we saw from Tonga—even these numbers do not give a full

FIGURE 3.2 Share of ever-partnered women who have experienced physical or sexual violence or both by an intimate partner, by ethnic group, in selected countries

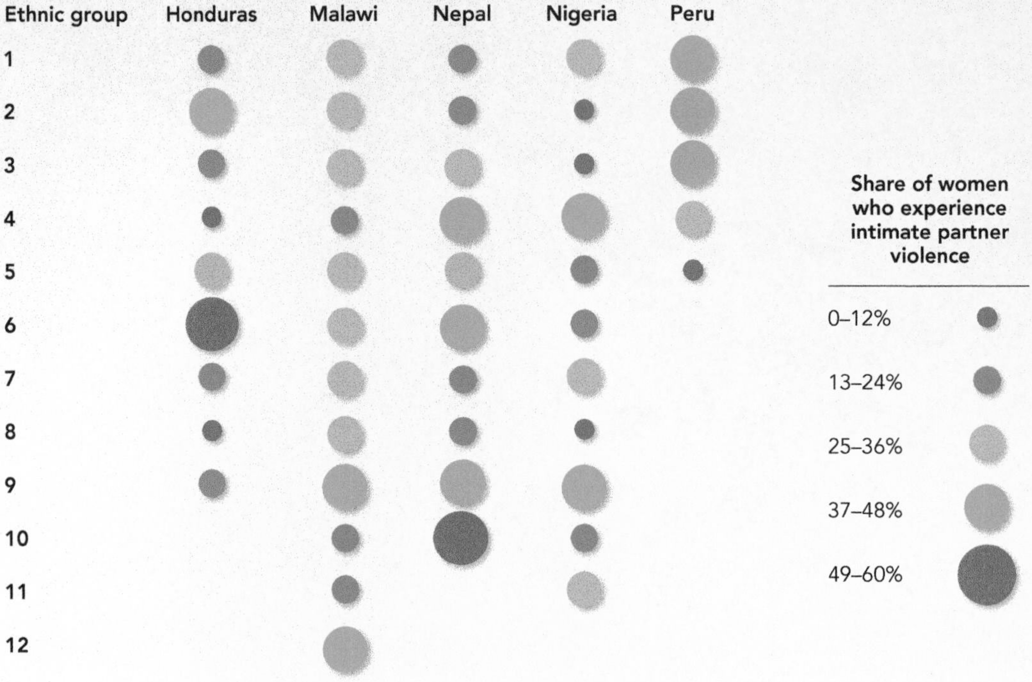

Source: Estimates based on Demographic and Health Surveys using the latest available data, 2008–12

picture. Women who experience intimate partner violence tend to experience multiple forms. In Latin America and the Caribbean, for example, most women who experienced physical IPV in the past 12 months also reported emotional abuse (ranging from 61 percent in Colombia to 93 percent in El Salvador). Women exposed to three or more controlling behaviors by their partners—such as efforts to limit their mobility and contact with friends and family—were also at much higher risk of experiencing physical or sexual partner violence (Bott et al. 2013). Less than half (43 percent) of women in our sample of 26 countries have experienced neither IPV nor controls on their behavior

(figure 3.3). More than 7 out of 10 women who have experienced IPV were also subject to at least one control. Such controlling behaviors are often a risk factor and precursor to a partner's use of physical violence (Campbell et al. 2003; Xu et al. 2005).

Abused women generally experience emotional violence more frequently than physical violence. In Mali—the only country in our DHS data set with frequency data—women report more than twice as many occurrences of emotional violence than of physical violence. Across our sample, about one-fifth of women experiencing physical abuse, one-fourth of those experiencing

Box 3.2   The domestic violence module of the Demographic and Health Surveys

Demographic and Health Surveys (DHS) support nationally representative data collection in the areas of population, health, and nutrition. A standardized domestic violence module was developed in 1998 and has since been included in 91 surveys. It collects data on the prevalence of physical, sexual, and emotional violence against women since the age of 15, by current and previous partners as well as by nonpartners within the household context, and it allows the experience of violence to be linked to a range of risk and protective factors and health outcomes.

In both stand-alone surveys developed specifically to measure violence and broader surveys (like DHS) that integrate a violence module, underestimation of the actual prevalence of violence is a concern. The DHS incorporated enhancements to protect respondents and optimize the accuracy of violence estimates, including offering multiple opportunities for disclosure by asking at multiple points about any experience of many types of violence and by generally placing the module toward the end of the questionnaire, which provides the greatest opportunity for a rapport to develop between interviewers and respondents. Further, the DHS adhere to strict ethical and safety guidelines aligned with the internationally recognized recommendations of the World Health Organization (WHO). Key precautions include anonymity of respondents (that is, names are never disclosed and are excluded from all data sets). The guidelines include providing specialized training for interviewers, observing strict informed-consent procedures, ensuring privacy during the interview, administering the module to only one eligible woman per household, not asking men in the same household questions about violence, and providing referrals to services.

Stand-alone surveys such as the *WHO Multi-country Study on Women's Health and Domestic Violence against Women* (García-Moreno et al. 2005) generally report higher prevalence than DHS, likely because of greater efforts to enhance disclosure in the questionnaire design and in interviewer training. However, in terms of risk and protective factors and gaps in help seeking, results from analyses of DHS data are comparable to those from the WHO study. DHS are the largest source for population-based data about violence and so constitute a large share of the available data on the prevalence of intimate partner violence. Further detail about the data sources used in this book can be found in chapter 7.

Sources: Bott et al. 2013; Ellsberg and Heise 2005; Kishor 2005; Kishor and Johnson 2004; WHO 2001.

Note: The full list of 91 surveys can be accessed at http://www.dhsprogram.com/What-We-Do/survey-search.cfm.

---

sexual abuse, and more than one-fourth (26 percent) of those experiencing emotional abuse report that the abuse occurs "often." Repeated victimization exposes women and girls to complex trauma, with cumulative and devastating effects on survivors' basic functioning across a range of activities in day-to-day life (Cloitre et al. 2009; Follette et al. 1996; Roth et al. 1997).

Coercion, forced sex, and rape

The ability to choose when to have sex and on what terms is a critical indicator of agency. Social norms dictate women's perceived and actual control over their own sexuality, meaning that power disparities can leave them unable to control whether, when, how, and with whom they have sex (Gee et al. 2009;

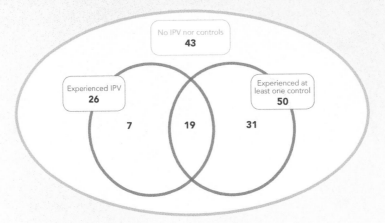

FIGURE 3.3 Share of ever-partnered women who have experienced physical or sexual violence or both by an intimate partner and at least one control on their behavior (percent)

Source: Estimates based on Demographic and Health Surveys for 26 countries using data, 2006–12.

Note: IPV = intimate partner violence. Controls include limiting a woman's contact with her family, not permitting her to meet female friends, and insisting on knowing where she is.

Gipson and Hindin 2007; Khawaja and Hammoury 2008). There is a continuum of volition related to sex, with willful participation at one end and forced sex and rape at the other end (Weissman et al. 2006). Even when a young woman chooses her partner, her choice may be constrained by her economic needs and the social expectations placed on her (McCleary-Sills, Douglas, et al. 2013). Poor women and girls, for example, may engage in transactional or commercial sex for lack of good alternate livelihoods (Hope 2007). Research across Sub-Saharan Africa shows that cross-generational sex between girls and older men may involve provision for girls' basic needs, such as school fees and food, in exchange for sex (Luke 2003; Pettifor et al. 2005).

Our analysis of 37 developing countries reveals extensive lack of agency:

- Almost one-third of women (33 percent) report that they cannot refuse sex with their partners—rising to over 70 percent of women in Mali, Niger, and Senegal.

- Over 44 percent say they could not ask their partner to use a condom.

Underpinning women's difficulty in refusing sex is the common assumption that consenting to sex at any point in the relationship establishes consent for the rest of the relationship, which also creates barriers to recognizing marital rape (Logan, Walker, and Cole 2013). The ability to refuse sex and to ask a partner to use a condom are closely correlated,[6] but in Sub-Saharan Africa and Latin America, higher shares of women say they can refuse sex than ask a partner to use a condom. These findings likely reflect attitudes that associate condom use with illicit sex and promiscuity and with perceived and real ethnic and religious prohibitions (Gupta and Weiss 1993). In many contexts, the higher confidence in refusing sex than in insisting on condom use may reflect a dislike of condoms among both men and women (Sarkar 2008).

The strongest correlate of women's sexual autonomy in a relationship is her level of education. Overall, 90 percent of women with a higher education say they can refuse sex, compared with 71 percent of women with a primary education and 51 percent of women with no education. Each additional year of education is associated with a 1 percent increase in the ability to refuse sex (see figure 4.1 in chapter 4). Compared to women with no education, those with a secondary education have a 10 percent higher probability of being able to refuse sex, all else being equal. These results suggest the importance of improving girls' education as an entry point for enhancing their agency.

Our analysis of DHS data shows a strong association between early sexual initiation and the likelihood that sexual initiation was forced. In some countries (notably Bangladesh and rural Ethiopia), high levels of forced first sex are likely related to early marriage rather than to violence by acquaintances or strangers (García-Moreno et al. 2005). On average, across 16 countries for which data are available, 11 percent of women report that their first sex was forced, ranging from 1 percent in Timor-Leste to 63 percent in the Democratic Republic of Congo. Our analysis shows that women who report that their first intercourse had been forced are twice as likely to have experienced recent IPV. National surveys by Together for Girls found that

significant shares of young women ages 18 to 24 experienced sexual violence before their 18th birthdays—26 percent in Haiti, 27 percent in Tanzania, 32 percent in Kenya, 33 percent in Zimbabwe, and 38 percent in Swaziland (Together for Girls 2013).

While not the focus of this chapter, more than 1 in 20 women globally—7 percent according to WHO (2013)—have suffered sexual violence by nonpartners. A recent study with more than 10,000 men across Asia and the Pacific revealed that prevalence varies widely—3 percent of men in rural Bangladesh and 27 percent in Bougainville, Papua New Guinea, reported having raped a woman who was not their partner (Jewkes et al. 2013). Although it is less common, men also reported their involvement in gang rapes: levels ranged from 1 percent of men in urban Bangladesh to 14 percent of men in Bougainville.

Reporting and responses

Around the world, the vast majority of women who experience violence never seek help or report the violence to anyone. Only 2 percent of women in India and East Asia, 6 percent in Africa, 10 percent in Central Asia, and 14 percent in Latin America and the Caribbean made any formal disclosure of their experience of violence (Palermo, Bleck, and Peterman 2014).

Our analysis of DHS data shows that across 30 countries, on average only 4 in 10 women exposed to violence sought any help, and only 6 percent sought help from authorities, such as police, lawyers, doctors, or religious authorities. Similarly, in Bangladesh, two-thirds of abused women did not seek help at all, only 2 percent ever sought help from institutions, and rural women were even less likely to seek help than urban women (Naved et al. 2006). Only 3 percent of women experiencing violence sought help from the police—ranging from 10 percent in Moldova and Ukraine to fewer than 1 percent in Bolivia, Burkina Faso, Haiti, Mozambique, Nigeria, and Zimbabwe.[7]

Studies in Bangladesh, Turkey, and the United States find that women are more likely to seek help from formal agencies as violence becomes more severe—beyond what they can endure or to the point at which they feel their lives or children's safety are in serious jeopardy (Ergöçmen, Yüksel-Kaptanoğlu, and Jansen 2013; Fugate et al. 2005; Naved et al. 2006). Likewise, our analysis suggests that on average 47 percent of women experiencing "severe" physical violence sought help, compared with 31 percent of those experiencing "less severe violence"—and the former were nearly twice as likely to seek help from the police. Across 28 European countries in a recent survey, one-third of women experiencing severe IPV sought some form of help, but only 14 percent of women reported their most serious incident of IPV to the police. Among European women who did not seek help for their most severe incident of physical IPV, the most common reasons were choosing to handle it on their own (55 percent) and not feeling it was serious enough to warrant reporting (34 percent) (EU Agency for Fundamental Rights 2014). Even in cases of severe violence, if help is sought at all, it is often as a last resort rather than as an opportunity for early intervention.

The barriers to reporting and to help seeking reflect social norms and systems that are not responsive to women's needs. Figure 3.4 underscores the host of socio-cultural and structural barriers that inhibit women's ability to report and seek help of any kind (McCleary-Sills, Namy, et al. 2013). DHS in six countries ask why women do not seek help. Many see violence as a "part of life." But a substantial number do not know how or where to report violence. In Burkina Faso, Côte d'Ivoire, the Dominican Republic, and Mali, the predominant reason was the belief that that there was no use doing so. Many women also said they were embarrassed to tell anyone, which underlines the stigma and blame that are often placed on survivors of violence.

> *Across 37 developing countries, almost one-third of women cannot refuse sex with their partner and over 40 percent cannot ask their partner to use a condom.*

In Mexico, the most common reasons women gave for not reporting violence included a perception that the violence was insignificant (29 percent), concern for their children (18 percent), embarrassment (14 percent), and fear of retaliation by their partners (14 percent) (Frías 2013). Only 8 percent of women cited not knowing they could press charges. Among a sample of Bangladeshi women, the most common reasons given were high acceptance of violence, fear of stigma, and fear of greater harm (Naved et al. 2006).

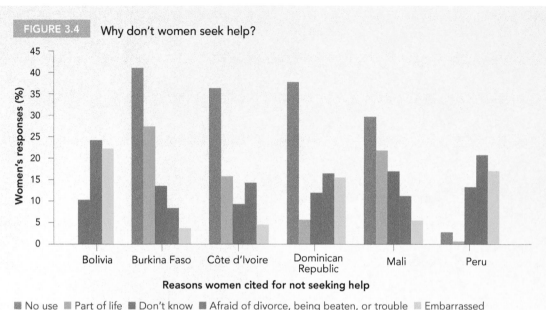

FIGURE 3.4 Why don't women seek help?

Reasons women cited for not seeking help

■ No use ■ Part of life ■ Don't know ■ Afraid of divorce, being beaten, or trouble ■ Embarrassed

Source: Estimates based on Demographic and Health Surveys using the latest available data, 2006–12.

Note: Sums might not total 100 percent; bars represent the percentage of women who chose that reason, but more than one option could have been selected. The "other" category is not shown.

The lack of help seeking represents an enormous missed opportunity to enhance women's agency through entry points in the justice and social service sectors. This challenge requires concerted attention from medical and social service providers, as well as police and the justice system. Although the existence and awareness of laws criminalizing IPV are important, they are not enough. Parallel efforts are needed to increase responsiveness to women's needs (Ellsberg et al. 2011). Box 3.3 provides an overview of a new World Bank initiative to address the needs of survivors and other vulnerable women through a multipronged approach in the Great Lakes region.

The magnitude of violence against women is a major development challenge. Each IPV incident brings costs at multiple levels, a theme we will cover in the next section.

Costs of violence

Intimate partner violence has devastating consequences for individuals, communities, societies, and economies. Tackling this challenge head-on would advance efforts to end extreme poverty and increase prosperity for all. This section documents evidence of the consequences of IPV at the individual, family, and economy levels.

Individual-level effects

Exposure to IPV has been linked with a multitude of adverse health outcomes, including acute injuries, chronic pain, gastrointestinal illness, and gynecological problems

Box 3.3 Serving survivors and empowering women in the Great Lakes

Poor and vulnerable women in the Great Lakes states (Burundi, the Democratic Republic of Congo, and Rwanda) face multiple and mutually reinforcing constraints, including high levels of violence, lack of say over their health, and limited economic opportunities. In the Democratic Republic of Congo alone, nearly three-quarters of women have experienced intimate partner violence. Although women and girls are particularly vulnerable during and after armed conflicts, there is growing recognition that sexual violence has become a wider social phenomenon, including through increasing levels of sexual partner violence.

To help respond, the World Bank Group has approved a US$107 million operation to address the needs of survivors of violence and of other vulnerable women in targeted communities, with activities spanning several sectors. The project is expected to offer the following support:

> Improved maternal, reproductive, and obstetric care

> Mental health services to reduce post-traumatic stress and to improve daily functioning

> Case management, referrals for survivors, and assistance in accessing the judicial system through civil society organizations

> Assistance through village savings and loans associations and cooperatives for survivors and other vulnerable groups

> Scale-up of one-stop centers for survivors of violence and provision of emergency contraception kits, antiretroviral drugs, and surgery equipment to boost the technical capacity of facilities to deliver specialized services

Finally, the program aims to build relevant capacities of a full range of professionals—including social workers, the police, and the military—and to engage community leaders as agents of change.

Source: Great Lakes Emergency Women's Health and Empowerment Project (P147489).

(Campbell 2002; Coker et al. 2008). Mental health consequences include increasing women's risk of depression, post-traumatic stress disorder, and substance abuse (Taft and Watson 2008). A recent systematic review found that IPV increases a woman's risk of experiencing depression two- to threefold (Beydoun et al. 2012). Survivors of violence are also 2.3 times more likely to have alcohol use disorders. IPV has also been linked to the risk of contracting human immunodeficiency virus (HIV) and other sexually transmitted infections, as well as the risk of attempting or completing an abortion (Campbell et al. 2000; Kaye et al. 2006; Maman et al. 2003).

Beyond the damage to health, violence reduces women's economic opportunities. For example:

■ Women exposed to partner violence in Vietnam have higher work absenteeism, lower productivity, and lower earnings than working women who are not beaten (Duvvury, Nguyen, and Carney 2012).

- In Tanzania, women in formal wage work who are exposed to severe partner abuse (both lifetime and current) have 60 percent lower earnings (Vyas 2013).

- In the late 1990s in Nagpur, India, women had to forgo, on average, seven days of paid work per violent episode (ICRW 2000).

Accessing treatment and support services can be expensive. In Uganda, for example, the average direct out-of-pocket expenditure related to an incident of IPV was estimated to be the equivalent of US$5 (ICRW 2009), about one-twelfth of the average monthly income in rural areas (Uganda Bureau of Statistics 2010). A 2011 household survey in Vietnam estimated that out-of-pocket expenditures for accessing services and replacing damaged property averaged 21 percent of women's monthly income (Duvvury, Nguyen, and Carney 2012).

Family-level effects

Violence brings dangers of short-term and long-term effects on children, who may witness frequent abuse. In Monterrey, Mexico, for example, half of abused women reported that their children routinely witnessed the abuse (Granados Shiroma 1996). Children exposed to violence at home show impaired socioemotional functioning and educational outcomes in adolescence and lower job performance, job stability, and earnings into adulthood (Holt, Buckley, and Whelan 2008). Research has consistently found greater health risks in children exposed to violence, such as higher infant mortality rates (Jejeebhoy 1998), lower vaccination rates (Kishor and Johnson 2004), and lower birth weight (Campbell 2002) compared to children whose mothers have not experienced

IPV. Children exposed to violence also face a greater likelihood of being abused themselves, an experience that increases their risk-taking behaviors in adolescence, including drinking, drug use, and early initiation of sex (World Bank 2003). Girls who witness their mothers being abused are twice as likely to experience IPV later, and boys show an increased risk of becoming perpetrators later in life (Kishor and Johnson 2004), hence the much higher risk of a continuing cycle of violence.

Child abuse and partner violence often occur in the same home. Evidence from six Latin American countries shows that children of women who have experienced IPV are more likely to experience beating, spanking, or slapping. This ranges from just over one-third of children in Paraguay, compared with fewer than one-quarter whose mothers reported no partner violence, to more than two-thirds of children of abused mothers in Colombia, compared with 58 percent of children of never-abused mothers (Eijkemans 2013).

There are also repercussions for the men who perpetrate IPV. In Vietnam, male perpetrators had higher work absenteeism following a violent episode (Duvvury, Nguyen, and Carney 2012). A similar study from Maine in the United States showed that 48 percent of offenders had difficulty concentrating at work, with 19 percent reporting a workplace accident or near miss because of preoccupation with their relationship (Lim, Rioux, and Ridley 2004).

Economywide effects

Beyond the human costs, violence incurs major economywide costs. Those costs include expenditures on service provision, forgone income for women and their families, decreased productivity, and negative effects on human capital formation.

Different models have been developed to estimate the economywide costs of IPV. Although these models vary in their core assumptions, they generally take into account some combination of direct and indirect costs that are both tangible (and can be monetized) and intangible (which cannot be readily monetized) (Day, McKenna, and Bowlus 2005). These estimates typically include costs related to service provision, out-of-pocket expenditures, and lost income and productivity. IPV incurs direct costs on services in the health, social service, justice, and police sectors. In the United States, health care costs among women experiencing physical abuse have been estimated to be 42 percent higher than among nonabused women (Bonomi et al. 2009). Notably, estimates typically do not include

costs associated with the long-term emotional effects, increased health care needs, and second-generation consequences.

Figure 3.5 presents estimated costs for a variety of countries, ranging from 1.2 percent to 3.7 percent of gross domestic product, equivalent to what many governments spend on primary education. It should be noted that the estimates are not directly comparable across countries because the methodologies and data vary. One recent study in the United Kingdom sought to account for the loss of life satisfaction because of IPV and arrived at estimates of about 10 percent of gross domestic product (Santos 2013).

The costs vary with the severity of violence. A recent study found that in Tanzania, compared with women who had never been abused by a partner, women currently experiencing IPV earned 29 percent less, and those

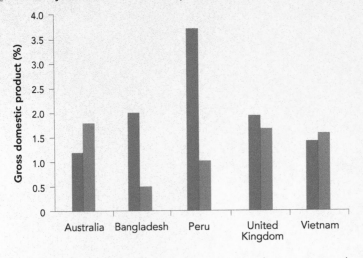

FIGURE 3.5 Economywide costs of intimate partner violence in selected countries

■ Costs of intimate partner violence ■ Spending on primary education

Sources: Duvvury et al. 2013; Horna 2013.

Note: Primary education expenditures (as % of GDP) calculated based on UNESCO Data: http://data.un.org/Data .aspx?q=primary+education+expenditure&d=UNESCO&f=series%3aXLEVEL_1_FSGOV.

currently experiencing severe IPV earned 43 percent less (Vyas 2013). In Chile and Nicaragua, severely abused women earned 61 percent and 43 percent less, respectively (Morrison and Orlando 1999).

Who is worst affected?

Hundreds of millions of women experience some form of intimate partner violence in their lifetimes, and many experience multiple forms over the course of their lives. Violence is not limited to specific regions of the world or to socioeconomic, religious, or ethnic groups. Understanding risk and protective factors and how they interact is critical to inform the design of programmatic responses.

Our analysis of pooled DHS data from 21 countries explored the risk and protective factors for violence in multivariate models controlling for individual and relationship characteristics. Among the strongest individual-level risk factors are family history of violence and attitudes toward wife beating:

- Women whose fathers beat their mothers have two and one-half times greater risk of experiencing IPV in their adult lives compared with women who did not witness IPV as children.

- Agreeing with any justification for wife beating increases the odds of violence by 45 percent.

These results also highlight important protective factors, including education and wealth:

- Women with some or completed secondary education have an 11 and 36 percent lower risk of violence, respectively, compared with women with no education.

- Compared to women living in poorer households, women in wealthier households have a 45 percent lower risk of violence.

Relationship characteristics determine risk

Characteristics of the partner and the relationship affect a woman's odds of experiencing violence. All else being equal, having a husband or partner with some education reduces the likelihood that a woman will experience violence, though the effect is less than that of her own education. Several relationship characteristics affect the odds of experiencing IPV:

- Being in a polygamous marriage increases the risk of IPV by 22 percent.

- Being married before age 18 increases the odds by 22 percent.

- Women who report that their husbands sometimes get drunk have an 81 percent higher risk, while having a husband who drinks often increases the risk nearly fivefold (4.8 times).

Poverty and lack of economic opportunities are associated with increased IPV (Buvinic, Morrison, and Shifter 1999). Such violence may stem from perpetrators' own sense of powerlessness or insecurity, especially when they feel unable to meet the roles socially assigned to them as men (Jewkes 2002). But that situational risk tells only part of the story. Triggers do not create violent behavior, and many men who live in poverty or are unemployed are not violent, even if they use alcohol.

Two recent multicountry studies have sought to understand the protective and risk factors for perpetration of violence. The International Men and Gender Equality Survey (IMAGES) found that attitudes toward gender equality are important, alongside witnessing parental violence, being depressed, and having been involved in fights (Barker et al. 2011). Analyses of IMAGES data across six countries undertaken for this report underline this point; we found that men had more than 10 percent lower odds of perpetrating partner violence for every one standard deviation increase in their Gender Equitable Men score.[8] Similar findings from the Partners for Prevention multicountry study in Asia highlight that most men do not perpetrate violence and that for those who do, the primary risk factors include witnessing or experiencing abuse as children and having gender-inequitable norms and practices (Fulu et al. 2013). Better understanding of these factors is needed to inform prevention efforts.

Increased access to income may affect risk

The relationship between women's economic opportunities and exposure to violence is complex and highly context dependent. Evidence from some studies shows employment and earnings reduce women's risk of violence, whereas others indicate that economic participation increases the risk. A systematic review found mixed evidence as to whether women's own incomes reduced or increased the likelihood of experiencing violence (Vyas and Watts 2009). And several studies have found no statistically significant support for either hypothesis (Lenze and Klasen 2013). In Bangladesh, working increased women's exposure to IPV, but only for women who had low education or were married young (Heath 2013). Our DHS analyses show that women's employment increases the odds of IPV exposure by about 25 percent on average, though less for women who work for cash than for those who work "in kind."

There is some evidence of social protection programs being associated with reduced risk of IPV, as we saw in chapter 2. But it is not always the case, and results are highly context specific. Here are some examples:

- In Ecuador, unconditional cash transfers to mothers reduced psychological partner violence against women with greater than primary education, but they were found to increase psychological violence against women with only a primary education or less or when their education level was equal to or higher than their partners' (Hidrobo and Fernald 2013).

- A randomized evaluation in Kenya found that unconditional cash transfers for the poor paid through mobile phones reduced IPV against women by 30 to 50 percent and reduced rape within marriage by 50 to 60 percent, with larger effects when transfers were made to women and larger amounts of money were given (Haushofer and Shapiro 2013).

- A study of Mexico's Oportunidades program found that women who received a cash transfer conditional on their children's attendance at school and health clinics were 40 percent less likely to experience physical abuse. But they were more likely to experience threats of physical harm than women who did not receive a transfer (Bobonis, González-Brenes, and Castro 2013).

How do we explain these apparent contradictions? On the one hand, conditional cash transfers targeted to women could lessen economic stress on the household; increase financial independence; and, through conditions, increase women's exposure to supportive services, such as health centers. In some cases, women's newfound resource control may reduce violence-inducing economic stressors on the household or even open the option to leave an abusive relationship (Farmer and Tiefenthaler 1997).

On the other hand, women's increased control over resources could also challenge traditional gender roles and aggravate violence, particularly when women are disadvantaged from the outset (Bhattacharya, Bedi, and Chhachhi 2009). Property ownership, particularly of land, may give women a more stable and tangible exit option than work or income—and has a range of other benefits, as we see in chapter 5—but may not be sufficient to offset other risk factors.

The mixed results across studies illustrate the complexity of the relationship between women's economic opportunities, cash transfer programs, and violence and underscore the need for careful consideration in program design, a topic to which we return later.

Community environment and norms determine risk

Various factors at the community level have been shown to increase individual women's risk of experiencing IPV. A systematic review of 36 studies from both developing and developed countries highlights socioeconomic disadvantage and residential instability as factors that erode the social fabric, thereby reducing the collective social controls that might otherwise keep violence in check (Perkins and Taylor 1996). In Colombia, high levels of unemployment and poverty in a community can affect the individual likelihood of violence (Pallitto and O'Campo 2005), and community-level norms in Jordan are very influential determinants of individual risk for IPV, alongside measures of women's empowerment. For example, in Jordanian communities with lower mean age at marriage, higher educational differences between spouses, and higher prevalence of polygyny, women are significantly more likely to experience IPV (McCleary-Sills 2013).

Fragility and armed conflict increase risk

Fragility and armed conflict increase women's risk of experiencing IPV and other forms of gender-based violence, including nonpartner rape. Gender-based violence against women and men is a weapon of war used to humiliate, terrorize, punish, and torture both combatants and civilians. A recent review found that in most conflict settings, between one in four and one in three women experience sexual violence (Spangaro et al. 2013), which includes rapes committed systematically by armed groups, rapes that take advantage of weakened policing and governance, and sexual exploitation and abuse (Wood 2006).

The incidence of intimate partner violence also increases in conflict contexts:

■ One of the highest rates of recent IPV recorded is in the Democratic Republic of Congo in 2007, where 64 percent of women reported experiencing physical or sexual IPV in the previous 12 months (Ministère du Plan 2008).

- In the West Bank and Gaza, women whose husbands were exposed to political violence were 89 percent more likely to have been physically abused by their partner (Clark et al. 2010).

- In Liberia, men's perpetration of violence against their partners was significantly associated with exposure to traumatic war-related events (Vinck and Pham 2013).

- In Colombia, the incidence of IPV was more than 12 percentage points higher in areas that had experienced intense conflict (Noe and Rieckmann 2013).

The state of the evidence: What works?

Programmatic and policy approaches to address intimate partner violence range from legislative reform and enforcement of protective laws to media campaigns, community- and school-based programming, and services for survivors. We undertook a systematic review of violence prevention reviews for this book, which concluded that the most promising interventions include multiple components and engage with different audiences and stakeholders (Arango et al., forthcoming). Although no single recipe will bring success across diverse social and geographic contexts, this review and other recent research identify core elements that are essential to prevent IPV and to alleviate its adverse repercussions. Interventions can be broadly grouped under social norm change, legal reform and responses, social support and services, economic empowerment, and integrated approaches.

Before we review what is known about the impacts of selected interventions and what promising approaches these lessons offer, it should be noted that the majority of available evaluation evidence comes from high-income countries. While informative, greater investment in documenting what works in developing countries is needed, particularly with respect to multisectoral interventions to prevent and respond to violence.

Boosting of positive gender norms

Chapter 2 underscored the importance of social norm change for expanding women's agency. Influencing norms is a critical entry point for addressing and challenging the deeply rooted inequalities that perpetuate IPV. Our systematic review of violence prevention reviews found that positive effects were strongest among interventions with elements targeting attitudes toward the acceptability of IPV, gendered expectations, and definitions of masculinity (Arango et al., forthcoming). This requires understanding which attitudes are most directly linked with violence and identifying potential levers of change, including community, opinion, and religious leaders.

In social contexts where IPV is not an accepted norm, fewer women report experiencing violence. As our analyses showed, women who condoned wife beating were more likely to be subject to violence. Although acceptance of wife beating is widespread globally, it is not an attitude held by the majority of people. Across 66 countries for which we have data, including several high-income countries, on average 75 percent of people feel that wife beating cannot be justified for any of five reasons: (a) if a wife goes out without telling her husband, (b) if she neglects their children, (c) if she argues with her husband, (d) if she refuses him sex, or (e) if she burns the food. However, variation exists across countries, and all of the countries surveyed demonstrated some degree of justification, ranging from less than 5 percent in Colombia, the Dominican Republic, Nepal, and Ukraine to rates exceeding 75 percent in Guinea, Mali, and Timor-Leste.

IMAGES data show that in the Democratic Republic of Congo, India, and Rwanda, all countries with high levels of IPV, most men agreed with the statement that a woman should tolerate violence to keep the family together. And that attitude is not isolated to men. Indeed, a recent review of 23 studies measuring IPV justification found that women tended to report a higher rate of violence justification than did men (Waltermauer 2012). A multicountry study of more than 10,000 men revealed that their most frequently cited reasons for committing

rape included sexual entitlement (73 percent), entertainment (59 percent), and as a punishment (38 percent) (Jewkes et al. 2013). Younger respondents also tend to report a higher rate of justification than did older respondents, underscoring that much more work is needed to change norms and attitudes among youth.

Figure 3.6 shows country variation in women's acceptance of violence, which falls among older age cohorts. In developing countries, 17 percent of female respondents in Latin American and the Caribbean, 25 percent in East Asia and the Pacific, and 40 percent in South Asia justify wife beating for at least one reason.

Majority opinions and reported attitudes about violence reflect social norms, which are both mirrored in and determined by the legal sanctions against violence. In countries with legislation against domestic violence, women's acceptance of wife beating is lower. Among the 31 countries

FIGURE 3.6   Share of women who condone wife beating, by age of respondent

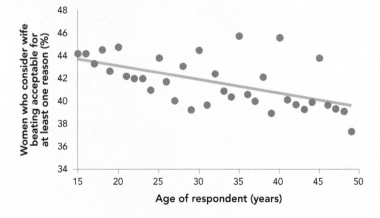

Source: Estimates based on Demographic and Health Surveys for 55 countries using data, 2001–12.

with such legislation, 40 percent of women condone domestic violence compared with 57 percent of women in the 12 countries in the sample without such legislation.[9]

The need to engage men and boys in interventions to promote positive norms around gender equality and to sensitize men to the repercussions of violence is receiving greater attention. Some key findings were highlighted in chapter 2. A variety of approaches have been used—social marketing, awareness campaigns, and edutainment (for example, themed television shows, radio programs, and theater)—as ways to reach a large number of people with messages about violence. But the message matters. A quasi-experimental evaluation of a mass media campaign in the United States found mixed results: among women, the perception of violence as severe, awareness of support services, and belief in services' effectiveness all increased. However, the result among men was the inverse: their perception of violence as severe actually fell by a wider margin (Keller, Wilkinson, and Otgen 2010).

Male engagement interventions have achieved attitudinal changes and decreases in self-reported use of violence. These interventions cover a diverse range of settings and approaches, from workplace training sessions to community-based dialogues and campaigns anchored in sports events (Instituto Promundo 2012). In Chile, educational workshops for young men on gender equality and the prevention of violence against women increased their knowledge about different forms of violence and their intention to reject violence against women.

Research suggests that messaging that promotes and reinforces positive norms—such as showing men modeling equitable and nonviolent behaviors—may be more effective in reaching men than messages condemning violence (Instituto Promundo 2012). Such messages promote the positive aspects of doing "the right thing" rather than asserting fear or shame for doing the wrong thing. And they give visibility to nonviolent, gender-equitable men who can be models of positive behavior. Evidence from Oxfam's "We Can" campaign in five countries showed that combined efforts of communication campaigns with activities by community change agents have the greatest success in changing attitudes and behaviors (Rajan and Chakrabarty 2010).

Another promising example is Soul City in South Africa. The initiative included the use of prime-time radio and television dramas and print materials to portray role models with positive attitudes and behaviors, including help-seeking and help-giving actions. Domestic violence was a major focus of the campaign. A pretest-posttest evaluation found that the intervention was associated with a 10 percent increase in respondents disagreeing that domestic violence was a private affair and a 41 percent increase in awareness of the domestic violence hotline. Notably, the intervention was specifically designed to support implementation of the national Domestic Violence Act by promoting widespread awareness of the protections and consequences defined in the new law, as well as offering greater access to necessary support services (Usdin et al. 2005). Additionally, research suggests that men can often underestimate the disapproval of both women and men of gender-based violent behaviors. Consequently, providing men with more accurate normative information can be effective in changing behaviors and attitudes toward violence by countering the misperception that such violence is widely accepted by their peers (Fabiano et al. 2003).

Community mobilization has been used to address rigid gender norms and attitudes, engaging and educating the wider community, including men and boys, on issues such as human rights, gendered power dynamics, reporting, political participation, and laws. One prominent example is SASA!, an approach developed and implemented in Uganda to transform gender relations and power dynamics and to address HIV and violence against women (see box 3.4).[10] Several factors explain the success of SASA!, including the careful theory-based and culturally tailored design and engagement of opinion leaders and the entire community. Intervention length is also important. The

global systematic review undertaken for this book confirmed that short-term and one-off interventions are less likely to show positive effects (Arango et al., forthcoming). Out of 26 interventions with a less than one-month duration that included violence prevention as an outcome, only one showed a statistically significant positive result. Although the duration and intensity of interventions appear to be important to their effectiveness, most evaluated interventions are short term. These findings emphasize that duration and intensity matter, particularly when it comes to changing deep-seated norms and behaviors.

Legal reform and responses

Ending gender-based violence depends on the commitment of states to enact and implement effective and gender-equitable

---

Box 3.4 Mobilizing communities against violence: Lessons from SASA!

SASA!, which means "Now!" in Kiswahili, is a program developed by Raising Voices and implemented in Uganda by the Center for Domestic Violence Prevention. It is the first community-based violence prevention program in Sub-Saharan Africa to be rigorously evaluated. The program employs multiple strategies to build a critical mass of engaged community members, leaders, and institutions, including local activism, media and advocacy, communication materials, and training. The Activist Kit that is central to SASA! community engagement and mobilization involves four phases: Start, Awareness, Support, and Action. The content evolves with each phase, with power as a central theme. Results from a randomized controlled trial show positive effects after almost three years of programming. Compared with control communities, people in SASA! communities have more gender-equitable attitudes and a reduced prevalence of past-year physical violence by an intimate partner. Compared with control communities, SASA! communities report the following striking results:

> Levels of past-year IPV are 52 percent lower.

> Twenty-eight percent more women and 31 percent more men believe it is acceptable for women to refuse sex.

> Social acceptance of IPV is 87 percent lower among men and 46 percent lower among women.

Source: Abramsky et al. 2014.

prevention and response mechanisms, including prohibitions, policies, and services. International attention has been growing since the early 1990s, as evidenced by several key global norms and movements. The 1993 World Conference on Human Rights recognized violence against women as a human rights violation. That same year, the Declaration on the Elimination of Violence against Women was the first international instrument to address violence against women explicitly, providing a framework for national and international action. The landmark 1994 International Conference on Population and Development called on governments to take legal and policy measures to prevent and respond to violence against women and girls.[11]

The international momentum to address violence has been reflected in national legislative reforms, especially over the past decade, as shown in figure 3.7. Three-quarters of the 100 countries included in *Women, Business, and the Law 2014* criminalize domestic violence and almost four-fifths (79) have legislation addressing sexual harassment in employment. But only 8 out of 100 countries have legislation against harassment in public places (World Bank and IFC 2013).

However, as shown in map 3.2, only 38 of these 100 countries have introduced specific laws or provisions that explicitly criminalize marital rape and sexual assault within marriage. In the 62 countries with no specific legislation, marital rape can still be tried under general rape legislation unless a spousal exemption provision exists. In Ghana, the spousal exemption was removed in 2007, and marital rape can now be prosecuted under the criminal code. Conversely, in Kenya and Malawi, marital

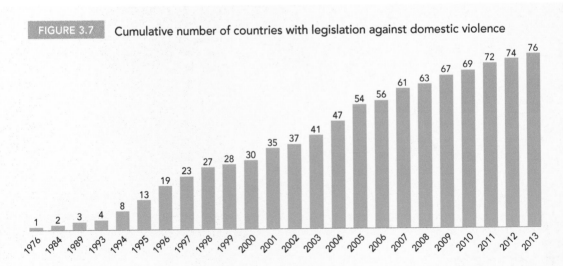

FIGURE 3.7   Cumulative number of countries with legislation against domestic violence

Source: World Bank and IFC 2013.

MAP 3.2   Countries with specific legislation criminalizing marital rape

Is there a specific marital rape law or provision?
■ Yes   ■ No   ■ No data

Source: World Bank, Women, Business, and the Law (database), http://wbl.worldbank.org/.

Note: According to the methodology used, which considers the laws governing the main business city of a country, the United States does not meet the criteria for having specific legislation or provisions criminalizing marital rape because New York state removed the marital exemption but has not yet introduced specific legislation criminalizing marital rape.

rape is exempt from criminal rape legislation and is not even considered a crime. The same is true in India, even after the recent reforms to respond to the Delhi bus rape and murder. The United Kingdom also removed the exemption for spousal rape from general legislation in 1991, but it has not yet introduced specific provisions or legislation.

Intimate partner violence remains outside the law in many countries, and in some cases, it is explicitly allowed. The Supreme Court of the United Arab Emirates ruled in 2010, for example, that a man has the right to physically discipline his wife as long as he does not leave physical marks (Elsaidi 2011).

Where laws do exist, better enforcement is critical and depends on several factors, including the capacity, training, and attitudes of police and legal personnel. Recent research from South Asia casts important light on some common challenges within the justice system. In India, nearly all police officers interviewed (94 percent) agreed that a husband is allowed to rape his wife. And judges in Bangladesh and India typically felt women abused by their spouses were partly to blame (Khan, Bhuiya, and Bhattacharya 2010). In Nepal, less than 5 percent of the police force is female, and in India, an overwhelming majority of police officers still view domestic violence as a private affair. Failure to prosecute remains a significant barrier to women accessing justice in many countries, including in Guatemala, where of the more than 20,000 cases of femicide and domestic violence filed in 2011, fewer than 3 percent of those that reached the courts resulted in a judgment (Musalo and Bookey 2013).

A well-functioning justice system, with appropriate sanctions against violence against women, can help deter future violence and is an important element of prevention efforts.

> *"A lot of men don't want to get on the wrong side of the police. So for a lot of them, when there's a court order, it's a deterrent."*
>
> —Female community member, Port Moresby, Papua New Guinea (Mukasa et al. 2014)

While legal reform and responses are a key entry point for increasing women's agency in this domain, it is clear that law alone is insufficient to prevent violence. Our analysis of DHS data points to the existence of national laws as an important protective factor: women who live in countries with domestic violence legislation have 7 percent lower odds of experiencing violence compared with women in countries without such laws.[12] Analysis also shows that each additional year that a country has had domestic violence legislation in place is associated with a reduced prevalence of about 2 percent. Although this finding underscores the promise of legislative reform as a preventive measure, alone it is not enough to eliminate violence.

In the Pacific, legislative reform and investment in response structures are bringing improvements in women's access to justice. The recent reforms in Papua New Guinea are promising (box 3.5).

Social support and services

The needs of women who experience violence depend greatly on their circumstances, their social and legal context, and their own desired outcomes. Services for survivors broadly fall into four domains (Mukasa et al. 2014):

- Physical health—medical care, safe housing, food, and clothing

---

Box 3.5 Increasing women's access to justice in Papua New Guinea

In Papua New Guinea, a Family Protection Bill was introduced to parliament in 2013 after extensive and inclusive stakeholder consultation. This effort was accompanied by the establishment of specialized Family and Sexual Violence Units and survivor-centered training to duty bearers and service providers, and prosecution efforts were strengthened through the creation of a Family and Sexual Offense Unit to support legal staff and to improve case management. The early results are promising. The number of female magistrates rose from 10 in 2004 to more than 900 in 2013. Since 2012, a record number of intimate partner violence cases have been heard in Papua New Guinea's courts, with two out of three resulting in a conviction or guilty plea. Of recent note are two landmark sexual violence cases involving police officers who received combined sentences of 30 years' imprisonment.

Sources: Mukasa et al. 2014; Office of the Public Prosecution 2012.

- Mental health—therapeutic and trauma counseling, building of self-efficacy and self-confidence, and reduction of internalized stigma

- Legal aid—literacy, advocacy, and filing of key documents

- Economic support—securing of land and property, employment, and income-generating activities

Such services are typically short term and are delivered by civil society groups and trained professionals. The primary aim may be to help stabilize survivors so they can file a claim and pursue a case. The evidence that these efforts improve women's psychological functioning is limited, suggesting that more substantial and repeated therapeutic interventions may be needed (Sims, Yost, and Abbott 2006). Emerging evidence from trials of longer-term and group-based interventions with survivors reveals promising models for improving coping skills, reducing symptoms of depression and post-traumatic stress disorder, and increasing self-efficacy (Bass 2013; Cohen 2013). World Bank funding in the Solomon Islands will support improved access to and quality of services for survivors of violence, as outlined in box 3.6.

As highlighted earlier, most survivors of violence never report or seek help, a gap that needs to be overcome. This gap highlights the importance of efforts to increase help-seeking behavior for health and other social services (Gulliver et al. 2012). The limited evidence about what works to increase help-seeking behavior has identified some promising areas, including grassroots outreach, secondary responder programs, and mass and interpersonal communication efforts. Community outreach workers who share health information can build trust with women in the community and can encourage help-seeking behaviors (Greene, Ennett, and Ringwalt 1999; Kelly et al. 2007). To date, however, evidence about effectiveness for prevention is lacking. Secondary responder programs pair a victim advocate with a police officer to meet with a victim and share information on services and legal options, as well as to warn the perpetrator of the consequences of continued abuse. Eight of 10 experimental or quasi-experimental studies, all in the

---

Box 3.6 Coordinated support for survivors of violence in the Solomon Islands

In the Solomon Islands, 64 percent of women have experienced physical or sexual partner violence or both. A World Bank grant supported the government's efforts to improve access to services for survivors by bringing together specialized organizations in a forum that allowed them to identify gaps and priority actions in supporting victims of violence.

As a next step, the grant will deliver a pilot project to strengthen frontline response and help coordinate referral services. Service providers will also be trained in sensitive and timely responses to the needs of survivors of violence. Finally, the project will help the government undertake a diagnostic study on capacity constraints in the institutions and services, and it will support training and data collection.

Source: Improving Services for Victims of Gender-Based Violence Project (CGAP13-16).

United States, found that such interventions increased the number of subsequent calls to the police, though there was no evidence of actual reductions in of violence (Davis, Weisburd, and Taylor 2008). And such interventions have limited scope since they are designed only for survivors who report violence in the first place.

Schools and workplaces can disseminate information by placing materials in safe and accessible locations (such as restrooms), distributing newsletters, and holding informational sessions. Awareness-raising campaigns and activities may help break the culture of silence and stigmatization around violence and urge survivors to seek help.

Innovative information and communication technology tools can play a role. In 2013, the World Bank Group supported two hackathons aimed at developing tools to respond to or prevent gender-based violence. The first encompassed countries in Latin America and the second focused on Nepal. A number of different mobile applications were developed, including an app for women who have experienced violence that provides information and resources on obtaining support, as well as an app that allows the user to notify friends or family if she or he is in a threatening situation (World Bank 2013).

Internet-based tools (for example, Internet Resources and Information for Safety [IRIS]) and a smartphone app (MyPlan) aim to increase safety-seeking behaviors by reducing survivors' decisional conflict about safety in their relationship. While the results of the impact evaluations are not yet available, preliminary findings are promising, showing that after even just one use, survivors have greater clarity about where and how to seek help and

less uncertainty about doing so. Increasing help-seeking behavior is a critical first step toward improving the response mechanisms and ensuring justice for survivors. These broad types of services are essential for women's well-being and should be integrated into service provision efforts for survivors of violence.

Economic empowerment (plus)

Increasing women's economic opportunities can be an important entry point for expanding their ability to prevent and leave violent relationships. Yet programs to promote economic opportunities rarely take the risks of violence systematically into account, and impact evaluations of effects on violence are rare. But emerging evidence suggests that economic empowerment and social protection interventions by themselves can have significant effects on IPV, depending on the nature of the program, the population, and the context. Interventions may be able to expand both women's economic opportunities and their agency by adding strategic design features that intentionally address gender-based violence (Schuler et al. 1996). We refer to this approach as "economic empowerment plus" and it has shown success in several African countries.

The IMAGE (Intervention with Microfinance for AIDS and Gender Equity) program in rural South Africa combined microcredit with participatory gender training, social support groups, and community mobilization. The results are encouraging (Pronyk et al. 2006, 2008):

- IPV fell by 55 percent
- Household poverty rates fell
- HIV-related communication improved, as did social capital

In Côte d'Ivoire, a group savings intervention combined with "gender dialogue groups" led to significant reductions in women's reports of economic abuse and their acceptance of wife beating compared with women who participated in only group savings meetings (Gupta et al. 2013). Women who attended more than 75 percent of sessions with their male partner were also less likely to report physical IPV. In Uganda, a vocational training program—paired with safe spaces for young women's interactions and information on health and risky behaviors—reduced the share of young women experiencing forced sex from 21 percent to nearly zero, while also increasing engagement in income-generating activities by 35 percent (Bandiera et al. 2012).

These evaluations hint at ways to promote agency in economic programs, but the overall evidence base is still too thin to determine the active ingredients of "economic empowerment plus" interventions for reducing violence. Promising components include gender and health training, ongoing groups that facilitate social support, safe spaces to interact with peers, community mobilization, and, in some cases, elements that engage male partners to encourage more equitable relationship dynamics as women's economic empowerment increases. Further testing of which combinations work best and under what circumstances is needed, as are analysis and scaling up.

Integration of violence prevention into other sectoral interventions

Violence is a complex issue, and consequences have adverse ripple effects on other spheres of an individual survivor's life, as well as effects on her family and community.

Greater access by women and girls to public spaces can enhance agency by increasing educational attainment, economic opportunities, and mobility. However with such opportunities may come risks of being exposed to violence. Evidence indicates that structural interventions—which aim to make environments safer and to interrupt the cycle of violence before it begins—offer promising lessons for prevention (Beyer, Wallis, and Hamberger 2013). Among these lessons are efforts to improve the safety of public spaces for women and children, including investments in lighting, safe transit, and safer, more gender-equitable school environments.

Preventing childhood exposure to and direct experience of violence is critical to break the intergenerational cycles of violence (Renner and Slack 2006). Chapters 1 and 2 have already highlighted the critical role of education. Recent reviews show some evidence of effective interventions, including in developing countries (Knerr, Gardner, and Cluver 2011; Mikton and Butchart 2009). Evidence from "girl-friendly" schools shows that adjusting the physical school environment can dramatically improve girls' attendance, retention, and achievement. Changes included the construction of sex-segregated latrines, clean water supplies, and an array of outreach activities to promote girls' education. In Burkina Faso, girls' enrollment increased by 5 percentage points over that of their male classmates (Kazianga et al. 2013). Both girls and boys showed improved test scores in the intervention schools, pointing to positive effects for boys and increasing their likelihood of school completion.

The fear, threat, and experience of violence are often obstacles to women's and

Box 3.7 Integrating responses to violence: Innovations in a transport project in Brazil

As part of a broader effort to develop a regional master plan for the metropolitan transport system, the government of Rio de Janeiro is looking to use trains and cable cars that connect many hillside shantytowns to increase access to job opportunities. With a loan from the World Bank, the government has integrated gender-responsive legal, social, and economic services within this system. The program will support the establishment of Women Reference and Service Centers—one-stop shops that will provide services, referrals, and information for survivors of violence. Electronic public information is used to promote the national law against domestic violence. Sustainable transport links to the Brazilian Women's House—a federal program that assembles several public services for women—will also be established as part of the effort. In addition, a women's police station, a women's clinic, and a child care center will be established. The project will also finance dissemination of information on improved security for women riders. Finally, the program will pilot vocational education and training for women who are at risk of violence.

Source: Urban Mass Transport: Gender Agency and Inclusion Project (P147695).

girls' engagement in civic, political, and economic spheres (Whitzman et al. 2013). Efforts to improve urban environments' safety for women and girls have included enhancements to police protocols and procedures, help lines, and efforts to promote bystander intervention (Bhatla et al. 2012). The World Bank is also investing in efforts to prevent and respond to violence through projects in other sectors, such as an innovative transport project in Brazil (box 3.7), to reduce the risk of violence.

* * *

Violence is one of the most pronounced manifestations of gender inequality across the globe. Addressing violence is critical for promoting women's agency and for a range of other gender outcomes and development goals. But violence is perpetuated by social norms and institutions that implicitly or explicitly condone this behavior. This means that eliminating violence requires appropriate prevention strategies, as well as response mechanisms that prioritize the needs of survivors. Effective approaches are likely to target multiple entry points—improved laws and policies, more gender-equitable attitudes, and safer social environments. This effort also requires better data for decision making. One recent advance is the international agreement on standard indicators for measuring violence against women, which will provide much-needed data on prevalence as well as monitoring of efforts to reduce violence, as discussed in chapter 7.

Notes

1. Calculations using data from *World Population Prospects* (United Nations 2013).

2. Our sample covered 40 percent of the world's population (50 percent if China is excluded). The variable analyzed here is the share of women who agree that wife beating is justified for at least one of five reasons: (a) going out without permission, (b) burning food, (c) neglecting children, (d) refusing sex, and (e) arguing with a husband.

3. Data are from the World Bank Group and International Finance Corporation database on Women, Business, and the Law, available at http://wbl.worldbank.org/.

4. They include (a) Resolution 1325, which recognizes the impact of conflict on women and girls, particularly their vulnerability to sexual violence; (b) Resolution 1820, calling for an end to sexual violence and recognizing sexual violence as a weapon of war; (c) Resolution 1888, which calls for strengthened leadership to end sexual violence, and (d) Regulation 1960, calling for the involvement of women and civil society organizations in implementing Resolution 1325 and establishing tools for action, monitoring, and reporting.

5. This definition is from the Council of Europe Convention on Preventing and Combating Violence against Women and Domestic Violence. The full text of the convention is available at http://conventions.coe.int/Treaty/EN/Treaties/Html/210.htm.

6. The correlation is $rs = 0.71$ (37), $p < 0.001$.

7. Figures are from our analysis of DHS data, available for 24 countries.

8. The findings were as follows: odds ratio of 0.89, 95 percent confidence interval: 0.80–0.97. See Fleming et al. (2013).

9. These population-weighted medians were calculated from DHS data.

10. For more information, see the Raising Voices website at http://raisingvoices.org/sasa/#tabs-419-0-3.

11. For more information about the conference, see the website of the United Nations Entity for Gender Equality and the Empowerment of Women at http://www.unwomen.org/en/what-we-do/ending-violence-against-women/global-norms-and-standards.

12. The countries that had both DHS data on domestic violence and data on legislation from the World Bank were Azerbaijan, Burkina Faso, Cameroon, Colombia, Côte d'Ivoire, Ghana, Haiti, Honduras, India, Kenya, Malawi, Mozambique, Nepal, Nigeria, Peru, the Philippines, Tanzania, Uganda, Ukraine, Zambia, and Zimbabwe.

References

Abramsky, Tanya, Karen Devries, Ligia Kiss, Janet Nakuti, Nambusi Kyegombe, Elizabeth Starmann, Bonnie Cundill, Leilani Francisco, Dan Kaye, Tina Musuya, Lori Michau, and Charlotte Watts. 2014. "Findings from the SASA! Study: A Cluster Randomized Controlled Trial to Assess the Impact of a Community Mobilization Intervention to Prevent Violence against Women and Reduce HIV Risk in Kampala, Uganda." *BMC Medicine* 12:122.

Agarwal, Bina, and Pradeep Panda. 2007. "Toward Freedom from Domestic Violence: The Neglected Obvious." *Journal of Human Development* 8 (3): 359–88.

Arango, Diana J., Matthew Morton, Floriza Gennari, Sveinung Kiplesund, and Mary Ellsberg. Forthcoming. "Interventions to Prevent and Reduce Violence against Women and Girls: A Systematic Review of Reviews." Women's Voice, Agency and Participation Research Series, World Bank, Washington, DC.

Bandiera, Oriana, Niklas Buehren, Robin Burgess, Markus Goldstein, Selim Gulesci, Imran Rasul, and Munshi Sulaiman. 2012. "Empowering Adolescent Girls: Evidence from a Randomized Control Trial in Uganda." London School of Economics and Political Science, London. http://econ.lse.ac.uk/staff/rburgess/wp/ELA.pdf.

Barker, Gary, Juan Manuel Contreras, Brian Heilman, Ajay Singh, Ravi Verma, and Marcos Nascimento. 2011. *Evolving Men: Initial Results from the International Men and Gender Equality Survey (IMAGES)*. Washington, DC, and Rio de Janeiro: International Center for Research on Women and Instituto Promundo.

Bass, Judith. 2013. "Group Cognitive Processing Therapy: A Specialized Mental Health Intervention That Supports Improvements in Well-Being for Sexual Violence Survivors." Presented at the Sexual Violence Research Initiative Forum, Bangkok, October 16.

Beydoun, Hind A., May A. Beydoun, Jay S. Kaufman, Bruce Lo, and Alan B. Zonderman. 2012. "Intimate Partner Violence against Adult Women and Its Association with Major Depressive Disorder, Depressive Symptoms, and Postpartum Depression: A Systematic Review and Meta-analysis." *Social Science and Medicine* 75 (6): 959–75.

Beyer, Kirsten, Anne Baber Wallis, and L. Kevin Hamberger. 2013. "Neighborhood Environment and Intimate Partner Violence: A Systematic Review." *Trauma Violence Abuse*, December 26.

Bhatla, Nandita, Pranita Achyut, Sancheeta Ghosh, Abhishek Gautam, and Ravi Verma. 2012. "Safe Cities Free from Violence against Women and Girls: Baseline Finding from the 'Safe Cities Delhi Programme.'" UN Women, New Delhi.

Bhattacharya, Manasi, Arjun S. Bedi, and Amrita Chhachhi. 2009. "Marital Violence and Women's Employment and Property Status: Evidence from North Indian Villages." Discussion Paper 4361, Institute for the Study of Labor, Bonn.

Bobonis, Gustavo J., Melissa González-Brenes, and Roberto Castro. 2013. "Public Transfers and Domestic Violence: The Roles of Private Information and Spousal Control." *American Economic Journal: Economic Policy* 5 (1): 179–205.

Bonomi, Amy E., Melissa L. Anderson, Frederick P. Rivara, and Robert S. Thompson. 2009. "Health Care Utilization and Costs Associated with Physical and Nonphysical-Only Intimate Partner Violence." *Health Services Research* 44 (3): 1054–67.

Bott, Sara, Alessandra Guedes, Mary Goodwin, and Jennifer Adams Mendoza. 2013. *Violence against Women in Latin America and the Caribbean: A Comparative Analysis of Population-Based Data from 12 Countries*. Washington, DC: Pan American Health Organization.

Brown, DeNeen L., and Ashley Surdin. 2009. "Chris Brown Pleads Guilty to Assault." *Washington Post*, June 23. http://www .washingtonpost.com/wp-dyn/content /article/2009/06/22/AR2009062200452 .html?wprss=rss_print/style.

Buvinic, Mayra, Andrew Morrison, and Michael Shifter. 1999. "Violence in Latin America and the Caribbean: A Framework for Action." Sustainable Development Department, Inter-American Development Bank, Washington, DC.

Campbell, Jacquelyn C. 2002. "Health Consequences of Intimate Partner Violence." *The Lancet* 359 (9314): 1331–36.

Campbell, Jacquelyn C., Daniel Webster, Jane Koziol-McLain, Carolyn Block, Doris Campbell, Mary Ann Curry, Faye Gary, Nancy Glass, Judith McFarlane, Carolyn Sachs, Phyllis Sharps, Yvonne Ulrich, Susan A. Wilt, Jennifer Manganello, Xiao Xu, Janet Schollenberger, Victoria Frye, and Kathryn Laughon. 2003. "Risk Factors for Femicide in Abusive Relationships: Results from a Multisite Case Control Study." *American Journal of Public Health* 93 (7): 1089–97.

Campbell, Jacquelyn C., Anne B. Woods, Kathryn Laughon Chouaf, and Barbara Parker. 2000. "Reproductive Health Consequences of Intimate Partner Violence: A Nursing Research Review." *Clinical Nursing Research* 9 (3): 217–37.

Clark, Cari Jo, Susan A. Everson-Rose, Shakira Franco Suglia, Rula Btoush, Alvaro Alonzo, and Muhammad M. Haj-Yahia. 2010. "Association between Exposure to Political Violence and Intimate-Partner Violence in the Occupied Palestinian Territory: A Cross-Sectional Study." 2010. *The Lancet* 375 (9711): 310–16.

Cloitre, Marylene, Bradley C. Stolbach, Judith L. Herman, Bessel van der Kolk, Robert Pynoos, Jing Wang, and Eva Petkova. 2009. "A Developmental Approach to Complex PTSD: Childhood and Adult Cumulative Trauma as Predictors of Symptom Complexity." 2009. *Journal of Traumatic Stress* 22 (5): 399–408.

Cohen, Rachel A. 2013. "Common Threads: A Recovery Programme for Survivors of Gender Based Violence." 2013. *Intervention* 11 (2): 157–68.

Coker, Ann L., James E. Ferguson, Heather M. Bush, Carol Jordan, and Leslie Crofford. 2008. "Intimate Partner Violence and Gynecologic Health: Focus on Women in Kentucky." Presented at the American Public Health Association Annual Meeting and Expo, San Diego, October 29.

Commission on the Status of Women. 2013. "Agreed Conclusions on the Elimination and Prevention of All Forms of Violence against Women and Girls." UN Women, New York. http://www.un.org/womenwatch/daw/csw/csw57/CSW57_Agreed_Conclusions_(CSW_report_excerpt).pdf.

Coomaraswamy, Radhika. 1999. "Integration of Human Rights of Women and the Gender Perspective: Violence against Women." Report of the Special Rapporteur on Violence against Women, Its Causes and Consequences, Addendum: Communications to and from Governments, United Nations, New York.

Davis, Robert C., David Weisburd, and Bruce Taylor. 2008. "Effects of Second Responder Programs on Repeat Incidents of Family Abuse: A Systematic Review." Australian Institute of Criminology, Canberra.

Day, Tanis, Katherine McKenna, and Audra Bowlus. 2005. "The Economic Costs of Violence against Women: An Evaluation of the Literature." Expert brief compiled in preparation for the secretary-general's in-depth study on all forms of violence against women, University of Western Ontario, London.

Duvvury, Nata, Aoife Callan, Patrick Carney, and Srinivas Raghavendra. 2013. "Intimate Partner Violence: Economic Costs and Implications for Growth and Development." 2013. Women's Voice, Agency, and Participation Research Paper 3, World Bank, Washington, DC.

Duvvury, Nata, Huu Minh Nguyen, and Patricia Carney. 2012. *Estimating the Cost of Domestic Violence against Women in Viet Nam.* Hanoi: UN Women.

Eijkemans, Gerry. 2013. "Breaking the Cycle: Addressing the Intersections between Violence against Women and Violence against Children." Pan American Health Organization, Washington, DC. http://www.unicef.org/easterncaribbean/ECAO_Addressing_the_intersections_between_Violence_againist_Women_and_Children.pdf.

Ellsberg, Mary, Brian Heilman, Sophie Namy, Manuel Contreras, and Robin Hayes. 2011. "Violence against Women in Melanesia and Timor-Leste: Progress Made since the 2008 Office of Development Effectiveness Report." Australian Agency for International Development, Canberra.

Ellsberg, Mary, and Lori Heise. 2005. *Researching Violence against Women: A Practical Guide for Researchers and Activists.* Washington, DC: World Health Organization and Program for Appropriate Technology in Health.

Elsaidi, Murad H. 2011. "Human Rights and Islamic Law: A Legal Analysis Challenging the Husband's Authority to Punish 'Rebellious' Wives." *Muslim World Journal of Human Rights* 7 (2): 1–25.

Ergöçmen, Banu Akadli, İlknur Yüksel-Kaptanoğlu, and Henrica A. F. M. Jansen. 2013. "Intimate Partner Violence and the Relation between Help-Seeking Behavior and the Severity and Frequency of Physical Violence among Women in Turkey." *Violence against Women* 19 (9): 1151–74.

EU (European Union) Agency for Fundamental Rights. 2014. *Violence against Women: An EU-Wide Survey.* Vienna, Austria: EU Agency for Fundamental Rights.

Fabiano, Patricia M., H. Wesley Perkins, Alan Berkowitz, Jeff Linkenbach, and Christopher Stark. 2003. "Engaging Men as Social Justice Allies in Ending Violence against Women: Evidence for a Social Norms Approach." *Journal of American College Health* 52 (3): 105–12.

Farmer, Amy, and Jill Tiefenthaler. 1997. "An Economic Analysis of Domestic Violence." *Review of Social Economy* 55 (3): 337–58.

Fleming, Paul J., Gary Barker, Jennifer McCleary-Sills, and Matthew Morton. 2013. "Engaging Men and Boys in Advancing Women's Agency: Where We Stand and New Directions." Women's Voice, Agency, and Participation Research Paper 1, World Bank, Washington, DC.

Follette, Victoria M., Melissa A. Polusny, Anne E. Bechtle, and Amy E. Naugle. 1996. "Cumulative Trauma: The Impact of Child Sexual Abuse, Adult Sexual Assault, and Spouse Abuse." *Journal of Traumatic Stress* 9 (1): 25–35.

Frías, Sonia M. 2013. "Strategies and Help-Seeking Behavior among Mexican Women Experiencing Partner Violence." *Violence against Women* 19 (1): 24–49.

Fugate, Michelle, Leslie Landis, Kim Riordan, Sara Naureckas, and Barbara Engel. 2005. "Barriers to Domestic Violence Help Seeking: Implications for Intervention." *Violence against Women* 11 (3): 290–310.

Fulu, Emma, Xian Warner, Stephanie Miedema, Rachel Jewkes, Tim Roselli, and James Lang. 2013. *Why Do Some Men Use Violence against Women and How Can We Prevent It? Quantitative Findings from the United Nations Multi-country Study on Men and Violence in Asia and the Pacific.* Bangkok: United Nations Development Programme, United Nations Population Fund, UN Women, and UN Volunteers.

García-Moreno, Claudia, Henrica A. F. M. Jansen, Mary Carroll Ellsberg, Lori Heise, and Charlotte Watts. 2005. *WHO Multi-country Study on Women's Health and Domestic Violence against Women.* Geneva: World Health Organization.

Gee, Rebekah E., Nandita Mitra, Fei Wan, Diana F. Chavkin, and Judith A. Long. 2009. "Power over Parity: Intimate Partner Violence and Issues of Fertility Control." *American Journal of Obstetrics and Gynecology* 201 (2): 148.e1–7.

Gipson, Jessica D., and Michelle J. Hindin. 2007. "'Marriage Means Having Children and Forming Your Family, So What Is the Need of Discussion?' Communication and Negotiation of Childbearing Preferences among Bangladeshi Couples." *Culture, Health, and Sexuality* 9 (2): 185–98.

Granados Shiroma, Marceka. 1996. *Salud reproductiva y violencia contra la mujer: Un análisis desde la perspectiva de género* [Reproductive health and violence against women: A gender perspective]. Nuevo Léon, Mexico: Asociación Mexicana de Población, Colegio de México.

Greene, Jody M., Susan T. Ennett, and Christopher L. Ringwalt. 1999. "Prevalence and Correlates of Survival Sex among Runaway and Homeless Youth." *American Journal of Public Health* 89 (9): 1406–9.

Gulliver, Amelia, Kathleen M. Griffiths, Helen Christensen, and Jacqueline L. Brewer. 2012. "A Systematic Review of Help-Seeking Interventions for Depression, Anxiety and General Psychological Distress." *BMC Psychiatry* 12 (1): 81–92.

Gupta, Geeta Rao, and Ellen Weiss. 1993. "Women's Lives and Sex: Implications for AIDS Prevention." *Culture, Medicine, and Psychiatry* 17 (4): 399–412.

Gupta, Jhumka, Kathryn L. Falb, Heidi Lehmann, Denise Kpebo, Ziming Xuan, Mazeda Hossain, Cathy Zimmerman, Charlotte Watts, and Jeannie Annan. 2013. "Gender Norms and Economic Empowerment Intervention to Reduce Intimate Partner Violence against Women in Rural Côte d'Ivoire: A Randomized Controlled Pilot Study." *BMC International Health and Human Rights* 13 (1): 46.

Guttenbeil-Likiliki, Ofa-Ki-Levuka. 2014. "Pacific Network against Violence against Women and Girls." Presentation at the United Nations 58th Commission on the Status of Women, New York, March 11. https://globalwomensinstitute.gwu.edu /sites/globalwomensinstitute.gwu.edu/files /downloads/WCCC%20Tonga-Likiliki%20 CSW%2003.2014.pdf.

Haushofer, Johannes, and Jeremy Shapiro. 2013. "Policy Brief: Impact of Unconditional Cash Transfers," Innovations for Poverty Action, New Haven, CT.

Heath, Rachel. 2013. "Women's Access to Labor Market Opportunities, Control of Household Resources, and Domestic Violence: Evidence from Bangladesh." *World Development* 57: 32–46.

Heise, Lori, Mary Carroll Ellsberg, and M. Gottemoeller. 1999. "Ending Violence against Women." Population Report, Series L, 11. Baltimore, MD: Johns Hopkins University School of Public Health.

Hidrobo, Melissa, and Lia Fernald. 2013. "Cash Transfers and Domestic Violence." *Journal of Health Economics* 32 (1): 304–19.

High-Level Panel of Eminent Persons on the Post-2015 Development Agenda. 2013. "A New Global Partnership: Eradicate Poverty and Transform Economies through Sustainable Development." United Nations, New York.

Holt, Stephanie, Helen Buckley, and Sadhbh Whelan. 2008. "The Impact of Exposure to Domestic Violence on Children and Young People: A Review of the Literature." *Child Abuse and Neglect* 32 (8): 797–810.

Hope, Ruth. 2007. "Addressing Cross-Generational Sex: A Desk Review of Research and Programs." Population Reference Bureau, Washington, DC.

Horna, Arístides Alfredo Vara. 2013. Los costos empresariales de la violencia contra las mujeres en el Perú: Una estimación del impacto de la violencia contra la mujer en relaciones de pareja en la productividad laboral de las empresas peruanas. Lima, Peru: Deutsche Gesellschaft für Internationale Zusammenarbeit (GIZ).

IASC (Inter-Agency Standing Committee). 2005. *Guidelines for Gender-Based Violence Interventions in Humanitarian Settings: Focusing on Prevention of and Response to Sexual Violence in Emergencies.* Geneva: IASC.

ICRW (International Center for Research on Women). 2000. "Domestic Violence in India: A Summary Report of a Multi-Site Household Survey." ICRW, Washington, DC.

———. 2009. "Intimate Partner Violence: High Costs to Households and Communities." ICRW, Washington, DC.

Instituto Promundo. 2012. "Engaging Men to Prevent Gender-Based Violence: A Multi-country Intervention and Impact Evaluation Study." Instituto Promundo, Washington, DC.

Jejeebhoy, Shireen J. 1998. "Associations between Wife-Beating and Fetal and Infant Death: Impressions from a Survey in Rural India." *Studies in Family Planning* 29 (3): 300–8.

Jewkes, Rachel. 2002. "Intimate Partner Violence: Causes and Prevention." *The Lancet* 359 (9315): 1423–29.

Jewkes, Rachel, Emma Fulu, Tim Roselli, and Claudia García-Moreno. 2013. "Prevalence of and Factors Associated with Non-partner Rape Perpetration: Findings from the UN Multi-Country Cross-Sectional Study on Men and Violence in Asia and the Pacific." *The Lancet Global Health* 1 (4): e208–18.

Kaye, Dan K., Florence M. Mirembe, Grace Bantebya, Annika Johansson, and Anna Mia Ekstrom. 2006. "Domestic Violence as Risk Factor for Unwanted Pregnancy and Induced Abortion in Mulago Hospital, Kampala, Uganda." *Tropical Medicine and International Health* 11 (1): 90–101.

Kazianga, Harounan, Dan Levy, Leigh L. Linden, and Matt Sloan. 2013. "The Effect of 'Girl-Friendly' Schools: Evidence from the BRIGHT School Construction Program in Burkina Faso." *American Economic Journal: Applied Economics* 3 (5): 41–62.

Keller, Sarah N., Timothy Wilkinson, and A. J. Otgen. 2010. "Unintended Effects of a Domestic Violence Campaign." *Journal of Advertising* 39 (4): 53–68.

Kelly, Patricia J., Janna Lesser, Esther Peralez-Dieckmann, and Martha Castilla. 2007. "Community-Based Violence Awareness." *Issues in Mental Health Nursing* 28 (3): 241–53.

Khan, M. E., Ismat Bhuiya, and Aruna Bhattacharya. 2010. "A Situation Analysis of Care and Support for Rape Survivors at First Point of Contact in India and Bangladesh." *Injury Prevention* 16 (suppl. 1): A160–61.

Khawaja, Marwan, and Nadwah Hammoury. 2008. "Coerced Sexual Intercourse within Marriage: A Clinic-Based Study of Pregnant Palestinian Refugees in Lebanon." *Journal of Midwifery and Women's Health* 53 (2):150–54.

Kishor, Sunita. 2005. "Domestic Violence Measurement in the Demographic and Health Surveys: The History and the Challenges." Prepared for the Expert Group Meeting, organized by the United Nations Division for the Advancement of Women, Geneva, April 11–14.

Kishor, Sunita, and Kiersten Johnson. 2004. *Profiling Domestic Violence: A Multi-country Study.* Calverton, MD: ORC Macro.

Knerr, Wendy, Frances Gardner, and Lucie Cluver. 2011. "Parenting and the Prevention of Child Maltreatment in Low- and Middle-Income Countries: A Systematic Review of Interventions and a Discussion of Prevention of the Risks of Future Violent Behaviour among Boys." Sexual Violence Research Initiative, Pretoria.

Lenze, Jana, and Stephan Klasen. 2013. "The Impact of Women's Labour Force Participation on Domestic Violence in Jordan." Discussion Paper 143, Courant Research Centre, Göttingen, Germany.

Lim, Kim C., John Rioux, and Ellen Ridley. 2004. "Impact of Domestic Violence Offenders on Occupational Safety and Health: A Pilot Study." Family Crisis Services and Maine Department of Labor, Augusta.

Logan, T. K., Robert Walker, and Jennifer Cole. 2013. "Silenced Suffering: The Need for a Better Understanding of Partner Sexual Violence." *Trauma Violence Abuse*, published online December 30.

Luke, Nancy. 2003. "Age and Economic Asymmetries in the Sexual Relationships of Adolescent Girls in Sub-Saharan Africa." *Studies in Family Planning* 34 (2): 67–86.

Maman, Suzanne, Jessie K. Mbwambo, Nora M. Hogan, Gad P. Kilonzo, Jacquelyn C. Campbell, Ellen Weiss, and Michael D. Sweat. 2003. "HIV-Positive Women Report More Lifetime Partner Violence: Findings from a Voluntary Counseling and Testing Clinic in Dar es Salaam, Tanzania." *American Journal of Public Health* 92 (8): 1331–37.

McCleary-Sills, Jennifer. 2013. "Jordanian Social Norms and the Risk of Intimate Partner Violence and Limited Reproductive Agency." *Journal of International Women's Studies* 2 (14): 12–29.

McCleary-Sills, Jennifer, Zayid Douglas, Annagrace Rwehumbiza, Aziza Hamisi, and Richard Mabala. 2011. "Vijana Tunaweza Newala: Findings from a Participatory Research and Action Project in Tanzania." International Center for Research on Women, Washington, DC.

———. 2013. "Gendered Norms, Transactional Sex, and Adolescent Pregnancy in Rural Tanzania." *Reproductive Health Matters* 21 (41): 97–105.

McCleary-Sills, Jennifer, Sophie Namy, Joyce Nyoni, Datius Rweyemamu, Adrophina Salvatory, and Ester Steven. 2013.

"Help-Seeking Pathways and Barriers for Survivors of Gender-Based Violence in Tanzania: Results from a Study in Dar es Salaam, Mbeya, and Iringa Regions." EngenderHealth/CHAMPION, Dar es Salaam.

Mikton, Christopher, and Alexander Butchart. 2009. "Child Maltreatment Prevention: A Systematic Review of Reviews." *Bulletin of the World Health Organization* 87 (5): 353–61.

Ministère du Plan. 2008. *République Démocratique du Congo: Enquête démographique et de santé, 2007*. Calverton, MD: Macro International.

Morrison, Andrew R., and Man'a Beatriz Orlando. 1999. "Social and Economic Costs of Domestic Violence: Chile and Nicaragua." In *Too Close to Home: Domestic Violence in the Americas*, edited by Andrew R. Morrison and María Loreto Biehl, 51–67. New York: Inter-American Development Bank.

Mukasa, Stella, Jennifer McCleary-Sills, Brian Heilman, Sophie Namy, Laura Brady, and Shawna Stich. 2014. *Review of Australian Aid Programs in the Pacific Aimed at Ending Violence against Women.* Washington, DC: International Center for Research on Women.

Musalo, Karen, and Blaine Bookey. 2013. "Crimes without Punishment: An Update on Violence against Women and Impunity in Guatemala." *Hastings Race Poverty and Law Journal* 10 (2013): 265–92.

Naved, Ruchira Tabassum, Safia Azim, Abbas Bhuiya, and Lars Åke Persson. 2006. "Physical Violence by Husbands: Magnitude, Disclosure, and Help-Seeking Behavior of Women in Bangladesh." *Social Science and Medicine* 62 (12): 2917–29.

Noe, Dominik, and Johannes Rieckmann. 2013. "Violent Behaviour: The Effect of Civil Conflict on Domestic Violence in Colombia." Discussion Paper 136, Courant Research Centre, Göttingen, Germany.

Office of the Public Prosecution. 2012. "Strongim Gavman Program Internal Progress Report." Australian Agency for International Development, Port Moresby, Papua New Guinea.

Palermo, Tia, Jennifer Bleck, and Amber Peterman. 2014. "Tip of the Iceberg: Reporting and Gender-Based Violence in Developing Countries." *American Journal of Epidemiology* 179 (5): 602–12.

Pallitto, Christina C., and Patricia O'Campo. 2005. "Community Level Effects of Gender Inequality on Intimate Partner Violence and Unintended Pregnancy in Colombia: Testing the Feminist Perspective." *Social Science and Medicine* 10 (60): 2205–16.

Pepin, Joanna. 2013. "Cultural Portrayals of Intimate Partner Violence: Analyzing Media Coverage of Celebrity and Sports' Figures Domestic Violence Relationships." Presented at a seminar at the University of Maryland, College Park, March 6.

Perkins, Douglas D., and Ralph B. Taylor. 1996. "Ecological Assessments of Community Disorder: Their Relationship to Fear of Crime and Theoretical Implications." *American Journal of Community Psychology* 24 (1): 63–107.

Pettifor, Audrey E., Helen V. Rees, Immo Kleinschmidt, Annie E. Steffenson, Catherine MacPhail, Lindiwe Hlongwa-Madikizela, Kerry Vermaak, and Nancy S. Padian. 2005. "Young People's Sexual Health in South Africa: HIV Prevalence and Sexual Behaviors from a Nationally Representative Household Survey." *AIDS* 19 (14): 1525–34.

Pierotti, Rachael S. 2013. "Increasing Rejection of Intimate Partner Violence: Evidence of Global Cultural Diffusion." *American Sociological Review* 78 (2): 240–65.

Pronyk, Paul M., James R. Hargreaves, Julia C. Kim, Linda A. Morison, Godfrey Phetla, Charlotte Watts, Joanna Busza, and John D. H. Porter. 2006. "Effect of a Structural Intervention for the Prevention of Intimate-Partner Violence and HIV in Rural South Africa: A Cluster Randomised Trial." *The Lancet* 368 (9551): 1973–83.

Pronyk, Paul M., Trudy Harpham, Joanna Busza, Godfrey Phetla, Linda A. Morison, James R. Hargreaves, Julia C. Kim, Charlotte H. Watts, and John D. Porter. 2008. "Can Social Capital Be Intentionally Generated? A Randomized Trial from Rural South Africa." *Social Science and Medicine* 67 (10): 1559–70.

Rajan, Anuradha, and Swati Chakrabarty. 2010. *Assessing Change: Regional Report of the Assessment of "We Can" Phase II.* London: Oxfam.

Rani, Manju, and Sekhar Bonu. 2009. "Attitudes toward Wife Beating: A Cross-Country Study in Asia." *Journal of Interpersonal Violence* 24 (8):1371–97.

Rani, Manju, Sekhar Bonu, and Nafissatou Diop-Sidibé. 2004. "An Empirical Investigation of Attitudes towards Wife-Beating among Men and Women in Seven Sub-Saharan African Countries." *African Journal of Reproductive Health* 8 (3): 116–36.

Renner, Lynette M., and Kirsten Shook Slack. 2006. "Intimate Partner Violence and Child Maltreatment: Understanding Intra- and Intergenerational Connections." *Child Abuse and Neglect* 30 (6): 599–617.

Roth, Susan, Elena Newman, David Pelcovitz, and Francine S. Mandel. 1997. "Complex PTSD in Victims Expose to Sexual and Physical Abuse: Results from the DSM-IV Field Trial for Posttraumatic Stress Disorder." *Journal of Traumatic Stress* 10 (4): 539–55.

Santos, Cristina. 2013. "Costs of Domestic Violence: A Life Satisfaction Approach." *Fiscal Studies* 34 (3): 391–409.

Sarkar, N. N. 2008. "Barriers to Condom Use." *European Journal of Contraception and Reproductive Health Care* 13 (2): 114–22.

Schuler, Sydney Ruth, Syed M. Hashemi, Ann P. Riley, and Shireen Akhter. 1996. "Credit Programs, Patriarchy, and Men's Violence against Women in Rural Bangladesh." *Social Science and Medicine* 43 (12): 1729–42.

Sims, Barbara, Berwood Yost, and Christina Abbott. 2006. "The Efficacy of Victim Services Programs: Alleviating the Psychological Suffering of Crime Victims?" *Criminal Justice Policy Review* 17 (4): 387–406.

Singh, Smriti. 2013. "Delhi Gang Rape: Case Diary." *Times of India*, September 13, http://articles.timesofindia.indiatimes.com/2013-09-13/india/41936569_1_mount-elizabeth-hospital-delhi-hc-safdurjung-hospital.

Spangaro, Jo, Anthony Zwi, Chinelo Adogu, Geetha Ranmuthugala, Gawaine Powell Davies, and Léa Steinacker. 2013. *What Is the Evidence of the Impact of Initiatives to Reduce Risk and Incidence of Sexual Violence in Conflict and Post-conflict Zones and Other Humanitarian Crises in Lower- and Middle-Income Countries?* London: EPPI-Centre, Social Science Research Unit, Institute of Education, University of London.

Stöckl, Heidi, Karen Devries, Alexandra Rotstein, Naeemah Abrahams, Jacquelyn C. Campbell, Charlotte Watts, and Claudia García-Moreno. 2013. "The Global Prevalence of Intimate Partner Homicide: A Systematic Review." *The Lancet* 382 (9895): 859–65.

Taft, Angela Joy, and Lyndsey F. Watson. 2008. "Depression and Termination of Pregnancy (Induced Abortion) in a National Cohort of Young Australian Women: The Confounding Effect of Women's Experience of Violence." *BMC Public Health* 8 (75): 1–8.

Together for Girls. 2013. "Building a Safer World for Children: Together for Girls Stakeholder Report 2010–2012." Together for Girls, Washington, DC.

Uganda Bureau of Statistics. 2010. *Uganda National Household Survey 2009/2010: Socio-economic Model.* Kampala: Uganda Bureau of Statistics.

Underwood, Carol, Joanna Skinner, Nadia Osman, and Hilary Schwandt. 2011. "Structural Determinants of Adolescent Girls' Vulnerability to HIV: Views from Community Members in Botswana, Malawi, and Mozambique." *Social Science and Medicine* 73 (2): 343–50.

UNFPA (United Nations Population Fund). 2007. "Ending Widespread Violence against Women." UNFPA, New York.

United Nations. 1993. "Declaration on the Elimination of Violence against Women." General Assembly Resolution A/RES/48/104, United Nations, New York. http://www.un .org/documents/ga/res/48/a48r104.htm.

———. 2013. *World Population Prospects: The 2012 Revision.* New York: United Nations.

Usdin, Shereen, Esca Scheepers, Susan Goldstein, and Garth Japhet. 2005. "Achieving Social Change on Gender-Based Violence: A Report on the Impact Evaluation of Soul City's Fourth Series." *Social Science and Medicine* 61 (11): 2434–45.

Vinck, Patrick, and Phuong N. Pham. 2013. "Association of Exposure to Intimate Partner Physical Violence and Potentially Traumatic War-Related Events with Mental Health in Liberia." *Social Science and Medicine* 77: 41–49.

Vyas, Seema. 2013. *"Estimating the Association between Women's Earnings and Partner Violence: Evidence from the 2008–2009 Tanzania National Panel Survey."* Women's Voice, Agency, and Participation Research Paper 2, World Bank, Washington, DC.

Vyas, Seema, and Charlotte Watts. 2009. "How Does Economic Empowerment Affect Women's Risk of Intimate Partner Violence in Low and Middle Income Countries? A Systematic Review of Published Evidence." *Journal of International Development* 21 (5): 577–602.

Waltermaurer, Eve. 2012. "Public Justification of Intimate Partner Violence: A Review of the Literature." *Trauma, Violence, and Abuse* 13 (3): 167–75.

Washington Post. 2013. "Saatchi Says He Is Divorcing Nigella Lawson." Washington *Post,* July 7. http://www.washingtonpost.com /lifestyle/style/saatchi-says-he-is-divorcing -nigella-lawson/2013/07/07/795ee4d8 -e730-11e2-aa9f-c03a72e2d342_story.html.

Weissman, Amy, Janine Cocker, Lisa Sherburne, Mary Beth Power, Ronnie Lovich, and Mary Mukaka. 2006. "Cross-Generational Relationships: Using a 'Continuum of Volition' in HIV Prevention Work among Young People." *Gender and Development* 14 (1): 81–94.

Whitzman, Carolyn, Crystal Legacy, Caroline Andrew, Fran Klodawsky, Margaret Shaw, and Kalpana Viswanath, eds. 2013. *Building Inclusive Cities: Women's Safety and the Right to the City.* London: Routledge.

WHO (World Health Organization). 2001. "Putting Women First: Ethical and Safety Recommendations for Research on Domestic Violence against Women." WHO, Geneva.

———. 2013. "Global and Regional Estimates of Violence against Women: Prevalence and Health Effects of Intimate Partner Violence and Non-partner Sexual Violence." WHO, Geneva.

Wood, Elizabeth Jean. 2006. "Variation in Sexual Violence in War." *Politics and Society* 34 (3): 307–42.

World Bank. 2003. *Caribbean Youth Development: Issues and Policy Directions.* Washington, DC: World Bank.

———. 2013. "Domestic Violence: Can Your Smartphone Save Your Life?" *News,* January 22. http://www.worldbank.org/en/news /feature/2013/01/22/domestic-violence -hackathon-smartphone-lifesaver.

World Bank and IFC (International Finance Corporation). 2013. *Women, Business, and the Law 2014: Removing Restrictions to Enhance Gender Equality.* London: Bloomsbury.

Xu, Xiao, Fengchuan Zhu, Patricia O'Campo, Michael A. Koenig, Victoria Mock, and Jacquelyn C. Campbell. 2005. "Prevalence of and Risk Factors for Intimate Partner Violence in China." *American Journal of Public Health* 95 (1): 78–85.

Chapter 4 Key messages

> Sexual and reproductive health and rights are important ends in themselves and can have valuable benefits for women's own health, nutrition, education, and livelihoods, and for the well-being of their children.

> Having agency over sexual and reproductive decisions includes being able to choose whether, when, and with whom to have sex; to ask a partner to use a condom; and to make decisions about childbearing and one's own health.

> Child marriage, high rates of adolescent pregnancy, and women's limited control over their own sexual and reproductive health decisions often reflect underlying gender inequalities and carry serious repercussions.

> Beyond access to contraceptive methods, promising interventions integrate multisectoral actions, such as sexual and reproductive health education, mentoring and peer group training, incentive programs, and activity clubs and sports.

> Broader structural and normative changes are critical and can be achieved by engaging community opinion leaders and gatekeepers to support changing norms.

CHAPTER 4

Control over Sexual and Reproductive Health and Rights

The nature of the challenge

The *World Development Report 2012* emphasized being able to decide whether, when, and with whom to have sex; whether, when, and whom to marry; whether or when to have children; and how many children to have as expressions of agency (World Bank 2011b). The intrinsic value of agency related to family formation has long been recognized by governments around the world. The Universal Declaration of Human Rights (1948) asserts that "Marriage shall be entered into only with the free and full consent of the intending spouses," and limits marriage to those "of full age." The right to sexual and reproductive health was recognized in 1994 by the Programme of Action of the International Conference on Population and Development (ICPD), and subsequently adopted by 179 governments (ICPD 1994). These positions stand alongside the Convention on the Elimination of All Forms of Discrimination against Women (CEDAW), which was discussed in chapter 1.

Enabling women's control over decisions about family formation also has instrumental value, as these decisions can affect investments in their education and economic opportunities as well as their health. Delaying marriage is associated with greater educational achievement and lower fertility, and lower fertility can increase women's life expectancy and benefit their children's health and education. Conversely, barriers to girls' and women's sexual and reproductive health have adverse repercussions—which can affect individuals, families, communities, societies, and economies—on a broad set of development outcomes (Grépin and Klugman 2013). Moreover, these impacts are often amplified by overlapping deprivations. For example, girls who marry before their 18th birthday are more likely to face restrictions on their mobility and financial decisions, as well as have a heightened risk of violence, of contracting HIV/AIDS or other sexually transmitted infections (STIs), and of early pregnancy (Bruce 2003; Hindin and Fatusi 2009; Nour 2009; Raj et al. 2010). And as we saw in chapter 1, the girls most likely to marry early are those with the least education and lowest economic status (Raj 2010).

Large shares of women and girls are constrained in exercising agency over these domains. What we see globally and investigate further in this chapter are high levels of unmet need for contraceptives, high numbers of unintended pregnancies, large gaps between expressed ideal family size and actual fertility, and inability to divorce because of financial dependency or legal restrictions. The starkest violation of girls' and women's agency addressed in this chapter is early marriage (forced and coerced sex were discussed in chapter 3). The many other manifestations of women's lack of sexual and reproductive agency, such as high levels of maternal mortality and morbidity, disproportionate risk of HIV/AIDS, and the challenges of accessing health services, have recently been explored in greater detail elsewhere and are beyond the focus of this chapter (see, for example, Grépin and Klugman 2013; Inelmen et al. 2012).

> *"The man brings the woman in his house [when he marries her]. How could she be his equal?"*
>
> —Men's focus group, Gliangou, Téra Department, Tillabéri Region, Niger (World Bank 2014)

As outlined in chapter 1 and explored further in this chapter, social norms and laws are important drivers of agency, and this is especially true in the context of sexual and reproductive decisions (see figure 1.1 in chapter 1, where social norms and laws, mediated through the household, affect agency and other gender equality outcomes). Interventions and policies that seek to change norms around acceptability of child marriage and modern contraceptives, for example, will be critical for increasing women's sexual and reproductive agency. While progressive laws can foster women's greater control over family formation decisions, in many countries laws reinforce constraints, as in the 29 countries where men are the legally designated heads of households. Indeed, 29 of the 188 states that have ratified CEDAW retain exceptions to the article requiring countries to eliminate discrimination in all matters related to marriage and family relations.

Gendered social norms surrounding sexuality are learned by girls and boys from their families and communities and affect their choices in adult life. In many cultures, it is considered inappropriate for women to learn "too much" about matters related to sexuality. For girls and women, though typically not boys and men, there is stigma around being sexually active (Fairhurst et al. 2004). Stigma and norms around purity can prevent girls from learning about sex and contraception, thereby giving men a prominent role in sex and contraceptive choices (McCleary-Sills, McGonagle, and Malhotra 2012). In Honduras, for example, in households where the husband makes the decisions regarding family size and family planning use alone, women are less likely to report that they currently or have ever used modern methods of family planning (Speizer, Whittle, and Carter 2005).

Which factors affect women's agency in sexual and reproductive decisions? We saw in chapter 3 that women's lack of education was associated with higher risks of violence. It is also associated with child marriage, early pregnancy, and the ability to negotiate within a sexual relationship, such as the ability to refuse sex with a partner or to ask a partner to use a condom (figure 4.1). Evidence suggests that economic and political opportunities

FIGURE 4.1 Education as a key driver of women's ability to exercise choice in sexual relationships

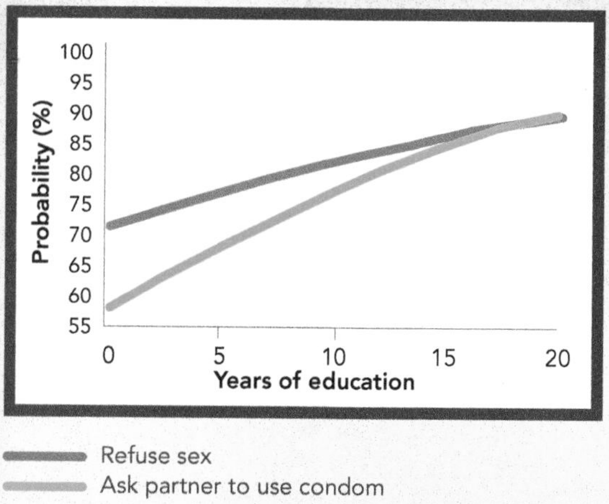

— Refuse sex
— Ask partner to use condom

Source: Estimates based on Demographic and Health Surveys for 37 countries, 2006–12: Albania, Armenia, Benin, Burkina Faso, Burundi, Cambodia, Cameroon, the Democratic Republic of Congo, the Republic of Congo, Côte d'Ivoire, the Dominican Republic, Ethiopia, Gabon, Ghana, Guyana, Haiti, Honduras, Lesotho, Liberia, Madagascar, Malawi, Mali, Mozambique, Namibia, Nepal, Niger, Nigeria, Rwanda, São Tomé and Príncipe, Senegal, Sierra Leone, Swaziland, Tanzania, Uganda, Ukraine, Zambia, and Zimbabwe.

also play a role. Where women are able to support themselves and to be active members of the community outside of the home, they have more decision-making power within the relationship itself (Duflo 2012).

The objective of this chapter is threefold. First, we highlight how women's ability to control their reproductive health and make decisions about family formation enhances their agency in other aspects of life, including education and access to economic opportunities. Second, the individual characteristics that affect women's and girls' ability to exercise agency in those domains are identified, and the impacts of overlapping disadvantage are explored. Third, evidence about what works in promoting women's exercise of their sexual and reproductive health and rights is reviewed. We build on several recent contributions, including those by the ICPD, the United Nations Population Fund, the Council on Foreign Relations, Women Deliver, and the International Center for Research on Women (ICPD 2014; Mathur, Greene, and Malhotra 2003; UNFPA 2013; Vogelstein 2013).

The next section reviews the magnitude of the challenge and the repercussions for women's health and well-being. We then highlight lessons learned and promising approaches. The final section summarizes the key findings and highlights important directions in the way forward.

How great is the challenge?

This section presents new analyses of women's ability to make choices about their sexuality and their sexual and reproductive health across 55 developing countries, which represent 40 percent of the world's population.

Fertility choices

In many countries today, women have far fewer children than they did four decades ago. Although many factors have had a role in this transformation, one of the main mechanisms through which this change has come about is women's use of contraception. For example, in Colombia, average fertility was six or seven children in 1960, whereas in 2009, it was closer to two. In 2005, 78 percent of Colombian women used contraception, compared to only 21 percent in 1970.[1]

Lower fertility has instrumental value, increasing women's life expectancy and enabling them to pursue economic opportunities (UNFPA 2013). Increased use of contraception reduces the number of high-risk births and lowers maternal mortality rates.[2] The beneficial impact of smaller family size on children's health and education is also well documented (UNFPA 2012b). Recent research also suggests that when fertility declines and the value of human capital in the economy increases, men are more willing to share household decision-making power with women to ensure their children get better education (Doepke and Tertlit 2009).

Yet many women are unable to realize their fertility preferences (ICPD 2014). Annually, in developing countries alone, about 80 million women have unintended pregnancies, which means that they had wanted to delay that pregnancy or not have it at all. Addressing the global unmet contraceptive need—defined as nonuse of contraception by women who do not want to get pregnant for at least two years—could avert 54 million unplanned pregnancies annually (Singh and Darroch 2012).

Unmet need may result from inadequate access to family planning methods because of factors such as distance, cost, insufficient supplies, and inconvenient hours. However, beyond ensuring adequate supply, increasing women's agency, education, and access to economic opportunities all can be important drivers of contraceptive use. A study in South Africa found that a woman's level of education and her control over her earnings are enabling factors for the voluntary use of modern contraceptive methods (Stephenson, Beke, and Tshibangu 2008). In Sub-Saharan Africa, women in wealthier households who are more educated are far more likely to use contraception than their less advantaged peers. Only 10 percent of women with no education and 10 percent of those in the poorest households use contraception, compared to 42 percent of women with secondary or higher education and 38 percent of women from the wealthiest households (UNFPA 2010). Across four African countries (Ghana, Namibia, Uganda, and Zambia), a woman's increased participation in household economic decision making, her ability to negotiate sexual activity, and a couple's agreement on fertility preferences were all associated with increased use of contraceptives that were either female-only methods (such as pills, intrauterine devices [IUDs], injectables, or implants) or methods that require some degree of cooperation from

"Each year, almost one in five women in developing countries become pregnant before turning 18, and 7.3 million girls under age 18 give birth."

partners (such as male and female condoms) (Do and Kurimoto 2012).

Open communication and joint decision making about family planning contribute to voluntary contraceptive use and the achievement of fertility intentions (Amatya et al. 1994; Ezeh 1993). Studies have shown that communication between partners is important for realizing women's choices about family formation and their sexual and reproductive health. Women who have difficulty communicating with their partners, or do so only infrequently, are less likely to use contraception or more likely to conceal its use (Biddlecom and Fapohunda 1998; Storey et al. 1999). In some cases, male partners restrict contraceptive use altogether (Casterline, Sathar, and ul Haque 2001; Kamal 2000). Communication with other family members can be important too. For example, women in urban slums in Karachi are more likely to use family planning following discussion with their mothers-in-law (Kadir et al. 2003).

To what extent are women involved in decisions about their fertility? Our analysis shows that across 55 developing countries, three-fourths of couples make joint decisions regarding contraception, whereas in 15 percent of cases, women make this decision themselves. Only a minority of women—about 1 in 14—report that their husband makes this decision alone. However, the regional averages vary: up to 1 in 16 women in South Asia and more than

> *"We do not use contraception. Otherwise people will think we're sterile."*
>
> —Women's focus group, Morey, Keita Department, Tahoua Region, Niger (World Bank 2014)

1 in 9 (11 percent) women in Sub-Saharan Africa say their husband makes the decision alone. In Liberia, nearly one-third of women say their husbands make this decision alone. On average, across 55 countries, 6 percent of women who are not current users report that they do not intend to use family planning in the future because their husbands or others are opposed, with Timor-Leste being the highest, at 22 percent.

These patterns help explain why women who want to delay or prevent pregnancy might choose to use more concealable methods such as injectables and IUDs. Women's covert use is generally motivated by a desire to keep partners, in-laws, or other family members from finding out that they are trying to prevent a pregnancy (Guttmacher Institute 2000). And women who are in violent relationships are more likely to report that their partners have tried to sabotage their use of contraception and that they have used a method covertly (Clark et al. 2008; Gee et al. 2009). However, enabling women to access and use contraceptives in secret is an inadequate and temporary solution—and one that carries risks. In some cases, women fear—or actually face—violence from their partner if their covert use of contraceptives is discovered (Bawah et al. 1999). In some contexts, enabling women's full control over family planning shows greater results; for example, unwanted births in Zambia were reduced only when women had individual control over contraceptive decision making (Ashraf, Field, and Lee 2010).

It is not just husbands and partners who limit women's agency over fertility decisions. Often family members and community leaders exert influence over these choices too, as in the following examples:

- In Jordan, women—young brides in particular—face significant pressure from their mothers-in-law to prove their fertility and bear children (Libbus and Kridli 1997).

- In Tanzania, family planning decisions are influenced by religious leaders and by male dominance over females (especially in polygynous relationships) (Keele, Forste, and Flake 2005).

Satisfying the unmet need for contraceptives and improving sexual and reproductive health services would also reduce the number of abortions. This is important because almost half of all abortions are unsafe (Sedgh et al. 2012), meaning that they are carried out by individuals lacking the necessary skills or in an environment that does not adhere to minimal medical standards.[3] These situations account for close to 13 percent of all maternal deaths. Young women face particular challenges in accessing abortion care and account for approximately 40 percent of, or as many as 3.2 million (UNFPA 2013), unsafe abortions worldwide (Shah and Ahman 2004).

Abortions are illegal or highly restricted in 53 countries (Center for Reproductive Rights 2014). Such restrictions have been directly linked to adverse health consequences (Guttmacher Institute and IPPF 2010). Procedural requirements can undermine access to services even where abortions are legal. Other, often related, barriers to accessing safe abortion care include social and religious stigma and travel and distance-related constraints.

Early sexual activity and pregnancy

Early sexual initiation puts girls at greater risk for HIV and other STIs, early pregnancy, and early childbearing (Hindin and Fatusi 2009). Every hour, 50 young women are newly infected with HIV (UNAIDS 2013a). In 2012, more than 5 million young people (ages 15 to 24) were living with HIV, with an estimated 2,400 new infections each day (UNAIDS 2012). In Sub-Saharan Africa, HIV prevalence among young people decreased by almost half between 2001 and 2012, but prevalence among young women remains more than double that among young men (UNAIDS 2013b).

Each year, almost one in five women in developing countries become pregnant before the age of 18, and 7.3 million girls under the age of 18 (2 million of whom are under age 15) give birth (UNFPA 2013). This is dangerous. In developing countries, pregnancy-related causes are the largest contributor to the mortality of girls ages 15 to 19, killing nearly 70,000 girls each year (UNFPA 2013). Early childbearing also increases the risk of childbirth complications such as obstetric fistula, which commonly occurs among young girls who give birth before their bodies are physically mature and causes chronic incontinence, often resulting in social exclusion, among other consequences.

Globally, over the past 15 years, adolescent fertility rates have dipped slightly, albeit with large variation across countries and regions. The average rate in developing countries is 10 percent, compared to 2 percent in developed nations (Population Reference

Bureau 2013). Sub-Saharan Africa has the highest regional rate—about 12 percent in 2010—and the rate is rising in Burundi, Chad, the Republic of Congo, Lesotho, and Zimbabwe (Haub 2013). Following current trends, the region will take nearly 50 years to reach Europe's current levels of adolescent fertility.

Overall, adolescent fertility in Latin America and the Caribbean (72 births per 1,000 women 15 to 19 years of age) is lower than in Africa (Haub 2013). The annual reduction in births between 1997 and 2010 was 2.7 percent in South Asia and 1.6 percent globally, compared with just 1.3 percent in Latin America and the Caribbean. The countries with the highest teenage pregnancy rates (the Dominican Republic, Guatemala,

Honduras, and Nicaragua) reported no change since 2000 (Azevedo et al. 2012).

Not surprisingly, early marriage is strongly correlated with early childbearing (Hindin and Fatusi 2009). The highest rates of adolescent births occur in West and Central Africa and South Asia, where early marriage rates are high (UNFPA 2013). Figure 4.2 shows the regional share of married adolescents who are, or who wish to become, pregnant. Married girls in Sub-Saharan Africa show higher levels of pregnancy intention than their counterparts in Asia and in Latin America and the Caribbean. These high levels of pregnancy desire may also reflect social pressures to prove fertility immediately after marriage (Bearinger et al. 2007).

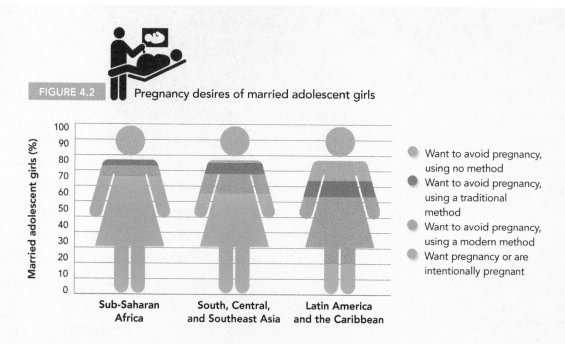

FIGURE 4.2 Pregnancy desires of married adolescent girls

Legend:
- Want to avoid pregnancy, using no method
- Want to avoid pregnancy, using a traditional method
- Want to avoid pregnancy, using a modern method
- Want pregnancy or are intentionally pregnant

Source: Guttmacher Institute and IPPF 2010.

Note: Girls ages 15 to 19 years.

Following from our earlier discussion about overlapping disadvantage, poor young women have fewer choices and opportunities (Guttmacher Institute and IPPF 2010). In several Latin American countries—including Bolivia, Colombia, the Dominican Republic, Haiti, Honduras, and Peru—adolescents who have more education, live in urban areas, and come from wealthier families are less likely to get pregnant (Azevedo et al. 2012). Mexican women who gave birth during adolescence were found to be more likely to depend on social assistance. This also highlights the potential long-term consequences for children born to young mothers, including low cognitive test scores, poor behavioral outcomes, grade repetition, and economic disadvantage (Levine, Pollack, and Comfort 2001).

At the same time, adolescents who are sexually active and wish to avoid pregnancy face a number of barriers to exercising agency over these decisions, including limited mobility and financial resources, lack of accurate information, stigma related to sexual activity before marriage, and restrictive policies (Singh and Darroch 2012). Whether married or unmarried, young women and girls around the world have greater difficulty than older women in accessing comprehensive contraceptive services and care (UNFPA 2010). The evidence on this point is striking:

■ Across 22 Sub-Saharan African countries for which data are available, adolescent girls have the lowest contraceptive prevalence rate; roughly only 1 in 10 adolescents who are married or in a union use any form of contraception, compared to roughly 1 in 4 women ages 30 to 44 (UNFPA 2010).

■ Young girls are also the least likely group to have reliable information on their rights and contraceptive options, they are the least likely group to use health facilities, and they generally have an incomplete understanding of how their reproductive system works (UNFPA 2010).

■ Unmarried girls are frequently denied care because providers require parental consent (UNFPA 2006; Zavodny 2004).

Research from East Asia and the Pacific suggests that restrictive laws—such as those requiring parental consent for HIV or STI testing or those permitting parental access to a minor's medical records without the child's consent—are a significant barrier to sexual and reproductive health services (UNESCO 2013). In Indonesia and Malaysia, only married women can access comprehensive sexual and reproductive services, and in Cambodia, parental consent is required for HIV testing of children under age 18 (UNICEF 2013a).

Where girls have greater educational and economic opportunities, evidence suggests that they are more likely to take up those opportunities than to have children in their teenage years. In Chile, extending the school day reduced teenage motherhood; an increase in full-day school enrollment of 20 percent reduced the likelihood of teen motherhood by 5 percent (Berthelon and Kruger 2011). Beyond the formal education system, life-skills courses also have dramatic impacts. For example, in Marathwada, India, attendance in life-skills classes increased the median age of marriage for girls in the area from 16 to 17 in just two years (ICRW 2006b). Elsewhere in rural

India, a three-year program that provided recruiting services to women resulted in more women choosing to enter the labor market or to obtain more schooling or post-school training than women getting married and starting families. When given the choice, women opted for greater economic opportunities (Jensen 2012).

Child marriage

Child marriage in developing countries remains pervasive, with one-third of girls being married before age 18 and one in nine being married before age 15 (UNICEF 2013b). If present trends continue, more than 142 million girls will be married before the age of 18 in the next decade—that is, 39,000 girls each day (UNFPA 2012a). This practice is driven by poverty, social norms, and pervasive discrimination against girls. CEDAW calls on all countries to take necessary action to eliminate child marriage and encourages lawmakers to set the minimum age of marriage at 18 years (United Nations 1967). Early marriage forces girls into adulthood and, frequently, motherhood before they are emotionally or physically mature—and often before they can complete their education.

Average regional prevalence of child marriage ranges from 21 percent in Africa and 17 percent in Latin America and the Caribbean to 8 percent in Eastern and Southern Europe (Raj and Boehmer 2013; see also map 4.1). These averages mask considerable variation across countries. Among the 111 countries with data, the prevalence of child marriage ranges from 2 percent in Algeria and Libya to as high as 74 and 75 percent in Niger and Bangladesh, respectively.

While the prevalence in India is not among the highest recorded, the sheer size of its population means that India has the highest number, accounting for one-third of the world's child brides.

Why is child marriage so common, often despite legal prohibitions? Social norms and expectations are again critical factors. Families may perceive marriage as a way to provide for their daughter's future, believing it will improve her economic and social circumstances. The reality, however, is that girls who marry young are more likely to remain poor even after marriage (Mathur, Greene, and Malhotra 2003).

There is often a large age difference between child brides and their husbands (UNICEF 2005). Such age gaps can disempower the wife (Jain and Kurz 2007). Research from a number of countries—including Cambodia, Colombia, Haiti, India, Kenya, Peru, South Africa, Turkmenistan, and Zambia—suggests that having a much older husband can dramatically increase the risk of intimate partner violence (UNICEF 2005). Similarly, in Peru (Flake 2005) and India (ICRW 2006a), girls who married before the age of 18 were twice as likely to experience violence compared with women who married later.

Growing evidence from Sub-Saharan Africa shows that girls who marry early are also at greater risk of contracting HIV or other STIs. Marriage before age 20 is considered a risk factor for HIV infection. For example, in Kenya and Zambia, HIV infection rates were found to be higher among married girls than among their unmarried, sexually active counterparts (Bruce 2007).

MAP 4.1   Child marriage prevalence in 111 countries

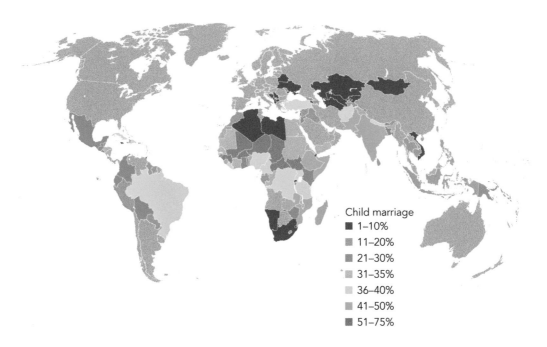

Child marriage
■ 1–10%
■ 11–20%
■ 21–30%
■ 31–35%
■ 36–40%
■ 41–50%
■ 51–75%

Sources: Estimates based on Demographic and Health Surveys, International Center for Research on Women reports, and United Nations Children's Fund statistics, using the latest available data for women ages 20 to 24, 2001–12.

Note: Countries in gray do not have comparable data available.

Similarly, in Uganda, the HIV prevalence rate for girls 15 to 19 years of age was higher for married girls (89 percent) than for unmarried girls (66 percent) (Kelly et al. 2003), and the age difference between spouses was a significant risk factor. Child brides are often unable to ask their husband to get an HIV test, to abstain from intercourse, or to demand that he use a condom (Clark 2004).

Using Demographic and Health Surveys for 37 developing countries, we find that women who marry after the age of 18 are 2 percent more likely to feel able to refuse sex than women who marry early. This small but significant difference grows as age at marriage increases. Each year marriage is delayed beyond age 18 is associated with higher odds of a woman being able to exercise agency to refuse sex. These results illustrate the important link between early marriage, adolescents' sexual and reproductive control, and experiences of intimate partner violence.

Our analysis of 55 countries shows that girls living in poor households are twice as likely to marry before the age of 18 compared with girls in higher-income households, as are rural girls compared with those from urban areas. A girl may be married off to pay debts or given away by her family in exchange for a wife for her brother (Mathur, Greene, and Malhotra 2003). Dowries are another driving force: in some cases, the younger the bride, the cheaper the dowry her family has to pay (Luffman 2012). Other local traditions may be at play; for example, in Bangladesh, the Kyrgyz Republic, and Somalia, there is still a practice of forcing girls who have been abducted and raped to marry the perpetrator to protect their families' honor (UN Women 2010).

Beyond poverty, we see other dimensions of overlapping disadvantage. Child marriage is closely associated with illiteracy, and more schooling tends to raise the age of marriage:

- Evidence from Bangladesh and Sub-Saharan Africa suggests that women who married early are over 5 percentage points less likely to be literate and over 8 percentage points less likely to have any secondary education (Field and Ambrus 2008; Nguyen and Wodon 2013).

- In Zimbabwe, only 4 percent of girls ages 15 to 19 who had attended primary school were married, compared to 40 percent of those who had received no education; in Haiti, the shares were 15 percent and 43 percent, respectively (UNICEF 2005).

- A study across 18 of the 20 countries with the highest prevalence of child marriage found that girls with no education were up to six times more likely to marry as children than girls who had received secondary education (ICRW 2006a).

- Across Africa, each additional year a girl is married before age 18 has been found to reduce her probability of literacy by

about 6 percentage points, the probability of having at least some secondary schooling by 8 percentage points, and the probability of secondary school completion by almost 7 percentage points (Wodon, forthcoming).

These patterns—of cultural norms, education, and links to poverty—begin to point to the layered challenges that policy makers need to address.

Whether divorce is socially acceptable and financially viable can also affect women's agency. Overall, divorce is still not widely accepted, and in some regions, it is becoming even less so, as in Latin America and the Caribbean and South Asia.[4] Although divorce is currently illegal only in the Philippines and Vatican City, in 13 out of the 70 countries for which data are available, women do not have equal rights to initiate a divorce. These countries include some middle-income and high-income countries, such as Israel, Jordan, and Malaysia (Htun and Weldon 2011). Beyond what the law says on paper, recent qualitative research across 20 countries found that the unequal division of assets and custody of children are significant obstacles to divorce, alongside opposition by families and communities, social isolation, and stigma (World Bank 2011a).

The foregoing has highlighted the nature of constraints on family formation and has hinted at some important emerging opportunities for action. The following section discusses the evidence on what works and identifies key priorities for moving forward.

> *"A man can easily divorce his wife because his decision is final. [On the other hand] it is difficult for a woman to obtain a divorce because people will try to reconcile the couple and, moreover, if she wants a divorce, she must reimburse the bride-wealth even if she had 10 children."*
>
> —Women's focus group, Toulou Karey, Loga Department, Dosso Region, Niger (Word Bank 2014)

Program and policy evidence: What works?

Several types of interventions have been shown to expand women's and girls' control over their sexual and reproductive decisions. These include interventions that promote more gender-equitable communication and decision making around sexual and reproductive health and that improve women's access to and the quality of reproductive health services and information. Interventions have also tested incentives for preventing child marriage and for supporting girls and their families. Interventions to expand education and economic opportunities offer promise when the need for safe spaces, life skills, and job skills are considered. Women's agency can also be supported through more progressive laws, including those related to marriage and property.

As discussed in chapter 2, a common factor across many successful approaches is an acknowledgment of the powerful role of gender norms. Approaches for effectively engaging men, boys, communities, and traditional authorities to change norms around sexuality, marriage, and reproduction have

been shown to contribute to the strengthening of women's agency (Fleming et al. 2013).

Engaging men and other gatekeepers

Paying attention to male attitudes and gender dynamics when designing family planning interventions is important because responsibility shared between women and men ultimately promotes greater agency for women in sexual and reproductive health decisions. Initiatives that engage men in sexual and reproductive health and contraceptive choices show promise, although they need to be carefully designed to avoid unintended consequences (Chant and Guttman 2000). In some cases, such interventions have been found to reinforce traditional power dynamics or to produce only modest behavioral change (McCleary-Sills, McGonagle, and Malhotra 2012; Rottach, Schuler, and Hardee 2009). In Ghana, for example, men who were educated about emergency contraception preferred this to longer-term methods and saw themselves as the primary decision makers on the issue, often without regard for their partners' preferences (L'Engle et al. 2009). But evidence of positive impacts is also emerging. Mass media campaigns are associated with higher approval of contraception and better communication between partners about use (Barker, Ricardo, and Nascimento 2007). The mass media campaigns that were evaluated as being most effective went beyond providing information and encouraged boys and men to talk about specific topics, such as gender-based violence (UNFPA 2013).

When the Male Motivator project sought to address men's limited engagement in fertility issues in Malawi, more than one-third of married women reported never having spoken to their husbands about family planning. Male outreach workers engaged men who were not using contraception in discussions about gender roles and norms, especially around the norm of having large families to demonstrate virility. As a result, contraceptive use increased significantly, which was attributed to greater ease and frequency of communication between partners, resulting in more joint decision making (Shattuck et al. 2011).

Interventions that engage other gatekeepers of women's health—older male and female family members and community leaders—can improve communication, especially between young people, couples, and other family members (Mwaikambo et al. 2011). As highlighted in box 4.1, working with customary leaders such as village chiefs can enhance adolescents' exercise of agency in their sexual and reproductive health.

Improving access to and quality of information and services

Improving the quality of services and availability of contraceptive methods can increase agency. Weak services often have low usage rates. A recent Egyptian study suggests that certain dimensions of quality are particularly important, including privacy during medical examinations and respect for patient confidentiality, as well as facility cleanliness, friendly staff, shorter wait times, and limited staff turnover (Rabie et al. 2013). Community-based distribution approaches can circumvent women's mobility constraints (McCleary-Sills, McGonagle, and Malhotra 2012). However, these may also have the unintended consequence of reinforcing gender inequalities.

Box 4.1 Engaging traditional gatekeepers in adolescent sexual and reproductive health in Malawi

Chapsinja, a rural area outside of Lilongwe, is known for customary practices such as initiation ceremonies, during which information is delivered to young people by traditional counselors or *akunjira*. A study by the Family Planning Association of Malawi (FPAM) documented that traditional counselors were strongly against condom use and that some of the messages they conveyed during the ceremonies likely contributed to the high prevalence of HIV/AIDS, sexually transmitted infections, adolescent pregnancies, and coerced sexual initiation rates for girls.

FPAM launched a community mobilization campaign to introduce sexual and reproductive health services and information. They worked with *akunjira* to transform existing rituals into opportunities for health-promoting messages. Girls and boys were encouraged to go to school and become sexually active only when they are socially, mentally, and physically mature. At the same time, young people were trained as peer educators and volunteer condom distributors in their communities. HIV testing has become more frequent, and according to preliminary results, HIV prevalence is declining. The Chapsinja senior chief now plans to serve as a bridge to chiefs in surrounding areas.

Source: Boehmova 2013.

For example, in Bangladesh, community-based distribution was found to reinforce women's seclusion by limiting interactions in the public space (McCleary-Sills, McGonagle, and Malhotra 2012).

Ensuring universal access to comprehensive adolescent-friendly services can reduce the likelihood of early pregnancies. Evidence from around the world shows that the friendliness of staff, quality of care, cost of services, and ease of getting to a facility are important determinants of adolescents' access to and use of sexual and reproductive health services (Erulkar, Charles, and Alford 2005; Kesterton and de Mello 2010). The 47th session of the ICPD in 2014 upheld the responsibility of governments to safeguard adolescents' rights to privacy, confidentiality, respect, and informed consent and to address the legal, regulatory, and social barriers adolescents face in receiving high-quality reproductive health information and care (Commission on Population and Development 2014).

Methods for measuring the acceptability of services can be incorporated into performance monitoring. Such measures can include client ratings of overall service satisfaction and such indicators as perceived respect for dignity, provision of satisfactory information and explanation, informed choice and consent, and availability of preferred contraceptive methods. These monitoring indicators link to mechanisms of social accountability, as highlighted in box 4.2.

Client awareness is important. In Peru, the FEMME (Foundations to Enhance Management of Maternal Emergencies) Project aimed to standardize care with new emergency obstetric guidelines. Among other things, these guidelines stressed

---

Box 4.2 Social accountability and service delivery

Social accountability mechanisms that help improve the quality of service delivery can improve women's ability to exercise agency over their own health and their health outcomes, as in the following examples:

> In Uganda, the introduction of a local accountability mechanism gave clients greater control over the delivery of primary health services, including through provision of information about staff performance. A year later, child survival rates improved, leading to a 33 percent reduction in under-five mortality.

> In Peru, a citizen surveillance program increased the number of births in health facilities by almost one-third in just one year, and increased access to culturally appropriate delivery options.

> Recent work from Orissa, India, identified three effective processes that had positive impacts on reproductive and maternal health: generating demand for rights and better services through information campaigns, leveraging intermediaries to legitimize the demands of poor and marginalized women, and sensitizing leaders and health providers to the needs of women.

Sources: Björkman and Svensson 2009; Díaz et al. 2001; Grépin and Klugman 2013; Papp, Gogoi, and Campbell 2012; World Bank 2011b.

women's rights as patients and their rights to privacy during care. As a result of the project, the maternal mortality rate declined by 49 percent in intervention facilities, compared to 25 percent in control facilities (Rottach, Schuler, and Hardee 2009).

Results-based financing (RBF)—whereby health service providers are paid according to their performance along a previously agreed-upon set of outcomes—has been used to expand women's options for reproductive health services and to improve sexual and reproductive health outcomes. In Rwanda, incentives have been introduced for community health workers that are based on their performance of certain functions, such as referrals of women for prenatal care, institutional delivery, referrals of new users of family planning, and the number of current users (World Bank 2013b). Preliminary results from several countries suggest that efficiency, equity, and accountability can be strengthened through the results-based approach, as in the following examples:

■ In Afghanistan, the number of women delivering their babies with the support of skilled birth attendants more than doubled from April 2010 to December 2012 in RBF-supported facilities (World Bank 2013c).

■ In Cameroon, the number of births attended by skilled professionals more than doubled between 2012 and 2013 in the regions involved in an RBF project (Robyn, Sorgho, and Zang 2014).

■ In Nigeria, coverage of institutional deliveries increased by 30 percentage points (to 39 percent), and coverage of prenatal care increased from 16 percent to 77 percent

in 2012, following the introduction of an RBF approach (World Bank 2013a).

More accessible family planning methods and information also made a difference in Ukraine, where removing barriers to providing sexual and reproductive health services led to a two-thirds decline in abortions since the early 1990s. This decline was attributed to policies and programs that prioritize young people's sexual and reproductive health, for example, through better training of staff, through the addition of specialized health facilities, and through public-private partnerships that increased the range of available contraceptive methods and reduced their cost (UNFPA 2013).

Vouchers can cut the costs of accessing services, which overcomes a critical barrier to exercising agency, particularly for young people. In Nicaragua, vouchers valid for three months can be used for one free consultation and a free follow-up visit for services such as counseling on family planning and prenatal care. Vouchers are distributed to adolescents and youth by nongovernmental organizations in markets, outside schools, in clinics, on the streets, and door to door, and they can be transferred to another adolescent (UNFPA 2013).

Innovations in information and communication technologies (ICTs) show promise in improving quality and access, including through enhanced social accountability, although more rigorous evaluations are needed in developing countries (Gurman, Rubin, and Roess 2012). Promising directions using mobile technology include the following:

■ Text messages can be a feasible method to send information and service referrals, especially for adolescents (Levine et al. 2008).

■ Reminders by text message have also been used to improve adherence to antiretroviral treatment and to increase births delivered by skilled attendants (Lester et al. 2010; Pop-Eleches et al. 2011).

■ Similarly, mobile solutions can improve patient awareness. For example, Project Masiluleke's text message campaign in South Africa, which promotes HIV/AIDS awareness, nearly tripled the volume of calls to a local HIV/AIDS helpline (United Nations Foundation–Vodafone Foundation Partnership 2009).

New partnerships using ICTs are emerging. In Nigeria, the World Bank Group is supporting an initiative using an SMS (short message service) platform, both to elicit citizen feedback on health services and to provide important maternal health information from the Mobile Alliance for Maternal Action.[5] In Tanzania, Vodafone and the Comprehensive Community Based Rehabilitation Hospital in Dar es Salaam have partnered to ensure that poor women can receive corrective surgery for obstetric fistula. Through this program, women from the poorest communities receive the funds for transport costs to the hospital through M-PESA, a mobile phone–based money transfer (UNFPA 2011; Vodafone Foundation 2011).

It has been shown that media can help to promote changes in perceptions about ideal family size and contraceptive use. In Brazil, soap operas have successfully promoted lower fertility by portraying smaller families as a positive norm. Over a 20-year period, fertility rates were significantly lower in communities exposed to such a show than in unexposed communities; the effect was greatest among women in lower socioeconomic groups and women in the middle or end of their fertile years (La Ferrara, Chong, and Duryea 2008). In the Arab Republic of Egypt, community norms—most notably desired family size and the community level of family planning use—are associated with changes in individual family planning use over time (Storey and Kaggwa 2009). This link is also reflected in fertility rates falling following several national media campaigns to promote child spacing and limited family size. As a result, the average number of births per woman declined from 5.3 in 1980 to 3.1 in 2005 (El-Zanaty and Way 2005).

Promoting alternatives to early marriage

Programmatic efforts to combat child marriage have gained momentum over the past two decades, with some encouraging results, albeit many still on a small scale. Most evaluated programs—18 out of 23 in a recent systematic review (Malhotra et al. 2011)—focus on girls themselves, through life-skills training, vocational and livelihood skills training, sexual and reproductive health education, communication campaigns, mentoring and peer group training, and "safe space" models. Several programs have changed knowledge, attitudes, and behavior in just a few years, although it is not yet clear which specific components are most influential (Malhotra et al. 2011).

Programs are increasingly addressing poverty, education, and lack of economic opportunities as drivers of child marriage (see box 4.3). We have seen clear evidence

Box 4.3 A promising approach to delaying marriage in Ethiopia

Ethiopia has high rates of child marriage. In Awi zone, in the rural Amhara region, one in five girls marry before age 15, and nearly half (44 percent) marry by age 17. Nearly all (92 percent) of these marriages are arranged by their families.

In 2004, the regional government partnered with the Population Council on a two-year project to delay marriage and keep girls in school. This program, Berhane Hewan ("Light for Eve"), provided families with cash conditioned on their daughters remaining unmarried and in school for the duration of the program. Other elements included social mobilization of girls led by female mentors, provision of school supplies, livelihood skills for out-of-school girls, and "community conversations" on early marriage and reproductive health.

Berhane Hewan was among the first projects targeting child marriage to be rigorously evaluated, and the results are promising. Girls (ages 10 to 14) enrolled in the program were only one-tenth as likely to be married as girls in the control site. Participants were also three times more likely to be in school. Married girls in the project site were three times more likely to be using contraception compared to married girls in the control site.

Source: Erulkar and Muthengi 2009.

that attending school reduces the likelihood of child marriage. It follows, then, that improving access to quality schooling and improving retention of girls in school are, among other things, important routes to preventing child marriage (Malhotra et al. 2011). Rising education levels have been a critical factor in increasing the age of marriage in a number of economies, including Indonesia; Sri Lanka; Taiwan, China; and Thailand (ICRW 2013).

Together these findings suggest that a program providing a conditional cash transfer (CCT) for early adolescents that transitions to an unconditional cash transfer (UCT) for older girls may yield the best results for both schooling and delaying pregnancy.

Given the links to poverty noted previously, it is no surprise that financial incentives can help combat child marriage. Payments to girls or their families are sometimes tied to investment in daughters' education and to the condition that they do not marry before age 18. In 1994, the Haryana government in India launched Apni Beti Apna Dhan (ABAD, or "Our Daughter, Our Wealth"), which gave poor families an incentive to keep their daughters in school and unmarried until the age of 18 and sought to increase family and community perceptions about the value of girls. A recent impact evaluation showed that girls enrolled in ABAD were significantly more likely to be in school and unmarried at age 18 than were girls in the control group, although the effects on attitudinal changes by parents about the value of girls were less clear (Nanda, Datta, and Das 2014).

Other evidence suggests that both CCTs and UCTs can play an important role:

- In Brazil, Colombia, and Peru, program experience suggests that conditional cash transfers (CCTs can be an effective instrument to delay marriage and child-bearing (Lopez-Calva and Perova 2012; Azevedo and Favara 2012), although the underlying mechanisms are not fully clear.[6]

■ Evidence from the Punjab Female School Stipend Program in Pakistan suggests that CCT effects on early childbearing were long lasting (Alam, Baez, and Del Carpio 2011).

■ An evaluation of a cash transfer program in Malawi found that teenage pregnancy and marriage rates were substantially lower in the UCT arm than in the CCT arm, because of the greater impact of uncondi-tional transfers among out-of-school girls (Baird, McIntosh, and Özler 2011). These findings suggest that a CCT program for early adolescents that transitions to a UCT for older girls may yield the best results for both schooling and early pregnancy.

Policies can also enable adolescents to make informed fertility choices and broaden their options. In a program in rural Egypt, girl-friendly spaces combined literacy and life-skills training with sports and changed girls' perceptions about early marriage. Evaluation results show an increase in liter-acy and school enrollment: nearly 70 percent of program participants entered or reen-tered school. After the project, participants expressed their intention to marry later, and girls reported increased self-confidence, with 65 percent feeling "strong and able to face any problem" (Brady et al. 2007, 2).

Successfully addressing child marriage requires locally developed solutions that are tailored to the context and reflect an under-standing of the social and religious motiva-tions for child marriage. Several programs successfully engage community and religious leaders in efforts to chip away at the norms that perpetuate the practice. Some programs engage not only teachers but also community leaders. Others use conditional cash trans-fers to improve public transportation to go to schools or improve the quality of schooling (Wodon, forthcoming). An important exam-ple is the Tostan program in Senegal, which mobilized communities to change norms and expectations around female genital cutting, child marriage, and the value of the girl child (see box 2.1 in chapter 2).

Programs can include one-on-one meetings with parents, community meetings and educa-tion sessions, committees and forums to guide services for girls, communication campaigns and public announcements, and pledges by community gatekeepers. The Maharashtra Life Skills Program in India engaged parents and other adults in committees to develop an ado-lescent life-skills curriculum. The results show the power of community engagement in chang-ing deeply entrenched social norms. In less than three years, girls' age at marriage increased by one year (from 16 to 17), and unmarried girls expressed greater self-confidence and an increased ability to negotiate with parents. Among young married women, knowledge and use of health services increased, and other decision makers showed greater support for women's reproductive health needs (Pande et al. 2006).

In Uganda, the Empowerment and Livelihoods for Adolescents (ELA) pro-gram illustrates the ways in which agency-enhancing goals can be included in economic empowerment. ELA targeted girls ages 14 to 20 and provided life-skills train-ing and local market–informed vocational training. The program significantly improved girls' agency over sexual and reproductive health decisions, with a 26 percent reduction in rates of early childbearing and a 58 percent reduction in rates of child marriage and cohabitation. A 50 percent increase in condom use was also reported among girls who were sexually active. The share of girls who reported engaging in sex against their will dropped from 14 percent to 7 percent (Bandiera et al. 2014).

Overall, multisectoral approaches are likely to be more effective than a single-stream intervention. This is because the risk factors for early pregnancy are closely intertwined— including, for example, lack of education or economic opportunities—and multiple vulnerabilities that place girls at risk of unintended pregnancies must be addressed together. Moreover, the prevalence of adolescent mothers among the poor points to the need for interventions to address other challenges. To help break an intergenerational pattern of poverty, improving the socioeconomic conditions of children born to young mothers can be critical (Azevedo et al. 2012).

Implementing legal responses

Although not sufficient on their own, legal reforms are important. Laws must be backed by enforcement, including clear mandates, procedures, and funding and accountability mechanisms. Where legal provisions are more progressive than social norms, knowledge and compliance may remain low. Child marriage has been illegal in Bangladesh since the 1920s, yet three-quarters of girls are married by their 18th birthday. In such contexts, a multipronged approach is needed (box 4.4).

Even where progressive laws exist, gaps in implementation and procedural requirements render services inaccessible in some countries. Take abortion services, for example. In 2009, the Supreme Court of Nepal ruled that the country's abortion law had not been sufficiently implemented because the cost was prohibitively high.[7] In 2011, the European Court of Human Rights found that, for the second time, Poland's lack of a comprehensive legal framework for implementation violated its obligation to ensure

Box 4.4 Closing the gap between laws and practice in the Arab Republic of Egypt

A recent review of laws and the code of medical ethics showed that Egypt recognizes most of women's key rights related to family planning and reproductive health. Reproductive rights are also recognized in the Standards of Practice for Service Providers in Family Planning. Yet the standards and guidelines are not legally binding and, therefore, cannot be relied on to enforce or pursue breaches of rights, such as denial of service, coercion over a woman's choice of contraceptive method, or denial of informed consent.

Women's lack of agency continues to be a challenge, with data from four regions showing that awareness of the right to autonomy is notably lower than other rights. In some instances, women are asked for spousal consent to receive sexual and reproductive services, although this is not required by law. In 2007, to help close this gap, Mansoura University launched joint medico-legal and ethics training courses for health and law students.

Source: Rabie et al. 2013.

access to safe abortion services.[8] In Ghana, despite progressive abortion laws, unsafe abortion continues to be one of the leading causes of maternal mortality in the country.[9]

Progressive laws on abortion, when implemented effectively, can save women's lives by broadening their options in the case of an unintended pregnancy, thereby minimizing their risk of dying from an unsafe procedure. Legalization in Bangladesh, Romania, and South Africa led to measurable declines in abortion-related mortality (Benson, Andersen, and Samandari 2011). In South Africa, the annual number of abortion-related deaths fell by 91 percent after liberalization of the abortion law (Jewkes and Rees 2005).

Legal interventions can also ensure the right to free and full consent to marry. Countries can enhance penalties for those who force girls and women into unions. Amendments to the penal code of the Kyrgyz Republic, for example, increased the penalties for the practice of bride kidnapping, in which women and girls are taken against their will for the purpose of marriage (UN Women 2012). The government can also enforce a minimum age of marriage by requiring birth certificates prior to issuing marriage registrations, although this in turn requires a functioning mechanism of compulsory birth registration (Center for Reproductive Rights 2013). Employing women in the justice system can also help to increase women's trust in the law and make them feel confident about seeking help.[10]

* * *

Sexual and reproductive autonomy are intertwined with women's agency and opportunities in life more broadly. Fertility decisions should be made on the basis of informed choices and life plans that women and girls themselves value. This is especially relevant for vulnerable adolescents, who may perceive motherhood as their only option for social mobility and recognition.

It is important to engage men, boys, and community and family opinion leaders as informed and responsible decision makers and as advocates for women's sexual and reproductive health and rights. Programs that target and engage only women and girls will bring only partial results.

Notes

1. These data are from the United Nations Entity for Gender Equality and the Empowerment of Women's Indicators and Statistics Database, http://unstats.un.org/unsd/demographic/gender/wistat/.

2. Statistics on unmet need understate the true demand for family planning. They often exclude unmarried women because, especially in conservative cultural contexts, it is more difficult to collect reliable information on such women.

3. This description accords with the World Health Organization's definition of *unsafe abortion*. For more information, see the organization's website at http://www.who.int/reproductivehealth/publications/unsafe_abortion/en/.

4. This finding is from the World Values Survey, 2010–14 (wave 6). For more information, see the survey's website at http://www.worldvaluessurvey.org.

5. For more information about the Mobile Alliance for Maternal Messages, see the organization's website at http://mobilemamaalliance.org/mobile-messages.

6. Teenage fertility may decrease through (a) increased knowledge about contraception and access to family planning services or (b) increased school attendance. Conversely, CCTs may increase adolescent fertility—just as with overall fertility—if the subsidies lower the costs of raising a child, at least in the short run.

7. The case was *Lakshmi Dhikta v. Government of Nepal*, Writ No. 0757, Jestha, 2066 (2009) (Supreme Court of Nepal). See the Center for Reproductive Rights' website on world abortion laws at http://worldabortionlaws.com/about.html.

8. The case was *R. R. v. Palando*, App. No. 27617/04, Eur. Ct. H.R., para. 267 (2011). See the Center for Reproductive Rights' website on world abortion laws at http://worldabortionlaws.com/about.html.

9. The nongovernmental organization Ipas describes the situation in Ghana on its website at http://www.ipas.org/en/Where-We-Work/Africa/Ghana.aspx.

10. See, for example, World Bank (forthcoming). In the report, women mention the lack of female justice providers as a key obstacle hindering women's right to due process.

References

Alam, Andaleeb, Javier Baez, and Ximena Del Carpio. 2011. "Does Cash for School Influence Young Women's Behavior in the Longer Term? Evidence from Pakistan." Policy Research Working Paper 5669, World Bank, Washington, DC.

Amatya, Ramesh, Halida Akhter, James McMahan, Nancy Williamson, Deborah Gates, and Yasmin Ahmed. 1994. "The Effect of Husband Counseling on NORPLANT Contraceptive Acceptability in Bangladesh." *Contraception* 50 (3): 263–73.

Ashraf, Nava, Erica Field, and Jean Lee. 2010. "Household Bargaining and Excess Fertility: An Experimental Study in Zambia." Working paper, Harvard University, Cambridge, MA.

Azevedo, João Pedro, and Marta Favara. 2012. "The Impact of Bolsa Família on the Incidence of Teenage Pregnancies in Brazil." Background paper for *Teenage Pregnancy and Opportunities in Latin America and the Caribbean*, World Bank, Washington, DC.

Azevedo, João Pedro, Marta Favara, Sarah E. Haddock, Luis F. López-Calva, Miriam Müller, and Elizaveta Perova. 2012. *Teenage Pregnancy and Opportunities in Latin America and the Caribbean on Early Child Bearing, Poverty, and Economic Achievement.* Washington, DC: World Bank.

Baird, Sarah, Craig McIntosh, and Berk Özler. 2011. "Cash or Condition? Evidence from a Cash Transfer Experiment." *Quarterly Journal of Economics* 126 (4): 1709–53.

Bandiera, O., N. Buehren, R. Burgess, M. Goldstein, S. Gulesci, I. Rasul, and M. Sulaiman. 2014. "Women's Empowerment in Action: Evidence from a Randomized Control Trial in Africa." Working Paper, The International Growth Center, London School of Economics. http://www.theigc.org/sites/default/files/Bandiera%20et%20al%202014.pdf

Barker, Gary, Christine Ricardo, and Marcos Nascimento. 2007. "Engaging Men and Boys in Changing Gender-Based Inequity in Health: Evidence from Programme Interventions." World Health Organization, Geneva.

Bawah, Ayaga, Patricia Akweongo, Ruth Simmons, and James Phillips. 1999. "Women's Fears and Men's Anxieties: The Impact of Family Planning on Gender Relations in Northern Ghana." *Studies in Family Planning* 30 (1): 54–66.

Bearinger, Linda H., Renee E. Sieving, Jane Ferguson, and Vinit Sharma. 2007. "Global Perspectives on the Sexual and Reproductive Health of Adolescents: Patterns, Prevention, and Potential." *The Lancet* 369 (9568): 1220–31.

Benson, Janie, Kathryn Andersen, and Ghazaleh Samandari. 2011. "Reductions in Abortion-Related Mortality Following Policy Reform: Evidence from Romania, South Africa, and Bangladesh." *Reproductive Health* 8 (39). http://www.reproductive -health-journal.com/content/8/1/39.

Berthelon, Matias, and Diana Kruger. 2011. "Risky Behavior among Youth: Incapacitation Effects of School on Adolescent Motherhood and Crime in Chile." *Journal of Public Economics* 95 (1–2): 41–53.

Biddlecom, Ann E., and Bolaji M. Fapohunda. 1998. "Covert Contraceptive Use: Prevalence, Motivations, and Consequences." *Studies in Family Planning* 29 (4): 360–72.

Björkman, Martina, and Jakob Svensson. 2009. "Power to the People: Evidence from a Randomized Field Experiment on Community-Based Monitoring in Uganda." *Quarterly Journal of Economics* 124 (3): 735–69.

Boehmova, Zuzana. 2013. "Malawi Family Planning and Nutrition Integration Assessment." World Bank, Washington, DC.

Brady, Martha, Ragui Assaad, Barbara Ibrahim, Abeer Salem, Rania Salem, and Nadia Zibani. 2007. "Providing New Opportunities to Adolescent Girls in Socially Conservative Settings: The Ishraq Program in Rural Upper Egypt." Population Council, New York.

Bruce, Judith. 2003. "Married Adolescent Girls: Human Rights, Health, and Developmental Needs of a Neglected Majority." *Economic and Political Weekly* 38 (41): 4378–80.

———. 2007. "Child Marriage in the Context of the HIV Epidemic." Transitions to Adulthood Brief 11, Population Council, New York.

Casterline, John, Zeba Sathar, and Minhaj ul Haque. 2001. "Obstacles to Contraceptive Use in Pakistan: A Study in Punjab." *Studies in Family Planning* 32 (2): 95–110.

Center for Reproductive Rights. 2013. "Child Marriage in South Asia: Stop the Impunity." Press release, November 10. http://reproductiverights.org/en/press -room/child-marriage-in-south-asia-press -release.

———. 2014. "The World's Abortion Laws 2014." Interactive map, http:// worldabortionlaws.com/map/.

Chant, Sylvia, and Matthew Guttman. 2000. "Mainstreaming Men into Gender and Development." Working paper, Oxfam GB, Oxford, U.K.

Clark, Cari Jo, Jay Silverman, Inaam Khalaf, Basem Abu Ra'ad, Zeinab Abu Al Sha'ar, Abdullah Abu Al Ata, and Anwar Batieha. 2008. "Intimate Partner Violence and Interference with Women's Efforts to Avoid Pregnancy in Jordan." *Studies in Family Planning* 39 (2): 123–32.

Clark, Shelley. 2004. "Early Marriage and HIV Risks in Sub-Saharan Africa." *Studies in Family Planning* 35 (3): 149–58.

Commission on Population and Development. 2014. "Assessment of the Status of Implementation of the Programme of Action of the International Conference on Population and Development." Statement from the 47th Session of the Commission on Population and Development, April 12. http://www .un.org/en/development/desa/population /pdf/commission/2014/documents/CPD47 _Resolution_12042014_cln.pdf.

Díaz, Margarita, Ruth Simmons, Juan Díaz, Francisco Cabral, Debora Bossemeyer, Maria Y. Makuch, and Laura Ghiron. 2001. "Action Research to Enhance Reproductive Choice in a Brazilian Municipality: The Santa Barbara Project." In *Responding to Cairo: Case Studies of Changing Practice in Reproductive Health and Family Planning*, edited by Nicole Haberland and Diana Measham, 355–75. New York: Population Council.

Do, Mai, and Nami Kurimoto. 2012. "Women's Empowerment and Choice of Contraceptive Methods in Selected African Countries." *International Perspectives on Sexual and Reproductive Health* 38 (1): 23–33.

Doepke, Matthias, and Michele Tertlit. 2009. "Women's Liberation: What's in It for Men?" *Quarterly Journal of Economics* 11 (92): 379–420.

Duflo, Esther. 2012. "Women Empowerment and Economic Development." *Journal of Economic Literature* 50 (4): 1051–79.

El-Zanaty, Fatma, and Ann Way. 2005. *Egypt Demographic and Health Survey 2005.* Cairo: Ministry of Health and Population.

Erulkar, Annabel, Onoka Charles, and Phiri Alford. 2005. "What Is Youth-Friendly? Adolescents' Preferences for Reproductive Health Services in Kenya and Zimbabwe." *African Journal of Reproductive Health* 9 (3): 51–58.

Erulkar, Annabel, and Eunice Muthengi. 2009. "Evaluation of Berhane Hewan: A Program to Delay Marriage in Rural Ethiopia." *International Perspectives on Sexual and Reproductive Health* 35 (1): 6–14.

Ezeh, Alex Chika. 1993. "The Influence of Spouses over Each Other's Contraceptive Attitudes in Ghana." *Studies in Family Planning* 24 (3): 163–74.

Fairhurst, Karen, Sue Ziebland, Sally Wyke, Peter Seaman, and Anna Glasier. 2004. "Emergency Contraception: Why Can't You Give It Away? Qualitative Findings from an Evaluation of Advance Provision of Emergency Contraception." *Contraception* 70 (1): 25–29.

Field, Erica, and Attila Ambrus. 2008. "Early Marriage, Age of Menarche, and Female Schooling Attainment in Bangladesh." *Journal of Political Economy* 116 (5): 881–930.

Flake, Dallan. 2005. "Individual, Family, and Community Risk Markers for Domestic Violence in Peru." *Violence Against Women* 11 (3): 353–73.

Fleming, Paul J., Gary Barker, Jennifer McCleary-Sills, and Matthew Morton. 2013. "Engaging Men and Boys in Advancing Women's Agency: Where We Stand and New Directions." Women's Voice, Agency, and Participation Research Paper 1, World Bank, Washington, DC.

Gee, Rebekah E., Nandita Mitra, Fei Wan, Diana F. Chavkin, and Judith A. Long. 2009. "Power over Parity: Intimate Partner Violence and Issues of Fertility Control." *American Journal of Obstetrics and Gynecology* 201 (2): 148.e1–7.

Grépin, Karen A., and Jeni Klugman. 2013. "Maternal Health: A Missed Opportunity for Development." *The Lancet* 381 (9879): 1691–93.

Gurman, Tilly, Sara Rubin, and Amira Roess. 2012. "Effectiveness of mHealth Behavior Change Communication Interventions in Developing Countries: A Systematic Review of the Literature." *Journal of Health Communication* 17 (suppl. 1): 82–104.

Guttmacher Institute. 2000. "Couples' Reports of Their Contraceptive Use: Do Husbands in Africa Overstate the Case?" *International Family Planning Perspectives* 26 (4): 203–4.

Guttmacher Institute and IPPF (International Planned Parenthood Federation). 2010. "Facts on the Sexual and Reproductive Health of Adolescent Women in the Developing World." Guttmacher Institute, New York.

Haub, Carl. 2013. "Trends in Adolescent Fertility: A Mixed Picture." Population Reference Bureau, Washington, DC. http://www.prb.org/Publications/Articles/2013/adolescent-fertility.aspx.

Hindin, Michelle J., and Adesegun O. Fatusi. 2009. "Adolescent Sexual and Reproductive Health in Developing Countries: An Overview of Trends and Interventions."

International Perspectives on Sexual and Reproductive Health 35 (2): 58–62.

Htun, Mala, and S. Laurel Weldon. 2011. "Sex Equality in Family Law: Historical Legacies, Feminist Activism, and Religious Power in 70 Countries." Background paper for *World Development Report 2012: Gender Equality and Development*, World Bank, Washington, DC.

ICPD (International Conference on Population and Development). 1994. *Programme of Action: Report of the International Conference on Population and Development.* ICPD, Cairo, September 5–13. http://www .unfpa.org/public/home/publications /pid/1973.

———. 2014. *Report of the Operational Review of the Implementation of the Programme of Action of the International Conference on Population and Development and Its Follow-up beyond 2014.* New York: ICPD.

ICRW (International Center for Research on Women). 2006a. "Child Marriage and Domestic Violence." ICRW, Washington, DC. http://www.icrw.org/files/images/Child -Marriage-Fact-Sheet-Domestic-Violence.pdf.

———. 2006b. "Delaying Age at Marriage in Rural Maharashtra, India." ICRW, Washington, DC. http://www.icrw.org /files/images/Delaying-Age-at-Marriage -in-Rural-Maharashtra-India.pdf.

———. 2013. "Child Marriage Facts and Figures." ICRW, Washington, DC. http://www.icrw .org/child-marriage-facts-and-figures.

Inelmen, Emine M., Giuseppe Sergi, Agostino Girardi, Alessandra Coin, Elena D. Toffanello, Fabrizio Cardin, and Enzo Manzato. 2012. "The Importance of Sexual Health in the Elderly: Breaking Down the Barriers and Taboos." *Aging Clinical and Experimental Research* 24 (3): 31–34.

Jain, Saranga, and Kathleen Kurz. 2007. "New Insights on Preventing Child Marriage." International Center for Research on Women, Washington, DC.

Jensen, Robert. 2012. "Do Labor Market Opportunities Affect Young Women's Work and Family Decisions? Experimental Evidence from India." *Quarterly Journal of Economics* 127 (2): 753–92.

Jewkes, Rachel, and Helen Rees. 2005. "Dramatic Decline in Abortion Mortality Due to the Choice on Termination of Pregnancy Act." *South African Medical Journal* 95 (4): 250.

Kadir, Muhammad Masood, Fariyal Fikree, Amanullah Khan, and Fatima Sajan. 2003. "Do Mothers-in-Law Matter? Family Dynamics and Fertility Decision-Making in Urban Squatter Settlements of Karachi, Pakistan." *Journal of Biosocial Science* 35 (4): 545–58.

Kamal, Nashid. 2000. "The Influence of Husbands on Contraceptive Use by Bangladeshi Women." *Health Policy and Planning* 15 (1): 43–51.

Keele, Jeremy, Renata Forste, and Dailan Flake. 2005. "Hearing Native Voices: Contraceptive Use in Matemwe Village, East Africa." *African Journal of Reproductive Health* 9 (1): 32–41.

Kelly, Robert, Ronald Gray, Nelson Sewankambo, David Serwadda, Fred Wabwire-Mangen, and Maria J. Wawer. 2003. "Age Differences in Sexual Partners and Risk of HIV-1 Infection in Rural Uganda." *Journal of Acquired Immune Deficiency Syndrome* 32 (4): 446–51.

Kesterton, Amy J., and Meena Cabral de Mello. 2010. "Generating Demand and Community Support for Sexual and Reproductive Health Services for Young People: A Review of the Literature and Programs." *Reproductive Health* 7: 25.

La Ferrara, Eliana, Alberto Chong, and Suzanne Duryea. 2008. "Soap Operas and Fertility: Evidence from Brazil." Research Department Working Paper 633, Inter-American Development Bank, Washington, DC. http:// www.iadb.org/res/publications/pubfiles /pubWP-633.pdf.

L'Engle, Kelly, Dawn Chin-Quee, Michele Lanham, Laura Hinson, and Heather Vahdat. 2009. "The Good, the Bad, and the Ugly: The Role of Men in Family Planning Decision Making—Male Partner's Roles in Women's Use of Emergency Contraception." Presented at the International Family Planning Conference: Research and Best Practices, Kampala, November 17. http://www.fpconference2009.org/media//DIR_169701/15f1ae857ca97193ffff82c9ffffd524.pdf.

Lester, Richard, Paul Ritvo, Edward Mills, Anthony Kariri, Sarah Karanja, Michael Chung, William Jack, James Habyarimana, Mansen Sadatsafavi, Menal Najafzadeh. 2010. "Effects of a Mobile Phone Short Message Service on Antiretroviral Treatment Adherence in Kenya (WelTel Kenya1): A Randomised Trial." *The Lancet* 376 (9755): 1838–45.

Levine, Deborah, Jacqueline McCright, Loren Dobkin, Andrew Woodruff, and Jeffrey Klausner. 2008. "SEXINFO: A Sexual Health Text Messaging Service for San Francisco Youth." *American Journal of Public Health* 98 (3): 393–95.

Levine, Judith A., Harold Pollack, and Maureen Comfort. 2001. "Academic and Behavioral Outcomes among the Children of Young Mothers." *Journal of Marriage and Family* 63 (2): 355–69.

Libbus, Kay, and Suha Kridli. 1997. "Contraceptive Decision Making in a Sample of Jordanian Muslim Women: Delineating Salient Beliefs." *Health Care for Women International* 18 (1): 85–94.

Lopez-Calva, Luis Felipe, and Elizaveta Perova. 2012. "The Impact of Conditional Cash Transfers on the Incidence of Teenage Pregnancies: Evidence from Peru." Background paper for *Teenage Pregnancy and Opportunities in Latin America and the Caribbean*, World Bank, Washington, DC.

Luffman, Laurinda. 2012. "Attitudes on Child Marriage Slow to Change in Nepal." SOS Children's Villages, Cambridge, U.K. http://www.soschildrensvillages.org.uk/news/archive/2012/06/attitudes-on-child-marriage-slow-to-change-in-nepal.

Malhotra, Anju, Ann Warner, Allison McGonagle, and Susan Lee-Rife. 2011. "Solutions to End Child Marriage: What the Evidence Shows." International Center for Research on Women, Washington, DC.

Mathur, Sanyukta, Margaret Greene, and Anju Malhotra. 2003. "Too Young to Wed: The Lives, Rights, and Health of Young Married Girls." International Center for Research on Women, Washington, DC.

McCleary-Sills, Jennifer, Alison McGonagle, and Anju Malhotra. 2012. "Women's Demand for Reproductive Control: Understanding and Addressing Gender Barriers." International Center for Research on Women, Washington, DC.

Mwaikambo, Lisa, Ilene Speizer, Anne Schurmann, Gwen Morgan, and Fariyal Fikree. 2011. "What Works in Family Planning Interventions: A Systematic Review." *Studies in Family Planning* 42 (2): 67–82.

Nanda, Priya, Nitin Datta, and Priya Das. 2014. "Impact of Conditional Cash Transfers on Girls' Education: Summary of Research Findings." International Center for Research on Women, Washington, DC.

Nguyen, Minh Cong, and Quentin Wodon. 2013. "Estimating the Impact of Child Marriage on Literacy and Education Attainment in Africa." World Bank, Washington, DC.

Nour, Nawal M. 2009. "Child Marriage: A Silent Health and Human Rights Issue." *Review of Obstetrics and Gynecology* 2 (1): 51–55.

Pande, Rohni, Kathleen Kurz, Sunayana Walia, Kerry MacQuarrie, and Safanga Jain. 2006. "Improving the Reproductive Health of Married and Unmarried Youth in India: Evidence and Effectiveness and Costs from Community-Based Interventions." International Center for Research on Women, Washington, DC.

Papp, Susan A., Aparajita Gogoi, and Catherine Campbell. 2012. "Improving Maternal Health through Social Accountability: A Case Study from Orissa, India." *Global Public Health* 8 (4): 449–64.

Pop-Eleches, Cristian, Harsha Thirumurthy, James Habyarimana, Joshua Zivin, Markus Goldstein, Damien de Walque, Lesley MacKeen, Jessica Haberer, Duncan Ngare, Davide Bangsberg, and John Sidle. 2011. "Mobile Phone Technologies Improve Adherence to Antiretroviral Treatment in a Resource-Limited Setting: A Randomized Controlled Trial of Text Message Reminders." *AIDS* 25 (6): 825–34.

Population Reference Bureau. 2013. "The World's Youth: 2013 Data Sheet." Population Reference Bureau, Washington, DC.

Rabie, Tamer, Zuzana Boehmova, Loraine Hawkins, Nahla Abdel Tawab, Sally Saher, and Atef El Shitany. 2013. "Transforming Family Planning Outlook and Practice in Egypt: A Rights-Based Approach." World Bank, Washington, DC.

Raj, Anita. 2010. "When the Mother Is a Child: The Impact of Child Marriage on Health and Human Rights of Girls." *Archives of Diseases in Childhood* 95 (11): 931–35.

Raj, Anita, and Ulrike Boehmer. 2013. "Girl Child Marriage and Its Association with National Rates of HIV, Maternal Health, and Infant Mortality across 97 Countries." *Violence against Women* 19 (4): 536–51.

Raj, Anita, Niranjan Saggurti, Danielle Lawrence, Donta Balaiah, and Jay G. Silverman. 2010. "Association between Adolescent Marriage and Marital Violence in Young Adulthood in India." *International Journal of Gynecology and Obstetrics* 110 (1): 35–39.

Robyn, Jacob, Gaston Sorgho, and Omer Zang. 2014. "Additional Financing: Concept Note Paper of the Performance Based Financing on Health in Cameroon." World Bank, Washington DC.

Rottach, Elisabeth, Sidney Ruth Schuler, and Karen Hardee. 2009. *Gender Perspectives Improve Reproductive Health Outcomes: New Evidence.* Washington, DC: Population Reference Bureau.

Sedgh, Gilda, Susheela Singh, Isabel Shah, Elisabeth Ahman, Stanley Henshaw, and Akinrinola Bankole. 2012. "Induced Abortion: Incidence and Trends Worldwide from 1995 to 2008." *The Lancet* 379 (9816): 625–32.

Shah, Iqbal, and Elisabeth Ahman. 2004. "Age Patterns of Unsafe Abortion in Developing Country Regions." *Reproductive Health Matters* 12 (24): 9–17.

Shattuck, Dominick, Brad Kerner, Kate Gilles, Miriam Hartmann, Thokozani Ng'ombe, and Greg Guest. 2011. "Encouraging Contraceptive Uptake by Motivating Men to Communicate about Family Planning: The Malawi Male Motivator Project." *American Journal of Public Health* 101 (6): 1089–95.

Singh, Susheela, and Jacqueline Darroch. 2012. "Adding It Up: Costs and Benefits of Contraceptive Services, Estimates for 2012." Guttmacher Institute and United Nations Population Fund, New York.

Speizer, Ilene, Lisa Whittle, and Marion Carter. 2005. "Gender Relations and Reproductive Decision Making in Honduras." *International Family Planning Perspectives* 31 (33): 131–39.

Stephenson, Rob, Andy Beke, and Delphin Tshibangu. 2008. "Contextual Influences on Contraceptive Use in the Eastern Cape, South Africa." *Health and Place* 14 (4): 839–50.

Storey, J. Douglas, Marc Boulay, Yagya Karki, Karen Heckert, and Dibya Man Karmacha. 1999. "Impact of the Integrated Radio Communication Project in Nepal, 1994–1997." *Journal of Health Communication* 4 (4): 271–94.

Storey, J. Douglas, and Esther Kaggwa. 2009. "The Influence of Changes in Fertility

Related Norms on Contraceptive Use in Egypt, 1995–2005." *Population Review* 48 (1): 1–19.

UNAIDS (Joint United Nations Programme on HIV/AIDS). 2012. "World AIDS Day Report." UNAIDS, New York.

———. 2013a. "AIDS by the Numbers." UNAIDS, New York.

———. 2013b. *Global Report: UNAIDS Report on the Global AIDS Epidemic 2013.* New York: UNAIDS.

UNESCO (United Nations Educational, Scientific, and Cultural Organization). 2013. *Young People and the Law in Asia and the Pacific: A Review of Laws and Policies Affecting Young People's Access to Sexual and Reproductive Health and HIV Services.* New York: UNESCO.

UNFPA (United Nations Population Fund). 2006. "Family Planning and Young People: Their Choices Create the Future." UNFPA, New York.

———. 2010. "How Universal Is Access to Reproductive Health? A Review of the Evidence." UNFPA, New York.

———. 2011. "Using Mobile Phones to Tackle Fistula in Tanzania." *UNFPA News,* May 23. http://www.unfpa.org/public/home/news/pid/7697.

———. 2012a. "Marrying Too Young: End Child Marriage." UNFPA, New York.

———. 2012b. *State of the World's Population: By Choice, Not By Chance—Family Planning, Human Rights, and Development.* New York: UNFPA.

———. 2013. *State of the World's Population 2013: Motherhood in Childhood.* New York: UNFPA.

UNICEF (United Nations Children's Fund). 2005. "Early Marriage: A Harmful Traditional Practice." UNICEF, New York.

———. 2013a. "Lost in Transitions: Current Issues Faced by Adolescents Living with HIV in Asia Pacific." UNICEF, New York.

———. 2013b. *State of the World's Children 2013: Children with Disabilities.* New York: UNICEF. http://www.unicef.org/sowc2013/.

United Nations. 1967. "Declaration on the Elimination of Discrimination against Women." UN General Assembly, 22nd Session, New York, November 7.

United Nations Foundation–Vodafone Foundation Partnership. 2009. "mHealth for Development: The Opportunity of Mobile Technology for Healthcare in the Developing World." United Nations Foundation, Washington, DC.

UN Women (United Nations Entity for Gender Equality and the Empowerment of Women). 2010. "Defining Other Forms of Forced Marriage: Bride Kidnapping." United Nations, New York.

———. 2012. "Marriages: Free and Full Consent in Entering a Marriage." United Nations, New York. http://www.endvawnow.org/en/articles/765-marriages-.html?next=766.

Vodafone Foundation. 2011. "Mobile for Good." Vodafone Group, Berkshire, U.K. http://www.vodafone.com/content/index/about/foundation/mobiles_for_good/ccbrt.html.

Vogelstein, Rachel. 2013. "Ending Child Marriage: How Elevating the Status of Girls Advances U.S. Foreign Policy Objectives." Council on Foreign Relations, New York.

Wodon, Quentin, ed. Forthcoming. *Child Marriage and Education in Sub-Saharan Africa.* Washington, DC: World Bank.

World Bank. 2011a. *Defining Gender in the 21st Century: Talking with Women and Men around the World—A Multi-country Qualitative Study of Gender and Economic Choice.* Washington, DC: World Bank.

———. 2011b. *World Development Report 2012: Gender Equality and Development.* Washington, DC: World Bank.

———. 2013a. "Health Results Innovation Trust Fund (HRITF): Initial Results." Presentation, Interagency Working Group, World Bank, Washington, DC, April 17.

———. 2013b. "Results-Based Financing for Health: Rwanda." World Bank, Washington, DC. http://www.rbfhealth.org/country /rwanda.

———. 2013c. "World Bank Group to Invest $700 Million by 2015 to Improve Women and Children's Health in Poor Countries." *News*, September 23. http://www.worldbank .org/en/news/press-release/2013/09/23 /world-bank-group-invest-700-million-2015 -improve-women-children-health-poor -countries.

———. 2014. "Voices of Men and Women regarding Social Norms in Niger." Poverty Reduction and Economic Management Africa Region Report 83296-NE, World Bank, Washington, DC.

———. Forthcoming. *Gender and Justice in Afghanistan*. Washington, DC: World Bank.

Zavodny, Madeline. 2004. "Fertility and Parental Consent for Minors to Receive Contraceptives." *American Journal of Public Health* 94 (8): 1347–51.

Chapter 5 Key messages

> Access to and control over land can expand women's agency, increasing self-esteem, economic opportunities, mobility outside of the home, and decision-making power.

> Fewer women than men report owning land or housing. More women who are married, divorced, or widowed report owning land than do single women. Women are more likely to report they own land jointly than individually.

> Social norms, customary practices, inaccessible and weak institutions, and, in many cases, women's lack of awareness of their rights are important barriers to the full realization of women's land rights.

> Three key areas of legislation—family law, inheritance law, and land law—affect the right to own and control property. Complex and sometimes contradictory sets of statutory laws, customs, and norms affect women's land ownership.

> Law reform and improved implementation, better gender-sensitive administration, and richer sex-disaggregated data are all needed to ensure women's land rights are fully realized.

CHAPTER 5

Control over Land and Housing

Women's control over land and housing as a development challenge

Access to and control over housing and land can expand women's agency and increase their access to a range of opportunities. The *World Development Report 2012* emphasized that assets are instrumental in increasing agency through boosting voice and bargaining power in household decision-making, access to capital, and overall economic independence (World Bank 2011). This chapter explores the benefits for women of owning and controlling land, presents new analysis about ownership patterns, and highlights evidence about what works to increase women's ownership. Access to movable assets and credit are clearly important for women's economic empowerment but are outside the scope of this book.

A growing global consensus recognizes the intrinsic and instrumental importance of securing rights to land and other productive resources in the eradication of poverty and reduction of gender inequality (Hanstad, Tran, and Bannick 2013). Equal rights to access, use, and control of land are enshrined in international agreements, such as the Universal Declaration of Human Rights and the Convention on the Elimination of All Forms of Discrimination against Women (CEDAW), and regional agreements, such as the Arab Charter on Human Rights. These rights have become increasingly important with the advent of large-scale land deals in developing countries. Women are often marginalized in such processes because they lack formal land rights and are not included in negotiations leading up to the leasing or sale of land (Behrman, Meinzen-Dick, and Quisumbing 2011).

Women's ability to exercise agency over land and housing is determined by the interplay of laws—including statutory, customary, and religious laws—and social norms.

Where good laws do exist, social norms that dictate men are the sole decision makers in the household may mean that those laws are not implemented. We focus on three key areas of legislation—family law, inheritance law, and land law—that affect the right to own and control property (Hallward-Driemeier and Hasan 2013). Together they govern the distribution of household property and assets, and discrimination against women in these areas can result in unequal property rights. Today, 37 of 143 countries included in *Women, Business, and the Law 2014* still have discriminatory laws in place (World Bank and IFC 2013).

Potentially transformative effects

Control over land and housing has instrumental value. Women who have more control over land—whether through inheritance, land titling, improved documentation, or stronger communal rights—tend to have greater self-esteem, respect from other family members, economic opportunities, mobility outside of the home, and decision-making power (Bhatla, Chakraborty, and Duvvury 2006; Rodgers and Menon 2012). Constraints on their land ownership can reduce the efficiency of land use (Udry 1996), can decrease women's economic

"When I have the feeling of security, that my land will not be taken away, I am able to grow food on it to feed my family and support my community. My community is more secure when I am secure."

—Parents of Children with Disabilities (ZPCD), Zimbabwe, Huairou Commission member (Scholz et al. 2013)

opportunities (Quisumbing and Maluccio 2003), and can exacerbate land conflict (Deininger and Castagnini 2008; Joireman 2008). Studies document that women's access to land and housing can affect girls' survival rates (Qian 2008), their nutritional status (Duflo 2003), and investment in girls' schooling (Luke and Munshi 2011), suggesting far-reaching benefits.

Amartya Sen (1990) has noted that female land ownership can increase a woman's contribution to the common good of the household, giving her a stronger voice. A broad selection of literature affirms this view, showing that enhanced ownership of assets, particularly land, raises household well-being through increased female bargaining power (Doss 2005; Smith et al. 2003). This increase can translate into greater participation in household spending decisions and stronger, more realistic exit options in the case of an unhappy or abusive relationship. Twenty years ago, Bina Argawal's study of rural South Asia identified gaps in land ownership and control as the most important contributor to disparities in economic well-being, social status, and empowerment (Agarwal 1994). More recent studies reinforce and extend this finding with the following associations:

- In Vietnam, women with a joint title are more aware of legal issues, are more likely to proactively seek a Land Tenure Certificate, have more say in the use and disposition of land, and are more likely to earn independent incomes than women who are not on the title (World Bank 2008).

- In Peru, squatter households given property titles experienced a 22 percent reduction in fertility rates, and females who received a joint title were two times less likely to have a child than females in families in which the title was in the male partner's name only. Receipt of titles also allowed women to seek paid work instead of spending time safeguarding their land against property invasion (Field 2007).

■ In Nepal, women who own land are significantly more likely to have a final say in household decisions, and children of mothers who own land are less likely to be underweight, with associated benefits for almost all maternal and child nutritional outcomes (Allendorf 2007).

■ In Ecuador, joint land ownership increased women's participation in household decisions about crop cultivation (Deere and Twymen 2012a, 2012b).

■ In rural Karnataka, India, ownership of land and housing improved women's mobility outside the home and their ability to make decisions about their work, health, and household spending (Swaminathan, Lahoti, and Suchitra 2012).

Our analysis of 15 countries suggests the overall level of gender equality in a country is correlated with the share of women who report owning housing (figure 5.1).

For single women, land ownership can provide independence. It may allow them to postpone marriage or stay in school longer. In India, for example, changes in the inheritance laws allowing unmarried daughters to inherit ancestral land delayed the age of marriage and increased investment in education for girls (Deininger, Goyal, and Nagarajan 2010; see also box 5.1).

Expanding women's ownership of land and housing is not a panacea, nor is land legislation alone. Access to credit, markets, education, extension services, technology, personal mobility, and public voice all influence women's ability to claim and make use of property rights (Spichiger et al. 2013).

What do ownership and control mean?

Ownership and *control* are defined in box 5.2. Generally, survey measures of ownership use self-reported ownership, which is obtained simply by asking respondents whether they own land. This means that land may be reported as "owned" even when this is not strictly the case legally. Questions about asset ownership more generally typically refer to the household and are only sometimes followed by inquiries about individual ownership, which is needed to conduct gender analysis. Questions about access and control may differ depending on the purpose of the survey. The Demographic and Health Surveys (DHS), for example, ask men and women individually about ownership of land and housing.

The different types of ownership and use rights outlined in box 5.2 affect the degree of women's control over land or housing, which in turn can have important bearing on household decision making and well-being. It is also important to recognize that joint ownership does not necessarily mean that women and men have equal management rights over the land or housing they own.

Land and housing rights may differ in urban versus rural areas. Increased urbanization means that owning housing in urban areas will become increasingly important for providing a place for women and their families to live as well as a potential source

FIGURE 5.1   Correlation between women's property ownership and gender equality

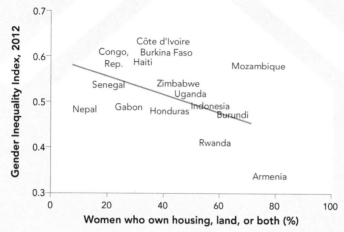

Sources: Demographic and Health Surveys data, 2010–12; United Nations Development Programme Gender Inequality Index (2012).

Box 5.1   Can control over land reduce gender-based violence?

Chapter 3 reviewed the extent and gravity of gender-based violence, focusing primarily on violence in the home. Women's asset ownership may provide exit options from unhappy or abusive relationships and can reduce vulnerability to domestic violence. In Kerala, India, a panel survey of ever-married women (that is, married women, widows, or divorcees) found that more than 70 percent of the women who owned land or housing and who had experienced long-term physical violence had left their husband and the matrimonial home, and few had returned. In contrast, almost all of the 20 percent of women who did not own such property went to live with their parents, and, ultimately, half returned to their husbands. Land and housing ownership also demonstrated a more secure exit option than employment: only one-third of women were employed, and the majority were in low-paying and irregular employment.

In West Bengal, India, women who did not own land or housing were more likely to report domestic violence than those who did—57 percent of women without property compared to 35 percent of women who were property owners. In contrast, in Sri Lanka, women who owned property did not report lower rates of intimate partner violence than women who did not own property. The mixed nature of these findings may be due in part to women acquiring property after marriage, when a pattern of violence may already be entrenched in the relationship, but further exploration is needed.

The introduction of joint titling in Ethiopia's Amhara region in 2000, supported by strong implementation, has meant that men are more reluctant to ask for a divorce because they risk the division of their property. However, whether this trend is beneficial for women or ties them to abusive relationships is unclear. It is important to bear in mind that most of the studies do not show causal relationships but instead demonstrate associations.

Sources: Agarwal and Panda 2007; Teklu 2005.

of income. In rural areas, agricultural land may be more important for men's and women's livelihoods and have greater benefits for women's agency than house ownership (Rakodi 2014). This is an area in which data and evidence are limited and further research is needed.

How large is the challenge?

Data on land ownership are scarce and often not comparable across countries, but available data suggest that women are disadvantaged. Women who own land are more likely to own it jointly, whereas men are more likely to own land alone. Often women can access land only through male relatives. A women's ability to inherit or hold onto land in the case of divorce is often limited, and daughters may not be entitled to inherit land. Our analysis of DHS data finds that women who are younger, are single, and have less education are more disadvantaged than others and that certain characteristics, such as being married or working, can increase women's likelihood of owning land and housing.

Box 5.2 What do we mean by ownership and control?

Clarifying the terms *ownership* and *control* in relation to land and housing is important.

Reported ownership indicates that a respondent reports owning land or housing (a question usually posed at the household level). However, even when a woman self-reports as a joint owner of a land parcel with her husband, often his name alone appears on the documentation.

Documented ownership indicates that an individual's name is on the relevant document, either alone or jointly with someone else. This document may be a formal land title or a customary certificate, certificate of sale, or inheritance documentation. Inclusion on a document provides a verifiable form of ownership; this is important for women in the wake of a divorce or a husband's death and also in the case of a sale or transfer of land.

Effective ownership is about decision-making power over how to use and dispose of property. Individuals may have partial ownership rights, such as user rights to cultivate, rent, and even bequeath land but still lack authority to sell the land.

In general, women's documented ownership of land is lower than self-reported ownership. For example, 8 percent of women and 15 percent of men are self-reported landowners in Ghana, which falls to 1 percent and 2 percent, respectively, among those with a formal ownership document.

Individuals can have control over land under customary law in a number of countries, including Malawi and Rwanda. Under customary law, individuals may have rights of use, with differing degrees of freedom to lease out, mortgage, bequeath, or sell. Land rights also may have a temporal or locational dimension: they may accrue only for a person's lifetime or some lesser period and may be conditional on the person residing on the land or locally. The extent to which an individual perceives herself to be an owner may affect her choices about the land and decision making more broadly.

Sources: Agarwal 1994; Doss 2012 ; Doss et al. 2011, 2013.

Existing disparities

A recent review of 17 microstudies from Sub-Saharan Africa suggests that regardless of indicator and country, women are disadvantaged relative to men in self-reported land ownership, documented ownership, management control, and decision-making authority over land. In Africa, the size of the gender gap varies by country and type of land and by type of landholding (Doss et al. 2013).

Our analysis of DHS data suggests that women are less likely to report owning land or housing than men in most of the 13 countries covered.[1] In some cases, the gaps are striking (figure 5.2). In several countries, the share of male landowners exceeds that of female landowners by a large margin, but the reverse is never true; where women report owning more land, as in Rwanda, the difference tends to be slight. With respect to housing, in a few countries, women's reported ownership is equal to or slightly greater than men's: In Burkina Faso, more than twice as many men than women (65 percent and 31 percent, respectively) report owning housing; in Mozambique, 64 percent of women and 59 percent of men report owning housing. In some countries, very few women *or* men own property: in Nepal, roughly one-quarter of men and less than one-tenth of women report owning housing.

Men's reporting of sole ownership is higher in all 13 countries, most notably in Burkina Faso, Burundi, Côte d'Ivoire, Honduras, Nepal, Senegal, and Uganda. Women tend to report owning land jointly rather than owning it alone, except in Honduras and Nepal (figure 5.3). In Armenia, Honduras, Indonesia, and Senegal, similar proportions of men and women report owning land jointly, but in the other countries, the share of women reporting joint ownership of land is much higher than that of men.

Widespread debate surrounds the merits of joint versus individual titles, but rigorous evidence is limited, and the patterns are complex and differ widely within and between countries. Social norms are important; contravening social norms by obtaining individual property rights may carry high social costs, making joint property rights more attractive (Jackson 2003). In Chandigarh, India, where joint titling was introduced in 2000, women reported valuing joint tenure because their husbands could not sell the property without their consent, and joint titling improved their self-esteem and access to financial and economic information and increased their involvement in household decision making (Datta 2006). In Heredia, Costa Rica, joint titles gave bargaining power to women during divorce proceedings but also meant that couples were more likely to stay in unhappy or violent relationships because neither could afford to buy out the other (Blanco Rothe et al. 2002).

The effects on women's decision-making power vary. In Mali, Malawi, and Tanzania, women with individual property ownership increased their agricultural decision-making power compared to women with joint ownership, but individual property ownership had little effect on nonagricultural decision making. In India, individual property ownership had little influence on agricultural and household decision making, and joint ownership had a negative correlation with women's inputs into household decision making. Social norms in India may mean that women with

FIGURE 5.2 Share of women and men who report owning housing and land

Women and men who own housing

Women and men who own land

Source: Estimates based on Demographic and Health Surveys data for 13 countries, latest year available.

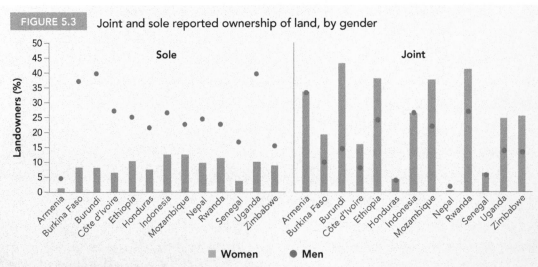

FIGURE 5.3 Joint and sole reported ownership of land, by gender

■ Women ● Men

Source: Estimates based on Demographic and Health Surveys data, latest year available, 2010–12.

higher social status who are property owners prefer to say that they are not involved in agricultural decision making. More data and evidence are needed (for example, on individual ownership at the plot level) to enhance our understanding of how individual and joint ownership affects women's role in household decision making (Doss et al. 2014).

Postconflict reconstruction may provide opportunities for reinforcing women's land rights. In the aftermath of the conflict in Rwanda, for example, the government initiated a policy of inclusive land reform to avert the possibility of future disputes over land. The resulting Matrimonial Regimes, Liberties, and Succession Law (2000) and Organic Land Law (2005) have improved inheritance rights and joint titling for women (UN Women 2013b).

Marital status and work

Our analysis of DHS data for 15 countries identifies some of the characteristics associated with women's land and housing ownership. Marital status, participation in labor markets, and geographic location influence whether women are likely to report owning property. Figure 5.4 shows that in rural areas, married women (including women who are formerly married or in de facto partnerships) have the highest probability of owning land and are

Social norms in India may mean that women with higher social status who are property owners prefer to say that they are not involved in agricultural decision making.

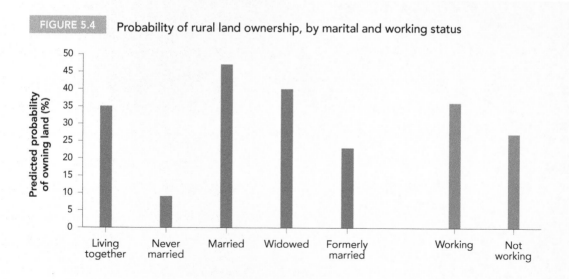

FIGURE 5.4   Probability of rural land ownership, by marital and working status

Source: Estimates using Demographic and Health Surveys data for 15 countries, latest years available, 2010–12.

Note: Figure shows predicted probabilities of land ownership in rural areas, controlling for age, work status, number of children, husband's education, marital status, various household characteristics, property regime (separate or community of property), and country fixed effects.

about five times more likely to own land than are women who have never married.[2] Working increases the likelihood of land ownership too. In some countries, the effect is particularly notable. Women who work in the Republic of Congo, for example, are 24 percent more likely to report owning land than women who do not work. Evidence from India also suggests that land ownership is a strong predictor of self-employment for rural women (Menon and Rodgers 2011). In urban areas, married women are three times more likely to report owning housing than never married women.

Laws and norms

Statutory laws, customs, and norms affect land ownership. Customary and local tenure systems are widespread. Worldwide, as many as 2 billion people live under customary tenure regimes (USAID 2013), and less than 10 percent of land in Africa is held under statutory land tenure (Cotula et al. 2009; Deininger 2003). These sets of laws and norms can be complex and sometimes contradictory. Most developing countries have hybrid or plural land tenure systems, where statutory property tenure rights exist alongside customary regimes. Customary tenure is often recognized under statutes or in constitutions; in Cambodia, the Land Law (2001) grants collective ownership rights to indigenous communities (Xanthaki 2003), and in Rwanda, the Organic Land Law (2005) recognizes customarily acquired land (Ali, Deininger, and Goldstein 2011).

Inheritance regimes reflect norms around women's property ownership and are often very complex. Key aspects include whether sons and daughters are treated equally and whether spouses have equal

inheritance rights to each other's estates, in addition to provisions governing those who pass away without a will. In 28 of 143 countries in the Women, Business, and the Law database (http://wbl.worldbank.org/), statutory inheritance laws differentiate between women and men. These countries include all those covered in the Middle East and North Africa and nine in Sub-Saharan Africa (Burundi, Guinea, Lesotho, Mali, Mauritania, Senegal, Sudan, Tanzania, and Uganda). Ten countries (Cameroon, Chile, the Democratic Republic of Congo, the Republic of Congo, Côte d'Ivoire, Ecuador, Gabon, Haiti, Mauritania, and the Philippines) limit married women's rights over property by requiring women to have their husband's permission to enter into a transaction concerning land (but lack a similar requirement for men).

Customary inheritance laws prevail constitutionally in more than one-quarter of countries in Sub-Saharan Africa and are often biased against women (Harrington and Chopra 2010). Customary land in Ghana is specifically excluded from statutory inheritance laws and, instead, usually devolves to a male heir in accordance with custom (Hallward-Driemeier and Hasan 2013). In some instances, judges may have a choice as to which law to apply. This is the case in Sri Lanka, where inheritance questions may be answered by the body of case law, Roman-Dutch law, Shari'a law, or customary law, depending on the ethnic group (Scalise 2009).

The reform of discriminatory inheritance laws can have broad positive effects. Females whose fathers died after the 1994 reform in India were 22 percentage points more likely to inherit land than those whose fathers died before the reform came into effect. The reform also had additional benefits for women's agency, including an increase in women's age at marriage relative to men and increased educational attainment (Deininger, Goyal, and Nagarajan 2010). However, implementation of the law is still weak, suggesting potentially more far-reaching results. For example, public officials may be ill informed, and women may lack awareness of their rights. Social norms can lead to women giving up their rights in return for protection from male relatives, and families may feel they have fulfilled their financial obligations to their daughters by providing a dowry on marriage (Landesa 2013).

Across plural legal systems, no clear pattern exists as to which source of law is more advantageous for women; this will depend on local context. Where discriminatory practices prevail, statutory laws may provide women with more secure rights than under custom. In other cases, women's rights may be better protected under customary tenure (Knight 2010). Statutory titling systems introduced in Kenya resulted in titles being held mostly in men's names only and failed to recognize women's customary rights to use the land (Harrington and Chopra 2010). Statutory laws can reinforce norms around women's traditional roles in land cultivation. In India, the Odisha Land Reforms Act allows only female heads of households to lease their land for cultivation on the premise that women should not have to engage in such activities directly (Doss et al. 2014). In many countries in Europe and Central Asia, privatization of farmland meant that the male head of household is the person listed formally on the title or deed, thereby reducing the de facto rights

of other family members (Stanley, Lamb, and De Martino 2013).

In Rwanda, a land tenure regularization pilot found that legally married women were more likely to have their informal land rights documented and secured and to be regarded as joint owners than women in customary unions. Analysis of the pilot program's effect showed the probability of having documented land ownership fell by nine percentage points for women in customary unions (Ali, Deininger, and Goldstein 2011). In response to these findings, the government changed the program to enable women in all types of unions to register land. This result suggests the wider social context, including social norms and customary practices, needs to be explicitly considered when introducing land tenure reform.

While the lack of statutory rights can leave women vulnerable to displacement or land grabbing in the event of widowhood or divorce, social norms can limit the effectiveness of statutory laws, depending on the woman's social position, education, and residency in a rural or urban area (Agarwal 1997). In some places, long-standing social norms shape women's access to rural land. It has been found that plow-intensive farming communities that were historically more dependent on male labor limit women's role in agricultural activity and their access to land (Alesina, Guilano, and Nunn 2013).

Discriminatory family laws can place control in the hands of men even in cases in which joint ownership is formally recognized, reflecting patriarchal social norms around men's and women's roles within the household. In 29 countries, married women cannot be the head of household or head of the family in the same way as a man. In the Democratic Republic of Congo, a married woman must obtain her husband's permission for all legal acts in which she incurs a personal obligation, including registering land in her name, and the husband has the right to administer joint marital property. In Cameroon, a husband can legally dispose of joint property without his wife's consent and can even administer his wife's personal property (World Bank and IFC 2013). These examples indicate the possible need for wide-reaching reforms of family laws as part of the process of land reform in order to achieve the intended effects.

Head-of-household provisions can also limit the effect of land titling programs. The Committee on the Elimination of Discrimination against Women (2011), in its Concluding Observations on Sri Lanka, for example, noted "discriminatory practices prevent women from acquiring ownership of land since only the 'head of household' is authorized to sign official documentation such as land ownership certificates and receive pieces of land from Government," because social norms mean that the head of the household is most often deemed to be male (Committee on the Elimination of Discrimination against Women 2014).

Default marital property regimes

The default marital property regime will automatically apply to distribution of assets upon death or divorce, unless the spouses choose otherwise. These laws and the manner in which they are implemented often reflect social norms around the allocation and control of household property and

directly affect access to land. In some countries, no alternative to the default regime exists. The main types of marital regimes are outlined in box 5.3.

Our analysis across 15 countries suggests that the type of marital property regime affects the reported levels of women's property ownership; women who live in countries with community of property regimes are more likely to report owning land and housing than those who live in countries with separation of property regimes. This is illustrated in map 5.1, with the size of the circles reflecting the share of property owned by women. In Burundi, Ethiopia, and Mozambique, countries with community of property regimes, more than three-fifths of women report owning property. In contrast, Nepal and Senegal, countries with separation of property regimes, have the smallest share—13 percent and 18 percent, respectively.

For married women, the probability of reporting land and housing ownership is 17 and 29 percentage points higher, respectively, if they live in a country with a community of property regime compared to a country with a separation of property regime (figure 5.5). And married women in urban areas are nearly three times more likely to own housing in those countries.[3] The probability of land ownership for unmarried women in a country with a community of property regime is higher too, most likely because such counties also have more gender-equal inheritance laws.

Research in Ecuador, Ghana, and Karnataka, India, supports these findings. In Ecuador, which has a partial community of property regime and inheritance laws that

Box 5.3   Main types of marital property regimes

Community of property regimes treat all assets, including land and housing, acquired during the marriage as the joint property of the couple, with the exception of inheritances or gifts specifically earmarked for one spouse. These regimes implicitly recognize nonmonetary contributions to the household, including domestic labor and child care. In our database, 87 countries have community of property regimes. Community of property regimes can be divided into three categories:

> *Full:* All property acquired before marriage is regarded as joint property.

> *Partial:* All property acquired before marriage remains the personal property of each spouse.

> *Deferred:* All property acquired during marriage is treated as individually owned during the marriage but is divided equally on divorce or death.

Separation of property regimes provide that all property is individually owned unless specified as jointly owned. In the event of marital dissolution, each spouse leaves with the property he or she brought into or acquired during the marriage. Specific legislation can be enacted to recognize nonmonetary contributions, but these provisions are rare. Of the 46 countries that have separation of property regimes, only 9 recognize nonmonetary contribution.

Sources: World Bank and IFC 2013.
Note: The Women, Business and the Law database covers 143 countries.

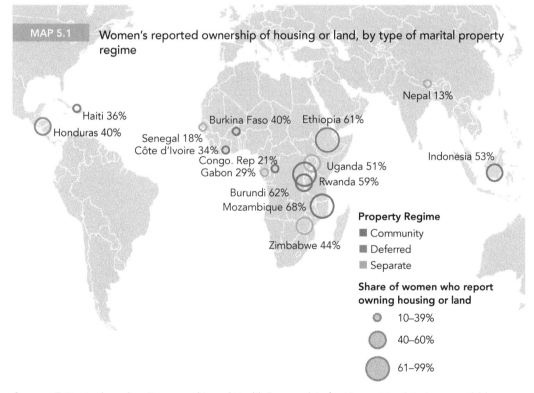

MAP 5.1   Women's reported ownership of housing or land, by type of marital property regime

Nepal 13%

Haiti 36%
Honduras 40%

Burkina Faso 40%   Ethiopia 61%

Senegal 18%
Côte d'Ivoire 34%

Congo. Rep 21%
Gabon 29%

Uganda 51%
Rwanda 59%

Indonesia 53%

Burundi 62%
Mozambique 68%

Zimbabwe 44%

Property Regime
■ Community
■ Deferred
■ Separate

Share of women who report owning housing or land
○ 10–39%
○ 40–60%
○ 61–99%

Sources: Estimates based on Demographic and Health Surveys data for 15 countries, latest year available, 2010–12, and World Bank and IFC 2013.

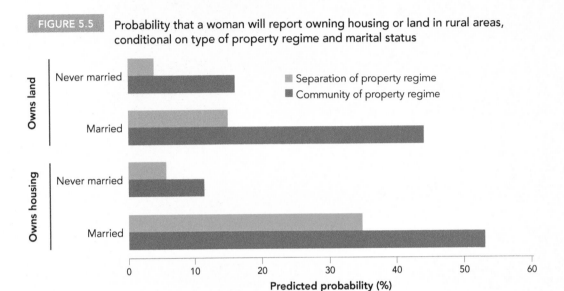

FIGURE 5.5 Probability that a woman will report owning housing or land in rural areas, conditional on type of property regime and marital status

Source: Estimates based on Demographic and Health Surveys data, latest year available.

Note: Figure shows predicted probabilities of housing and land ownership in rural areas, controlling for age, work status, number of children, husband's education, marital status, various household characteristics, property regime (separation or community of property), and country fixed effects.

provide for all children to inherit equally, women's share of a couple's wealth is around 44 percent. In comparison, in Ghana and Karnataka, which both have separation of property regimes and inheritance practices that are male biased, women's share of a couple's wealth is much lower—19 percent and 9 percent, respectively (Doss et al. 2012).

Weak implementation of laws

Social norms, customary practices, the inaccessibility and weak capacity of institutions, and women's lack of awareness of their rights all pose important barriers to the realization of women's land rights. Qualitative work undertaken in Niger as background for this book found that women tend to

accept a range of normative constraints on their rights. Legally, they can buy land, but the few women who did so were strongly criticized for not following customary ways and were told they were dishonoring their families (World Bank 2014). In Tanzania, the Land Act (1999) abolishes customary discriminatory practices and makes local land authorities responsible for protecting women, but implementation of the law has been slow and uneven (Spichiger et al. 2013). Most countries in Europe and Central Asia have laws that require property to be divided equally among heirs regardless of gender; however, some groups require women to relinquish their inheritance in favor of male relatives (Stanley, Lamb, and De Martino 2013). In Honduras, the World Bank Group is working with the government to overcome implementation challenges to enable women's access to equal property rights (box 5.4).

Land administration systems can help to ensure women's land rights are effectively implemented. Special provisions can ensure that women and other family members enjoy equal rights under land reforms where men are assumed to be the head of the household. Monitoring sex-disaggregated land administrative data can help flag implementation issues, but often these data are difficult to access and not well maintained.

The state of the evidence: What works?

Improving women's ownership and control of land and housing requires institutional change, as shown by the cogs in our framework in figure 1.1, where social norms, laws,

---

Box 5.4 Expanding women's access to land rights in Honduras

In 2003, the Honduras Land Administration Program (Programa de Administración de Tierras de Honduras, or PATH) was launched to address gaps in formalization of property rights, promote a more dynamic land market, increase investments in land, and reduce social instability resulting from conflict over land. Increasing formal property ownership for women was also seen as critical for improving rural productivity. At that time, about 30 percent of the country's land was registered, of which women owned less than 13 percent.

A World Bank Group–supported gender audit revealed that despite provisions allowing for joint titling, few women were named on a land title. The audit identified three primary constraints: limited awareness of legal rights among women and land administration personnel; land registries and other municipal offices that lacked capacity and procedural guidance on ways to implement the laws; and social norms that dictated that men were the head of household, thereby resulting in titling in their names alone.

To address these gaps, PATH held almost a dozen stakeholder workshops in different municipalities. Participants included local authorities, community leaders, and indigenous peoples' organizations, and the aim was to facilitate better understanding of the program among beneficiaries and the importance of gender-responsive design. The resulting gender strategy employed the following methods to improve implementation:

› The guiding documents and instruments were revised so that implementation included specific objectives for strengthening women's access to land.

› A media campaign, including a radio program on the gender situation of women in indigenous communications, was initiated, with materials targeted at men and women of all ages to convey clear messages on the importance of land titling and ways to use titles to advance economic opportunities.

› Project indicators were strengthened to include joint titling. The revised results and monitoring framework includes such targets as 30 percent of new titles to include women and 25 percent of individuals receiving training in alternative dispute resolution and in territorial planning and natural resource management to be women.

Source: World Bank 2012.

> *"Women cannot buy land because of social norms that forbid it."*
>
> —Men's focus group, Alpha Koura, Département of Dosso, Région of Dosso, Niger (World Bank 2014)

and household decisions interact to affect gender equality outcomes. Any intervention intended to improve women's access to and control over land therefore needs to begin with an analysis of how existing legislation and social norms affect the distribution of property between husbands and wives and between sons and daughters. We identify two broad areas of focus—ensuring gender equality under the law and ensuring effective implementation of laws and land policies.

Ensuring gender equality under the law

Gender equality in the distribution and ownership of land should be clearly specified in country constitutions and land administration laws. Constitutional protections can provide oversight of all sources of law and for redress against discrimination. In 2014, for example, the Nigeria Supreme Court voided Igbo customary law, which prevented girls from inheriting their father's estate, as unconstitutional (Vanguard 2014). Any divergence between different sources of law can be addressed under the constitution. The Constitution of Uganda, Article 33, for example, prohibits "laws, cultures, customs, or traditions which are against the dignity, welfare, or interest of women." Beyond this, strengthening family, inheritance, and land laws for women; reforming discriminatory laws; and harmonizing statutory, customary, and religious laws are all critical.

Promoting gender equality in family, inheritance, and land laws

Community of property regimes can provide solid legal ground for advancing married women's ownership of property and for securing women's property rights on dissolution of a marriage. Clear consent requirements should be in place for transfer or sale, requiring the informed written consent of both spouses. Separation of property regimes should recognize nonmonetary contributions to family wealth and provide for equal division on divorce or death. Marital property regimes should also extend to cover those in de facto relationships. Family, inheritance, and land laws all interact. We have seen that reforms to marital property laws and land laws can be undermined by discriminatory inheritance laws. Similarly, head of household laws, which limit women's rights across a range of spheres, including property ownership, should be repealed (UN Women 2013b). Laws in other areas can also address women's property rights. In Brazil, India, and Serbia, for example, national domestic violence legislation now provides that victims of domestic violence may stay in the marital home, regardless of who owns it (Rolnik 2013).

Inheritance laws should ensure that property rights are transmitted equitably across generations. As the example of India demonstrates, equalizing entitlements under inheritance laws can dramatically improve girls' and women's lives and potentially transform social norms. Discretion to circumvent women's inheritance rights through a will should be restricted. In Ethiopia, the Land Use and Administration Proclamation (2000) requires that the transfer of land through inheritance is legal only if the wife has signed the husband's will, a provision that serves to protect the widow's interests (Teklu 2005).

Social norms mean that widows are often pressured to waive their rights in return for protection from male family members. Laws that prevent women from giving up their rights for a specified period of time following a spouse's death can help offset such familial or community pressure. In Jordan, for example, a recent law prevents women from handing over their inheritance for three months following receipt and requires them to formally register the housing and land in their name (World Bank 2013). The legal grounds for divorce and the allocation of property rights on divorce in family laws should be reviewed so that joint titling does not become a constraint to exit. This is especially important for women living in abusive relationships.

Reform of land administration laws can also have positive effects. Mandatory joint titling has led to a marked increase in married women's land ownership in Rwanda, for instance (Ali, Deininger, and Goldstein 2014). Laws should ensure that the surviving spouse has, at a minimum, occupancy and use rights over the marital home as well as rights to movable and immovable property. Namibia's Communal Land Reform Act (2002) gives surviving spouses who reside in rural areas the right to remain on communal land that had been allocated to the deceased. This right is not affected by remarriage.

Harmonizing statutory, customary, and religious regimes

Experience from more than 40 World Bank Group land reform projects in Europe and Central Asia over the past two decades has demonstrated that challenges associated with social norms and culture cannot be solved by legal reform alone (Stanley, Lamb, and De Martino 2013). This underlines that understanding local context and realities in the field, including customs and traditions and the way statutory rights play out, is essential for the design of effective land reform policies and interventions. Country gender assessments are a useful tool to advance this understanding (see box 5.5).

Where constitutional and legal reforms strengthen the rights of women but conflict with norms and custom, changes in customary tenure systems need to be accommodated.[4] As far as possible, protections afforded under constitutional and statutory law should be extended to include situations covered by custom. Some examples include the following:

- In South Africa, the community of property regime applies to customary marriages as well as civil marriages (Hallward-Driemeier and Hasan 2013).
- In the Lao People's Democratic Republic, where strong matrilineal rights exist, the World Bank Group worked with the Lao Women's Union to ensure that existing customary rights were reflected in the new land registration systems.[5]
- The Uganda National Land Policy commits to reform customary law, modify the rules of transmission under customary land tenure, guarantee gender equality and equity, and ensure that the decisions of traditional land management institutions uphold constitutional rights and obligations on gender equality (UN Women 2013b).

Box 5.5 Tools to guide gender land assessments

The World Bank's (2010) "Toolkit for Integrating Gender-Related Issues in Land Policy and Administration Projects" provides guidelines for a gender analysis of the socioeconomic and cultural conditions in the project area, including with regard to statutory and customary property rights, land policies and legislation, land administration institutions, and land market transactions. In the West Bank and Gaza, for example, such an analysis identified that inheritance is determined according to Shari'a law and proof of ownership is issued by the Shari'a court. However, customary practice has encouraged women to cede their shares to their brothers. A gender analysis of the local conditions led the project design to counteract this type of pressure by issuing titles that include the names of all rightful heirs and specify their shares.

Landesa's "Women's Land Tenure Framework for Analysis: Inheritance" provides a framework for assessing women's ability to inherit land in a specific country, state, or community. Collaboration between the state and progressive traditional authorities can identify options for upholding women's land rights in customary tenure areas. In Foshan City, Guangdong Province, China, for example, the local government took action to address land rights of women who married someone from another village. Using clear guidance and principles based on relevant Chinese laws, the district government set up a working group of government officials to review village rules and work together with villagers to change the local provisions that discriminate against women's equal rights to land. Judicial procedures were applied to enforce compliance. After one year of the administrative and judicial intervention, 95 percent of married women in the district (about 18,000 women) were granted equal land rights.

Sources: Giovarelli and Scalise 2013; PLAAS 2011; UN Women 2013b; World Bank 2010.

Ensuring effective implementation of laws and land policies

Policy reforms and programmatic interventions must be coupled with awareness raising for women, men, and local leaders (including customary and religious leaders) on women's rights as well as on the benefits of women's land ownership. In Aceh, Indonesia, for example, the RALAS (Reconstruction of Aceh Land Administration System) project worked with local Shari'a courts to produce a manual that provided guidance on inheritance rights and helped protect widows from dispossession (Bell 2011).

An initial gender assessment can also help identify potential implementation challenges associated with social norms. In some cases, implementation challenges can be as obvious as allowing space for a second name on a land title or adjusting the ways in which acreage is distributed to address inequalities that may result from gender differences in seemingly unrelated legislation, such as retirement age, as in Vietnam (box 5.6).

An obvious key to the successful implementation of land rights is the commitment, willingness, and capacity of government staff and agencies. Establishing gender units within land administration units and appointing a lead gender focal point within land registries can help (World Bank 2010). Female representation in land administration institutions can also be mandated by law, as in the Uganda Land Commission, in district land boards, and in parish-level committees (UN Women 2013b). Women should also be involved in the design of national land policies and in the monitoring of their implementation. In Pernambuco, Brazil, women formed local committees to monitor the land titling program and make their needs known (Hallward-Driemeier and Hasan 2013). Similarly, in Nicaragua, a World Bank Group project involving demarcation of indigenous lands included participatory workshops to identify the most important factors affecting women and engaged women in the cadastre process. The project includes targets for the number of new titles given to women in the monitoring and results framework. Project results suggest

the gender strategy has raised awareness of gender inequality in land access across all agencies involved and has increased women's access to services through the provision of additional opening hours and hotlines for women (Stanley, Weiss, and Vyzaki 2013).

Awareness and training programs are important for ensuring that women and men, as well as land administration officials, are aware of what rights women and men have. Some examples include the following:

- In Tanzania, a World Bank Group study exploring the barriers to formalization of land titles in Dar es Salaam found that demand for land titles, when offered at affordable prices, was very high. When affordability was combined with a campaign emphasizing the importance of women being registered as joint landowners and offering discounts for female registration, the share of households that

Box 5.6 Lessons from Vietnam's land reform process

Vietnam's 1993 Land Law did not appear to discriminate because it used neutral language such as "individuals" and "users" when referring to targeted beneficiaries of the reforms. The 2000 Family and Marriage Law also provided for equal spousal rights to assets and property, including land. In practice, however, gender disparities resulted. Initially, the Land Use Certificates had space for only one name, which was to be filled in by the household head (generally the husband). The unintended consequence was that fewer women had their names on certificates. Gender disparities also resulted from the allocation of acreage based on the ages of household members, whereby working-age individuals received the largest shares. Because female households tended to have fewer adults of working age, they received on average less land than male-headed households. The legal retirement age for women was also five years earlier than that for men. In practice, this led to women ages 55 to 59 being allocated half the amount of land allocated to men of the same age.

Vietnam has made progress in remedying these disparities. For example, a 2001 government decree stipulated that the names of both husband and wife should be included on the certificate if the land is jointly owned, and the 2003 Land Law mandates joint titling.

Sources: Menon, Rodgers, and Kennedy 2013; Gender and Land Rights Database of the Food and Agriculture Organization of the United Nations, http://www.fao.org/gender/landrights/home/en/.

indicated they would include both husband and wife on the title increased from 24 percent to 89 percent (Ali et al. 2013).

- In Romania, the World Bank's Complementing European Union Support for Agricultural Restructuring Project included a communication and mediation specialist in field teams to provide information on social issues. Local leaders were also involved in public awareness campaigns, and special meetings were organized just for Roma women (Stanley, Lamb, and De Martino 2013).

- In Rwanda, the National Land Centre has undertaken training of local land committees across the country. The effort included making a video showing how women's rights should be recorded (UN Women 2011).

Local awareness-raising campaigns and community dialogue can also be effective ways to build understanding and support for women's land rights. There are several examples from Eastern Europe and Central Asia:

- In the Kyrgyz Republic, men and women were trained as community-based advisers to provide free advice to villagers on the process of applying for land ownership (UN Women 2013b).

- A land reform project in Tajikistan in 2007 sponsored by the U.S. Agency for International Development included support for a group of women who mounted a legal challenge to the decision of a local official to revoke their land rights. The women were successful, and the court's decision was used around the country to educate communities and local officials about respecting women's land rights (World Bank 2010).

- In Moldova, Joint Information and Services Bureaus offer a one-stop shop for advice on the job market, health care, agriculture, and land laws. The bureaus centralize at least nine key service providers in one office, thereby reducing time spent visiting multiple locations, and they have helped more than 10,000 women, primarily from remote rural areas (UN Women 2013a).

* * *

Control over land and housing affects women's agency across a range of domains, including household decision making and access to economic opportunities. Improving women's property rights can have transformative impacts on social norms and women's status at home and in the community. More and better sex-disaggregated data are needed to highlight gaps in ownership and access, and to inform policy and program design. Data availability and gaps are reviewed in chapter 7. A broad approach can help ensure that beneficial customary and communal rights are recognized and respected, coupled with reforms to promote gender equality and enable effective implementation.

Notes

1. DHS data are limited to the women between the ages of 15 and 49 and do not cover older women.

2. The probabilities are married women, 47 percent; widowed, 40 percent; living together, 35 percent; formerly married, 23 percent; never married, 9 percent.

3. For urban married women, the probability of owning housing if she lives in a country with a community of property regime is 44 percent compared to 15 percent in a country with a separation of property regime. The equivalent figures for women who never married are 16 percent in a country with a community of property regime compared to 4 percent in a country with a separation of property regime.

4. This recommendation is consistent with guidelines of the Committee on World Food Security (2012).

5. The projects were the Lao PDR Land Titling Project (1997–2005) and Land Titling Project II (2004–09).

References

Agarwal, Bina. 1994. "Gender and Command over Property: A Critical Gap in Economic Analysis and Policy in South Asia." *World Development* 22 (10): 1455–78.

———. 1997. "Bargaining and Gender Relations: Within and Beyond the Household." *Feminist Economics* 3 (1): 1–51.

Agarwal, Bina, and Pradeep Panda. 2007. "Toward Freedom from Domestic Violence: The Neglected Obvious." *Journal of Human Development* 8 (3): 359–88.

Alesina, Alberto, Paola Guilano, and Nathan Nunn. 2013. "On the Origins of Gender Roles: Women and the Plough." *Quarterly Journal of Economics* 128 (2): 469–530.

Ali, Daniel Alayew, Matthew Collin, Klaus Deininger, Stefan Dercon, Justin Sandefur, and Andrew Zeitlin. 2013. "Are Poor Slum-Dwellers Willing to Pay for Formal Land Title? Evidence from Dar es Salaam." Case Study, World Bank, Washington, DC.

Ali, Daniel Ayalew, Klaus Deininger, and Markus Goldstein. 2011. "Environmental and Gender Impacts of Land Tenure Regularization in Africa: Pilot Evidence from Rwanda." Policy Research Working Paper 5765, World Bank, Washington, DC.

———. 2014. "Environmental and Gender Impacts of Land Tenure Regularization in Africa: Pilot Evidence from Rwanda." *Journal of Development Economics* 110 (2014): 262–75.

Allendorf, Keera. 2007. "Do Women's Land Rights Promote Empowerment and Child Health in Nepal?" *World Development* 35 (11): 1975–88.

Behrman, Julia, Ruth Meinzen-Dick, and Agnes R. Quisumbing. 2011. "The Gender Implications of Large-Scale Land Deals." IFPRI Policy Brief 17, International Food Policy Research Institute, Washington, DC.

Bell, Keith. 2011. "Lessons from the Reconstruction of Post-Tsunami Aceh: Build Back Better through Ensuring Women Are at the Center of Reconstruction of Land and Property." *Smart Lessons*, August.

Bhatla, Nandita, Swati Chakraborty, and Nata Duvvury. 2006. *Property Ownership and Inheritance Rights of Women for Social Protection: The South Asia Experience—Synthesis Report of Three Studies.* Washington, DC: International Center for Research on Women.

Blanco Rothe, Lara, Ana Victoria Naranjo Porras, Yamileth Ugalde Benavente, and Felicia Ramírez Agüero. 2002. "Equidad de género y derechos de propiedad: Una investigación exploratoria sobre el impacto genérico de programas de titulación conjunta en Costa Rica—El caso de Guararí, Heredia." Fundación Arias para la Paz y el Progreso Humano, San José, Costa Rica.

Committee on the Elimination of Discrimination against Women. 2011. "Concluding Observations of the Committee on the Elimination of Discrimination against Women: Sri Lanka." Committee on the Elimination of Discrimination against Women, 48th session, New York, January 17–February 4, 2011. http://www.refworld.org/docid/533e8d224.html.

Committee on World Food Security. 2012. "Voluntary Guidelines on the Responsible Governance of Tenure of Land, Fisheries, and Forests in the Context of National Food Security." Food and Agriculture Organization of the United Nations, Rome.

Cotula, Lorenzo, Sonja Vermeulen, Rebeca Leonard, and James Keeley. 2009. *Land Grab or Development Opportunity? Agricultural Investment and International Land Deals in Africa*. London: International Institute for Environment and Development.

Datta, Namita. 2006. "Joint Titling: A Win-Win Policy? Gender and Property Rights in Urban Informal Settlements in India." *Feminist Economics* 12, (1–2): 271–98.

Deere, Carmen Diana, and Jennifer Twyman. 2012a. "Asset Ownership and Egalitarian Decision Making in Dual-Headed Households in Ecuador." *Review of Radical Political Economics* 44 (3): 1–8.

———. 2012b. "Land Ownership and Farm Management in Ecuador: Egalitarian Family Farming Systems and Gendered Constraints." Gender Asset Gap Project Working Paper 11, Centre for Public Policy, Indian Institute of Management Bangalore, Bangalore, India.

Deininger, Klaus. 2003. *Land Policies for Growth and Poverty Reduction*. Washington, DC: World Bank.

Deininger, Klaus, and Raffaella Castagnini. 2008. "Incidence and Impact of Land Conflict in Uganda." Policy Research Working Paper 3248, World Bank, Washington, DC.

Deininger, Klaus, Aparajita Goyal, and Hari Nagarajan. 2010. "Inheritance Law Reform and Women's Access to Capital: Evidence from India's Hindu Succession Act." Policy Research Working Paper 5338, World Bank, Washington, DC.

Doss, Cheryl. 2005. "The Effects of Intrahousehold Property Ownership on Expenditure Patterns in Ghana." *Journal of African Economies* 15 (1): 149–80.

———. 2012. "Intrahousehold Bargaining and Resource Allocation in Developing Countries." Background paper for *World Development Report 2012: Gender Equality and Development*, World Bank, Washington, DC.

Doss, Cheryl, Carmen Diana Deere, Abena D. Oduro, and Suchitra J. Y. 2012. "The Rural Gender Asset and Wealth Gaps: Evidence from Ghana, Ecuador, Uganda and Karnataka, India." Indian Institute of Management Bangalore, Bangalore, India.

Doss, Cheryl, Carmen Diana Deere, Abena D. Oduro, Hema Swaminathan, Suchitra J. Y., Rahul Lahoti, William Baah-Boateng, Louis Boakye-Yiadom, Jackeline Contreras, Jennifer Twyman, Zachary Catanzarite, Caren Grown, and Marya Hillesland. 2011. "The Gender Asset and Wealth Gaps: Evidence from Ecuador, Ghana, and Karnataka, India." Indian Institute of Management Bangalore, Bangalore, India.

Doss, Cheryl, Sung Mi Kim, Jemimah Njuki, Emily Hillenbrand, and Maureen Miruka. 2014. "Women's Individual and Joint Property Ownership: Effects on Household Decisionmaking," IFPRI Discussion Paper 01347, International Food Policy Research Institute, Washington, DC.

Doss, Cheryl, Chiara Kovarik, Amber Peterman, Agnes R. Quisumbing, and Mara van den Bold. 2013. "Gender Inequalities in Ownership and Control of Land in Africa: Myths versus Reality." IFPRI Discussion Paper 01261, International Food Policy Research Institute, Washington, DC.

Duflo, Esther. 2003. "Grandmothers and Granddaughters: Old-Age Pensions and

Intrahousehold Allocation in South Africa." *World Bank Economic Review* 17 (1): 1–25.

Field, Erica. 2007. "Entitled to Work: Urban Property Rights and Labor Supply in Peru." *Quarterly Journal of Economics* 122 (4): 1561–602.

Giovarelli, Renee, and Elisa Scalise. 2013. "Women's Land Tenure Framework for Analysis: Inheritance." Landesa, Seattle, WA.

Hallward-Driemeier, Mary, and Tazeen Hasan. 2013. *Empowering Women: Legal Rights and Economic Opportunities in Africa.* Washington, DC: World Bank.

Hanstad, Tim, D. Hien Tran, and Matt Bannick. 2013. "Why Land Should Be Part of the Post-2015 Development Agenda." Landesa, New Delhi. http://www.landesa.org/why-land-should-be-part-of-the-post-2015-development-agenda/.

Harrington, Andrew, and Tanja Chopra. 2010. "Arguing Traditions: Denying Kenya's Women Access to Land Rights." Justice for the Poor Research Report 2, World Bank, Washington, DC.

Jackson, Cecile. 2003. "Gender Analysis of Land: Beyond Land Rights for Women?" *Journal of Agrarian Change* 3 (4): 453–80.

Joireman, Sandra. 2008. "The Mystery of Capital Formation in Sub-Saharan Africa: Women, Property Rights, and Customary Law." *World Development* 36 (7): 1233–46.

Knight, Rachael S. 2010. "Statutory Recognition of Customary Land Rights in Africa: An Investigation into Best Practices for Lawmaking and Implementation." FAO Legislative Study 105, Food and Agriculture Organization of the United Nations, Rome.

Landesa. 2013. "The Formal and Informal Barriers in the Implementation of the Hindu Succession (Amendment) Act 2005 in the Context of Women Agricultural Producers of Andhra Pradesh, Bihar, and Madhya Pradesh." UN Women, New York.

Luke, Nancy, and Kaivan Munshi. 2011. "Women as Agents of Change: Female Income and Mobility in India." *Journal of Development Economics* 94 (1): 1–17.

Menon, Nidhiya, and Yana Rodgers. 2011. "How Access to Credit Affects Self-Employment: Differences by Gender during India's Rural Banking Reform." *Journal of Development Studies* 47 (1): 48–69.

Menon, Nidhiya, Yana Rodgers, and Alexis Kennedy. 2013. "Land Reform and Welfare in Vietnam: Why Gender of the Land-Rights Holder Matters." http://www.worldbank.org/content/dam/Worldbank/document/Gender/Vietnam%20Land%20Rights%20and%20Women%20Yana%20et%20al.pdf.

PLAAS (Institute for Poverty, Land, and Agrarian Studies). 2011. "Securing Women's Access to Land: Linking Research and Action—An Overview of Action-Research Projects in Southern Africa." Synthesis Report 15, International Land Coalition, Rome.

Qian, Nancy. 2008. "Missing Women and the Price of Tea in China: The Effect of Sex-Specific Earning on Sex Imbalance." *Quarterly Journal of Economics* 123 (3): 1251–85.

Quisumbing, Agnes R., and John A. Maluccio. 2003. "Resources at Marriage and Intrahousehold Allocation: Evidence from Bangladesh, Ethiopia, Indonesia, and South Africa." *Oxford Bulletin of Economics and Statistics* 65 (3): 283–327.

Rakodi, Carole. 2014. "Expanding Women's Access to Land and Housing in Urban Areas." Women's Voice, Agency, and Participation Research Paper 8, World Bank, Washington, DC.

Rodgers, Yana, and Nidhiya Menon. 2012. "A Meta-analysis of Land Rights and Women's Economic Well-Being." Brandeis University, Waltham, MA. http://people.brandeis.edu/~nmenon/Draft01_Survey_of_Land_Rights_and_Women.pdf.

Rolnik, Raquel. 2013. "Report of the Special Rapporteur on Adequate Housing as a Component of the Right to an Adequate Standard of Living, and on the Right to

Non-discrimination in This Context." United Nations, New York.

Scalise, Elisa. 2009. "Women's Inheritance Rights to Land and Property in South Asia: A Study of Afghanistan, Bangladesh, India, Nepal, Pakistan, and Sri Lanka," Rural Development Institute, Seattle, WA.

Scholz, Birte, Patricia Chaves, Fati Al Hassan, and Jacqueline Leavitt. 2013. "Grassroots Women and Tenure Security: Key to Empowerment and Resilient Communities." Huairou Commission, New York.

Sen, Amartya K. 1990. "Gender and Cooperative Conflict." In *Persistent Inequalities: Women and World Development*, edited by Irene Tinker, 123–149. Oxford, U.K: Oxford University Press.

Smith, Lisa C., Usha Ramakrishnan, Aida Ndiaye, Lawrence Haddad, and Reynaldo Martorell. 2003. *The Importance of Women's Status for Child Nutrition in Developing Countries*. Washington, DC: International Food Policy Research Institute.

Spichiger, Rachel, Rikke Brandt Broegaard, Rasmus Hundsbæk Pedersen, and Helle Munk Ravnborg. 2013. "Land Administration, Gender Equality, and Development Cooperation: Lessons Learned and Challenges Ahead." DIIS Report 2013:30, Danish Institute for International Studies, Copenhagen.

Stanley, Victoria, Tony Lamb, and Samantha De Martino. 2013. "Property Rights for Women in the ECA Region: Results from Recent World Bank Projects." Agriculture and Environmental Services Department Note 1, World Bank, Washington, DC.

Stanley, Victoria, Eli Weiss, and Marialena Vyzaki. 2013. "Supporting Women through Agriculture Projects in the Latin America and Caribbean Region." Agriculture and Environmental Services Department Note 4, World Bank, Washington, DC.

Swaminathan, Hema, Rahul Lahoti, and Suchitra J. Y. 2012. "Women's Property, Mobility, and Decision Making: Evidence from Rural Karnataka, India." IFPRI Discussion Paper 01188, International Food Policy Research Institute, Washington, DC.

Teklu, Askale. 2005. "Land Registration and Women's Land Rights in Amhara Region, Ethiopia." IIED Research Report 4, International Institute for Environment and Development, Addis Ababa.

Udry, Christopher. 1996. "Gender, Agricultural Production, and the Theory of the Household." *Journal of Political Economy* 104 (5): 1010–46.

UN Women (United Nations Entity for Gender Equality and the Empowerment of Women). 2011. *Progress of the World's Women: In Pursuit of Justice*, 2011–2012. New York: UN Women.

———. 2013a. "Reaching Out with Public Services across Rural Moldova." United Nations, New York. http://www.unwomen .org/ca/news/stories/2013/10/reaching -out-with-public-services-across-rural -moldova.

———. 2013b. "Realizing Women's Rights to Land and Other Productive Resources." United Nations, New York.

USAID (U.S. Agency for International Development). 2013. "The Future of Customary Tenure: Options for Policymakers." Property Rights and Resources Governance Briefing Paper 8, USAID, Washington, DC.

Vanguard. 2014. "Nigeria: Inheritance Rights for Girl Child." *All Africa Reports*, April 24. http://allafrica.com/stories /201404240350.html.

World Bank. 2008. "Analysis of the Impact of Land Tenure Certificates with both the Names of Wife and Husband in Vietnam." World Bank, Hanoi.

———. 2010. "Toolkit for Integrating Gender-Related Issues in Land Policy and Administration Projects." World Bank, Washington, DC.

————. 2011. *World Development Report 2012: Gender Equality and Development.* Washington, DC: World Bank.

————. 2012. "Women's Economic Empowerment in Latin America and the Caribbean: Policy Lessons from the World Bank Gender Action Plan." World Bank, Washington, DC.

————. 2013. *Opening Doors: Gender Equality and Development in the Middle East and North Africa.* Washington, DC: World Bank.

————. 2014. "Voices of Men and Women regarding Social Norms in Niger." Poverty Reduction and Economic Management Africa Region Report 83296-NE, World Bank, Washington, DC.

World Bank and IFC (International Finance Corporation). 2013. *Women, Business, and the Law 2014: Removing Restrictions to Enhance Gender Equality.* London: Bloomsbury.

Xanthaki, Alexandra. 2003. "Land Rights of Indigenous Peoples in South-East Asia." *Melbourne Journal of International Law* 4 (2): 467–96.

Chapter 6 Key messages

> Women's voices and leadership are too often denied by a combination of adverse attitudes and norms.

> Women's combined strength, through collective action and women's movements, can play a central role in building momentum for progressive legal reform, changing adverse social norms, and promoting accountability.

> Women's political participation can positively affect the range of policy issues considered and prioritized, can influence the types of solutions proposed, and can enhance perceptions of government legitimacy.

> Women still represent less than one-quarter of parliamentarians worldwide. However, major gains in women's political participation have been made in some regions and countries, such as Nicaragua, Rwanda, and South Africa.

> Promising directions for enhancing women's political participation are emerging, including creating quotas to help change stereotypes and providing financing and training to help level the playing field.

> The landscape for engaging in politics and collective action is being rapidly transformed by new technologies such as the Internet and social media, although gaps in access must be overcome.

CHAPTER 6

Amplifying Voices

Why women's voice and participation matter

To have a voice is to be a citizen (Drèze and Sen 2002). Having a voice means having the capacity to speak up and be heard and being present to shape and share in discussions, discourse, and decisions. Full and equal participation requires that everyone have a voice. Participation in decision making enables women to voice their needs and challenge gender norms in their community—individually and collectively (Kabeer 2013). If women's participation is to be transformative, their voices need to be heard in a broad range of decision-making forums, from households to national parliaments. Women's movements can play a pivotal role in building the momentum for progressive policy and legal reform. Digital technologies such as mobile phones and the Internet provide new avenues for greater voice, increased access to knowledge, and the potential for developing wider social and professional networks.

The extent to which women are able to participate in public decision making and make their voices heard is shaped by social norms, the legal framework, and the nature of formal political institutions such as political parties and parliamentary structures. This is reflected in the interaction of formal and informal institutions in our framework in figure 1.1. At the same time, women's greater voice can seek to change discriminatory social norms, as in the case of Malala Yousafzai, from Pakistan (see box 6.1) and can be a force for progressive legal reform (see box 6.2). Women's greater voice and participation can also affect other areas of women's lives, including economic opportunities and access to services.

We identify three main routes for amplifying women's voices. Starting with women themselves, we explore the role of the media and new information and communication technologies (ICTs) for expanding voice

> *"Nothing, arguably, is as important today in the political economy of development as an adequate recognition of political, economic, and social participation and leadership of women."*
>
> —Amartya Sen (1999b, 203)

and participation. Second, we consider not only women's combined strength but also the central role that women's groups can play in promoting gender equality, poverty reduction, and shared prosperity. Finally, we explore women's representation in formal institutions, where some, albeit slow, progress has been made in most countries and regions. Collective action and women's participation in community-level decision making can also lead to greater accountability, an area we touch on briefly in the policy section of this chapter.

Tackling poverty and boosting shared prosperity demand that everyone have the opportunity to participate fully in all aspects of life. Public discussion is an important vehicle for social change and economic progress. At the same time, political and social participation has intrinsic value for individual well-being.

Evidence about the instrumental value of women's participation in public discourse is growing. Autonomous women's movements, for example, have been influential in the passing of legislation on gender-based violence at the national level, as explored in chapter 3. Women's political participation can positively influence the range of policy issues considered and prioritized

and the types of solutions proposed. Some dimensions are clear:

■ Women's participation results in greater responsiveness to citizen needs, often increasing cooperation across party and ethnic lines and delivering more sustainable peace (Markham 2013).

■ When more women are elected to office, policy making increasingly reflects the priorities of families and women (Jones 2005; Schwindt-Bayer 2006). In Rwanda and South Africa, an increase in the number of female lawmakers led to progressive legislation on land inheritance and reproductive rights (Ballington and Karam 2005).

■ Recent cross-country analysis found that when at least one-quarter of members of parliament are women, laws that discriminate against women, such as laws that restrict women from being head of household, are more likely to be repealed (Hallward-Driemeier, Hasan, and Rusu 2013).

■ Around the world, women lawmakers are often perceived as more honest and more responsive than their male counterparts; a study of 39 countries found that a higher female presence in legislatures is correlated with higher perceptions of government legitimacy among men and women (Schwindt-Bayer and Mishler 2005).

Conversely, as the World Bank (2013a) among others has shown, exclusion and lack of voice can reinforce disparities and lead to fewer or poorer services that address the specific needs of women and girls. To be prevented or stymied from participating in the political life of the community is a major deprivation (Sen 1999a), and, as noted in chapter 1, voicelessness is a social dimension of poverty.

Driving social change for women's agency: The role of ICTs

Information and communication technologies, such as the Internet and mobile phones, are potentially powerful tools for increasing women's voice and participation in both formal and informal public spaces. ICTs can increase women's and girls' access to knowledge and information beyond their immediate environment and enable wider social and professional networks. By providing new ways of connecting people and creating new ways for opinions to be heard, ICTs can be used to overcome the restricted mobility and social exclusion from public spaces that is often experienced by women and girls. They can also provide spaces for collective action to attract supporters and build momentum. ICTs can help shape the aspirations and hopes of the next generation of women and girls, including their economic opportunities, expectations of gender roles, and leadership abilities.

The rapid expansion of ICTs globally is well known. Indeed, today more people can access a mobile network than energy and clean water (Nique and Arab 2013). There are currently an estimated 6.8 billion active mobile cellular subscriptions worldwide, and almost 40 percent of people globally had access to the Internet in 2013, compared with only 10 percent a decade ago. And yet women in developing countries are less likely than men to have access to the Internet, and 21 percent (or 300 million) fewer women than men in developing countries have access to a mobile phone (GSMA and Cherie Blair Foundation for Women 2010).

Using ICTs to increase voice and participation

The landscape for engagement in politics and public action is rapidly being transformed by new technologies, as the case of Malala Yousafzai illustrates (box 6.1). Internet and mobile technology have the potential to mobilize people around an issue

---

Box 6.1 "I believe in the power of the voice of women"

"When I was a girl in Swat [Pakistan], only a few of us were speaking, but our voice had an impact. And now not only I but millions of girls are speaking through our voice, through raising our books and pens.

My father said, 'Do not do one thing with your daughters—do not clip their wings. Give them the same right the boys have.'

Bad people came, and they took all normal life from us ... they had so many rules as to what we could do. We could not go to market.

We fought for our rights. I wrote the blog for the BBC and wrote my diary. Not only was I speaking, many of my friends were talking to the media and to news channels. Media was like a messenger, telling what we are saying to the world. We spoke, we wrote and raised our voices. We spoke, and we achieved our goal. Now Swat is now a peaceful place. Girls are going back to school and are allowed to go to the market."

Source: Malala Yousafzai in conversation with Jim Yong Kim, World Bank, Washington, DC, December 2013.

on a scale previously unimaginable (Evans and Nambiar 2013). Collective action online can range from petitions or educational forums to antiharassment initiatives and flash mobs (Postmes and Brunsting 2002). People with Internet access can gather voices and support globally for local causes. Websites such as Avaaz.org and Change.org allow users to formulate and circulate their own online petitions globally. A petition opposing the eviction of Masai villagers to make way for a game park in Tanzania, for example, garnered 1.7 million signatures and resulted in the government changing its policy (Kielburger and Kielburger 2013).

Information and communication technologies are being used to address threats to women's security by gathering information and providing women with a means to take preventive actions. In some large cities, innovative crowdsourcing tools have been developed. HarassMaps in Cairo and Mumbai allow incidents of harassment to be reported anonymously online or through mobile devices and then linked to city maps, giving women an overview of potential hotspots for sexual harassment. Hollaback!, which now operates in 70 cities across 24 countries, provides women and girls with a public forum in which to voice their experiences of public harassment. Through the exchange of experiences, participants reported a change in their previous acceptance of such behavior (Dimond et al. 2013). As more people access the Internet and smartphones, such crowdsourcing and online socialization tools hold promise.[1]

Addressing the digital divide

As a conduit to greater political participation and public action, ICTs have limitations; some

key facts need to be borne in mind. In 2013, nearly 8 in 10 Internet users (77 percent) lived in developed countries (ITU 2013). And a large gender divide in access, use, ownership, and development of ICT products persists, especially in Sub-Saharan Africa (43 percent fewer women and girls have access than men), the Middle East and North Africa (34 percent fewer women and girls have access), and South Asia (one-third fewer women and girls have access) (Intel and Dalberg Global Development Advisors 2012).

In developing countries, both men and women face barriers to ICT access, notably inadequate infrastructure and high costs. However, social norms can further restrict women's access (Cecchini and Scott 2003). In the Arab Republic of Egypt and India, for example, 12 percent of women stated that they did not access the Internet more often because they did not think it was appropriate, and more than 8 percent did not access it more often because family or friends would disapprove (Intel and Dalberg Global Development Advisors 2012). At home, husbands might regulate the family's use of radios, mobile phones, the Internet, and televisions. In some cases, husbands determine whether and how wives can use a mobile phone. In Afghanistan, more than half the women who did not have access to a phone cited lack of permission from family members as a major obstacle (USAID 2013). Tensions can arise and result in physical or verbal abuse. In Zambia, for example, a recent study found that many women reported social and economic benefits from mobile phones, but phones also created conflict between spouses and in some cases reinforced traditional gender power differences (Wakunuma 2012).

Collective action as a catalyst for change

Beyond individual actions and informal networks, collective action mobilizes people around shared concerns, which can include combating discrimination. Mobilization can take a variety of forms. It can be regular or sporadic and can take place through an organization, through government entities, or entirely outside formal structures. It can be localized or transnational; it can be induced from outside or evolve organically (Evans and Nambiar 2013).

Collective action can enhance women's voice and agency and reduce gender disparities through a number of channels. It can be used to increase accountability, by providing a platform for participatory budgeting, expenditure tracking, and community scorecards, thereby giving citizens voice and helping them claim resources through bottom-up pressure (Evans and Nambiar 2013).

Other actions may involve informing and educating people about civil rights, providing spaces for women's and girls' groups or peer support networks, or campaigning for reforms of discriminatory laws or practices, as in the following examples:

- In Nigeria, the Legislative Advocacy Coalition on Violence against Women campaign contributed to the passage of the Violence against Persons (Prohibition) Bill in 2013. The new law includes a more comprehensive definition of *rape*, stricter sentences, compensation for victims of rape and other sexual offenses, protection from further abuse through restraining orders, and a fund to support victim rehabilitation (Kombo, Sow, and Mohamed 2013).

- In Malawi, Let Girls Lead's Adolescent Girls' Advocacy and Leadership Initiative significantly contributed to the drafting and enactment of local bylaws to eradicate child marriage. The iniative included advocacy with village chiefs and traditional leaders. Adolescent girls interviewed after the bylaws came into effect reported cases of girls leaving marriages and returning to school, and they noted that the new penalties and associated community disapproval were deterring child marriage (Let Girls Lead 2014).

A growing body of evidence suggests that when women participate in self-help groups and other participatory development programs, increased agency accompanies economic outcomes (Beath et al. 2010; Blattman et al. 2013; Kandpal and Baylis 2013; Meier zu Selhausen 2012; Oxfam 2013). In Africa, for example, the following examples are notable:

- In Mali and Tanzania, women members of agricultural producer self-help groups benefit from increased mobility, and in Ethiopia, members reported enhanced control of household expenditures. In Mali, along with greater autonomy over the use of agricultural incomes, group members were consulted more on community and organizational decision making (Evans and Nambiar 2013).

- In western Uganda, members of a joint microfinance and coffee cooperative generally have higher incomes and have used their group status to effect broader change, including around the tolerance of gender-based violence and joint land titling (Meier zu Selhausen 2012).

But the benefits of self-help groups and other participatory development projects can be limited. Groups can at times exclude poor, less educated, or otherwise more marginalized women. A study of community forest groups in South Asia showed that low participation by women was driven by long-standing beliefs about women's roles, and women sometimes lost out as a result of decisions made by the groups (Agarwal 2001). In Bangladesh, studies of collective action in health and education have shown that elite groups were most motivated to participate and enjoyed the most benefits (Mahmud 2002). Programs aimed at increasing civic participation can inadvertently exclude less networked and resourced women. A project in Kenya that aimed to address low levels of community participation among women through leadership, management, and agricultural training was found to mostly benefit women of higher socioeconomic status, who enrolled in higher numbers. The project failed to reach more disadvantaged women, especially older women (Gugerty and Kremer 2008).

Even when income gains occur as a result of collective action, the link between material gain and agency is not always straightforward. For example, an impact assessment of a women's income generation support project in Uganda found that while household incomes increased, there was little evidence that women became more empowered in terms of participating in household decision making or avoiding intimate partner violence (Evans and Nambiar 2013).

A recurring theme in this book is the importance of normative change, and

collective action can be a tool for driving such wider social and political changes. There is a long history of mobilization led by women for public action to change gender-based norms, combat discrimination, and secure women's rights. Collective action may begin with a narrow focus but then evolve to address broader issues. For example, the Self Employed Women's Association (SEWA) in India began focusing on labor regulations and expanded into women's political leadership. In Botswana, the women's group Emang Basadi (Stand Up Women) initially mobilized to oppose discriminatory citizenship laws and evolved into a broader campaign to reform family laws and introduce domestic violence legislation. But there are cases where women's collective action seeks to entrench existing gender biases. For example, conservative women's networks in Mali opposed progressive provisions in the new Family Code, which would have benefited many women by outlawing polygamy and requiring all marriages to be registered. They were unsuccessful, however, and a new, more progressive Family Code was passed in 2012 (Hallward-Driemeier and Hasan 2013).

Women's movements have often played a pivotal role in progressive policy and legal reform. Autonomous women's movements, together with women's machineries (women's ministries and their equivalents), can effectively translate international norms into institutional reforms and are associated with more progressive policy regimes to address violence against women (Weldon and Htun 2013). The fact of being autonomous allows movements to take on issues that political parties and other associations may find too politically sensitive. For example, political parties often have little appetite

Box 6.2 Women's movements that drive reforms

In India, the women's movement helped secure wide-ranging reforms in the aftermath of the heinous attack of a young student on a bus in Delhi in December 2012. India's women's groups and their male allies used the attack and the inadequate response from India's authorities to highlight the customary violence against women that has been ignored by a culture of impunity and silence. Galvanized by these mass protests, a committee was set up and headed by a former chief justice to review antirape provisions and make recommendations for state action. Previously in India, women's networks had used the Convention on the Elimination of All Forms of Discrimination against Women (CEDAW) to press for sexual harassment legislation. In 1997, the Indian Supreme Court relied on the constitution and India's obligations under CEDAW to recognize the right to gender equality and a working environment free from sexual harassment and abuse. The court produced the first guidelines on sexual harassment and employment, which ultimately led in 2007 to legislation prohibiting sexual harassment in the workplace.

Litigation is another powerful tool women's movements have used to challenge unconstitutional discriminatory laws and to address gaps in legal frameworks. One example is the successful challenge to discriminatory customary inheritance laws in Botswana in 2013. And in the Arab Republic of Egypt, tireless mobilization by women's groups in the wake of the revolution led to a new decree that established the right of Egyptian women whose husbands are from West Bank and Gaza to pass on their Egyptian citizenship to their children. In El Salvador, Asociación de Madres Demandantes helps women enforce court-ordered child support payments, and its work has attracted national attention and led to several measures guaranteeing greater support for children.

Sources: Caivano and Hardwick 2008; Hasan and Tanzer 2013; UN Women 2011.

for challenging norms and behaviors perceived as private—including those affecting marriages or personal relationships or those concerning morality.

Recent research across 70 countries found that countries with the strongest feminist movements tend, other things being equal, to have more comprehensive policies on violence against women than those with weaker or nonexistent movements (box 6.2). Autonomous women's movements were found to be more important than left-wing parties, the numbers of women legislators, or even national wealth (Weldon and Htun 2013).

Women's groups can be particularly important in conflict-affected states to help secure access to justice. Umoja Wa Akina Mama Fizi (United Women of Fizi) promotes women's rights and raises women's consciousness in the Democratic Republic of Congo, training members to document human rights abuses and conducting workshops on citizenship, rights, and gender-based violence for rural women (Evans and Nambiar 2013). Women are also increasingly playing active roles in wider social movements, as in Egypt, where female political activists and reporters contributed to the revolution side by side with men. In 2007, the International Civil Society Action Network worked with the Association of War Affected Women in Sri Lanka to build a groundbreaking cross-party coalition of female politicians to ensure participation in the peace process in Sri Lanka. Group members visited South Africa to share experiences on constitution drafting and conflict resolution and participated in a Harvard University training course on negotiation skills and coalition building (Anderlini et al. 2010).

The potential of women's political voice and participation

Women remain underrepresented in key public institutions in most of the world. Greater representation of women in local and national government can influence both policy considerations and budget allocations:

- In a poll of members of parliament from 110 countries conducted between 2006 and 2008, female parliamentarians were more likely to prioritize social issues such as child care, equal pay, parental leave, and pensions; physical concerns such as reproductive rights, physical safety, and gender-based violence; and development matters such as poverty reduction and service delivery (IPU 2008).

- Data from 19 member countries of the Organisation for Economic Co-operation and Development found that having more women legislators resulted in higher total educational spending (Chen 2008). In Sweden, an increase in the number of women in parliament led to a rise in budget allocations to education (Markham 2013).

Women's parliamentary caucuses and committees can build collaboration on gender issues across political parties:

- In Uganda, the Women's Parliamentary Association engages directly in the legislative process, creating awareness campaigns, sharing information, and building networks with nongovernmental organizations and women's groups (Evans and Nambiar 2013).

- In Pakistan, the women's parliamentary caucus contributed to police reforms by visiting women's police stations and reporting on findings. The caucus also meets regularly with the Afghan women's parliamentary caucus and works on joint implementation of a peace process between the two countries (South Asian Regional Secretariat of Women Parliamentarians 2013).

- In Brazil, the women's caucus sponsored legislation to establish a gender quota, a law on violence against women, and the inclusion of funds for social programs and gender equality initiatives into the budget (Evans and Nambiar 2013).

Although evidence on the effect of women's participation in local government is sparser, Mansuri and Rao (2013) find a growing body of evidence from India that shows women's participation has positively affected social norms, as well as investments in public services. In India, since 1992, one-third of all seats on village councils (*gram panchayats*) and one-third of all presidencies are reserved for women (Mansuri and Rao 2013). The documented effect of these quotas includes the following:

- More investment in drinking water infrastructure and better availability of public goods (Chattopadhyay and Duflo 2004; Duflo and Topalova 2004)

- Less corruption, with men and women reporting they are less likely to pay a bribe when the gram panchayat president is a woman (Chattopadhyay and Duflo 2004)

Box 6.3 "If anyone listens, I have a lot of plans": Women in Afghanistan

Afghanistan's National Solidarity Program (NSP) mandates participation of women in community development councils. Evidence of the mandate's effect suggests that increasing women's participation in community development processes can improve women's mobility and enable access to a range of information, including legal rights. In most places, the NSP increased women's mobility by giving them socially acceptable places to visit on a regular basis and by showing men that women's mobility had a positive effect on women's personal growth.

A woman from Parwan Province reported: "NSP allowed women to come out of their houses and gather in groups. This has helped a great deal. The more women come out, the less people will talk."

At the same time, men's perceptions have changed: "After we allowed the women's *shura* (council) to become active, people do not make negative comments anymore, and if they do, nobody pays attention."

Mandating female participation improved both men's and women's attitudes toward female participation in community affairs (by 20 percent and 8 percent, respectively) and increased the likelihood that women would be involved in income-generating activities by some 13 percent.

Sources: Azarbaijani-Moghaddam 2010; Beath, Christia, and Enikolpov 2013.

- Positive effects on parents' aspirations for their daughters (narrowing the gap between fathers' and mothers' aspirations for their daughters) and simultaneous positive effects on the aspirations of girls themselves (Beaman et al. 2012)

- Increased reporting of crimes against women and increased police responsiveness (Iyer et al. 2012)

Requiring female participation in decision making can help counter exclusion and combat stereotypes (box 6.3; Mansuri and Rao 2013). Evidence from the United States, for example, suggests that living in a state with competitive female political candidates can increase women's self-efficacy (Atekeson 2003).

Underrepresentation and biased gender norms

Women remain underrepresented in key public institutions in most of the world. Discriminatory social norms can inhibit women's effective participation in politics at national and local levels. Weak networks, limited access to campaign financing, lower levels of education, greater family responsibilities, and fewer opportunities for acquiring political experience can all also hamper women's participation in public decision-making forums (UN Women 2005). This section examines participation rates in national parliaments and the judiciary and highlights the links with underlying social norms and perceptions.

As of 2014, women hold 22 percent of parliamentary seats globally. This is almost double the rate in 1997, at just 12 percent, but still far from parity (figure 6.1). As of January 2014, there were 18 women heads of state and government, which is about 10 percent (UN Women 2014). However, significant regional and country variation exists, and progress is evident: in

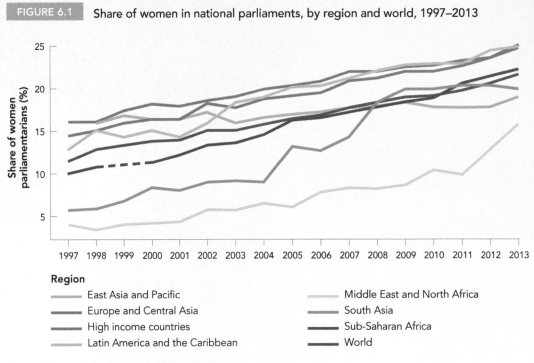

FIGURE 6.1 Share of women in national parliaments, by region and world, 1997–2013

Region

— East Asia and Pacific

— Europe and Central Asia

— High income countries

— Latin America and the Caribbean

— Middle East and North Africa

— South Asia

— Sub-Saharan Africa

— World

Source: Estimates based on World Bank 2013c.

Note: Data not available for East Asia and Pacific in 1997 and Sub-Saharan Africa in 1999.

the Nordic countries, women hold 42 percent of parliamentary seats; in Rwanda, the share is close to two-thirds (64 percent); and in Andorra, Cuba, Nicaragua, Senegal, the Seychelles, and South Africa, the share exceeds 40 percent (IPU 2014a).

Overall across developing regions, the Middle East and North Africa has the lowest levels of representation, at 16 percent, and Latin America and the Caribbean has the highest, at 25 percent (the same as the high-income country average).

Even when women enter parliament, they are less likely to hold ministerial posts, are mostly confined to social portfolios when they do so, and rarely hold high official positions (World Bank 2011).[2] In 2013, only about 14 percent of all presiding officers of parliament or one of its houses were women (IPU 2014b). Women are also underrepresented in the justice sector, including in constitutional courts (box 6.4).

Data on women's participation at the local level, although scarce, indicate even lower representation. The proportion of women among locally elected councilors, for example, ranges from a low of 8 percent in North Africa to a high of 30 percent in Sub-Saharan Africa (UNSD 2010). Fewer than 5 percent of mayors globally are women, and many countries, including Afghanistan, Egypt, and Morocco, have only one or two women

Box 6.4 Underrepresentation of women at senior levels in the justice sector

Globally, women account for 27 percent of judges. In some countries, women judges are restricted in their judicial duties. In the Islamic Republic of Iran, for example, women judges are unable to issue and sign final verdicts.

In nearly two-thirds of the 123 countries for which there are data, women comprise less than 25 percent of justices in constitutional courts (map B6.4.1). But there is significant country and regional variation. In Rwanda, Sierra Leone, and Zambia, more than half of justices are women. At 60 percent, Sierra Leone has the highest share of female constitutional judges in the world, and the chief justice is a woman. With six female chief justices—in Gabon, Ghana, Niger, Nigeria, Sierra Leone, and Zambia—Sub-Saharan Africa has more female chief justices than any other region.

MAP B6.4.1   Share of female justices in constitutional courts

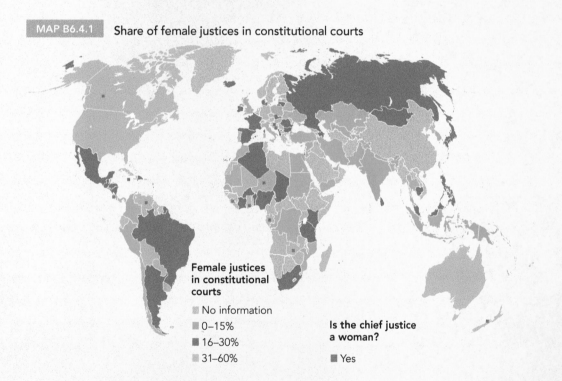

Female justices in constitutional courts

- No information
- 0–15%
- 16–30%
- 31–60%

Is the chief justice a woman?

- Yes

Sources: Estimates for 123 countries based on Kar 2008; OECD 2012; UNICEF 2011; UN Women 2011; World Bank and IFC 2013.

Box 6.5 Differing levels of political engagement

The World Values Survey asks women and men in 86 countries (representing nearly 90 percent of the world's population) about how often they discuss political matters with friends. Across all regions of the world, reports of such discussions were higher among men than women (figure B6.5.1). People were most engaged in East Asia and the Pacific, where one in five reported "frequent" conversations about politics, but the share of men (30 percent) was more than double that of women (13 percent).

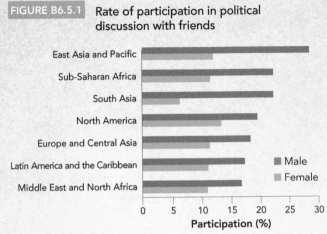

FIGURE B6.5.1 Rate of participation in political discussion with friends

Source: Estimates based on World Values Survey data, latest years available, 1994–2009.

serving in this position nationwide (Fleishman 2009; Motevalli 2013; UNSD 2010; York 2009). In the 77 countries with data, fewer than one in five mayors are women, with the exceptions of Mauritius, New Zealand, Serbia, and Latvia with 40 percent, 26 percent, 26 percent, and 25 percent, respectively (UNSD 2010).

Similarly, women's participation in local groups, such as community management groups, may also be more limited than men's. Although group membership is common in some developing countries, this does not necessarily translate into effective participation (Agarwal 2001). Globally, women are also less likely than men to participate in informal political discussions. Data gathered on engagement in political discussions with friends shows that across all regions, more men report having such conversations (see box 6.5).

Attitudes toward female leadership that affect women's political participation

Social norms often reinforce the notion that men are better leaders than women and limit the capacity for women to aspire to public roles. On average across 86 countries, most men (53 percent) and a sizable proportion of women (41 percent) assert that men make better political leaders than do women (Breznau et al. 2011). An earlier survey of 46 countries found that most respondents in North America, Latin America and the Caribbean, and Europe rated men and women as equally good leaders. In contrast, the majority of participants in Bangladesh, Ethiopia, Kuwait, Mali, Pakistan, and the West Bank and Gaza, preferred men as leaders (Horowitz 2007). These attitudes can limit women's political aspirations. For example, evidence from the United States shows that despite comparable

FIGURE 6.2   Attitudes toward women leaders reflected in the share of women in parliament

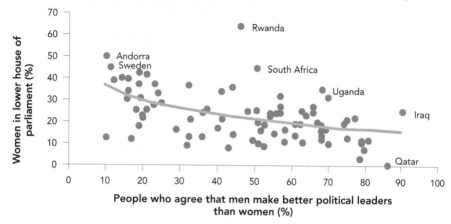

Sources: Estimates for 87 countries based on World Values Survey data, 1996–2012 latest years available and IPU 2013.

backgrounds, accomplished women are less likely to believe they meet the criteria to run for office than do men (Fox and Lawless 2011).

But attitudes vary, and people in some regions seem to place particular value on female politicians. In Latin America and the Caribbean, for example, 54 percent of men and 70 percent of women in 2007 agreed women had done a better job than men had in politics. The belief that women make equally good leaders as men is correlated with the percentage of female representation in parliament (figure 6.2). Countries where fewer respondents say that men make better political leaders tend to have the highest share of women parliamentarians— including Andorra, Argentina, Canada, Finland, the Netherlands, and Sweden— while countries where about 80 percent of respondents believe men make better political leaders have lower shares of women parliamentarians, including Egypt, the Islamic Republic of Iran, Iraq, Jordan, Ghana, Mali, and Qatar (World Bank 2013a).

Quotas that reduce barriers to women's participation

Quotas may help change stereotypes and attitudes regarding women as leaders and increase women's overall engagement in politics and civic life. In Rwanda and South Africa, political quotas have had a major effect on increasing women's representation. The Rwandan Constitution (Article 76, Section 2) guarantees women 30 percent of all government seats, and women now compose 64 percent of parliamentarians (IPU 2014a). Before the African National Congress established a 30 percent quota for female candidates in 1994, South Africa ranked 141st in the world in the percentage of legislative seats held by women. Just six years later, the country ranked 10th and currently ranks 8th in the world, with women holding 42 percent of parliamentary seats and 40 percent of ministerial positions (Haussmann, Tyson, and Zahidi 2012).

At the gram panchayat level in India, quotas for women and scheduled castes have weakened prevailing stereotypes around women's fitness to participate as political leaders and shifted social norms. After just seven years' exposure, men in villages with women leaders were no longer biased against them, and parents' aspirations for their daughters were higher. After the quotas ended, women continued to run for and, in many cases, win elections (Beaman et al. 2012).

Similarly, a recent study across 32 villages in India assessing trends in women's political involvement (including voting patterns, knowledge about rights, and participation in local-level political and social activities) finds that women's involvement is significantly higher after three years of having had women leaders and increases further after five years (Sathe et al. 2013). This suggests that quotas can take time to work.

Quotas can also be used to increase women's representation in the judiciary. For example, the Future Judges Program in Jordan has a minimum quota of 15 percent female participants and aims to triple the number of female judges by 2014. By 2013, women were 17 percent of all judges, compared to 7 percent in 2010.

But positive effects are not assured and will depend on the experience of the women leaders and the nature of local hierarchies. For example, women in panchayats were less effective in locations where upper castes owned most of the land (Ban and Rao 2009). Likewise, in Burundi in 2010, legislative quotas increased the share of women parliamentarians to 30 percent, but women continued to align themselves across partisan lines and failed to address institutional or legal gender discrimination (Evans and Nambiar 2013).

Implications for policy

As this chapter has demonstrated, it is important to include women in decision making at all levels—national and local politics, community-level decision making, and collective action processes. ICTs can facilitate this inclusion, but there are challenges and barriers and much that we still do not know.

Increasing access to ICTs and making content relevant

ICTs can be a driving force in providing new spaces and mediums for expanded participation of women in the public sphere, but some limitations must be overcome. A broad policy approach that focuses on access to ICTs—cell phones, Internet, and social media—and the quality of content is required.

Greater access to ICTs can be achieved in part by reducing costs and creating safe spaces where women can access hardware and training. Ownership of computers and smartphones for both women and men in many parts of the world remains a long way off. Alternative public access points can help fill this gap. This approach can include leveraging existing public domains such as libraries, health centers, schools, and community centers. Public libraries, for example, are often safe, trusted places for women and girls to visit, and many already have computer access points and training programs that could be leveraged to meet gender access objectives (Gomez 2012). In Copán, Honduras, for example, a local library provides technology training and digital literacy programs to local girls and women (Beyond Access 2012). Many of the girls trained in the program subsequently become library volunteers, training others in the community.

Leveraging both public and private sectors is integral for creating a media network that is relevant and accessible to women and girls. This requires supporting the creation and the development of online content that meets the needs and interests of women and girls, especially content developed by women and girls. Fostering collaboration between technology providers, manufacturers, content producers, and end users to provide women-tailored content will be critical (Broadband Commission Working Group on Broadband and Gender 2013). Service providers can team up with women's groups to produce tools and services that meet the needs of women and provide new spaces for online or mobile collaboration. So far, little evidence exists on successful approaches, and more research is needed to fully understand what interventions work and how such partnerships can best be achieved.

Greater use of ICTs for participatory mapping can provide valuable information on mobility and access to public spaces by highlighting specific constraints facing women and girls. Using ICTs in this way can provide a low-cost alternative for monitoring and assessment, including assessments on the perceptions of violence. For example, mapping applications in urban townships in South Africa provide information about travel distances and safe spaces for girls and boys. The mapping was subsequently used to provide recommendations for public service provision, including the creation of safe spaces where adolescent girls could meet and build networks (see box 6.6).

Supporting collective action

Women's movements play a pivotal role in building the necessary momentum and consensus for progressive policy and legal reform. The appropriate role for development agencies in supporting collective action processes is not always clear; however, some evidence suggests that such processes are more effective when they develop organically rather than as the result of top-down support. Nonetheless, development agencies and partners can help support policy reforms that create the space for collective action to operate and can help foster stronger dialogue among collective action groups and policy makers.

Development agencies can support knowledge exchange among groups within and across countries and can provide financial support to pilot innovative and locally driven programs that use collective action processes to help shift norms and behaviors (Evans and Nambiar 2013). Support to women's groups for specific interventions should embody large elements of local problem solving and learning by doing, which can be achieved in part by devolving responsibility to and empowering the groups with local legitimacy as frontline implementers (box 6.7).

Formal quotas or inclusion mandates are often needed in self-help groups and other collective participatory processes to counter exclusion and prevailing stereotypes (Mansuri and Rao 2013). Such mandates can ensure broader representation within groups and enable greater access by those who may otherwise be marginalized.

Increasing accountability

Social accountability mechanisms disseminate information, promote dialogue and negotiation, and provide forums through which the voices of previously excluded groups, such as women and girls, can be heard (George 2003;

Box 6.6 Mapping and creating safe spaces for girls in South Africa

The daily activities of adolescents in South Africa are overshadowed by social, economic, and physical risks that constrain their access to the public sphere and limit their economic opportunities. In particular, the threat of gender-based violence looms large for girls. As a result, they are encouraged to stay close to their home and limit their movements and activities to safe spaces.

In 2004–05, the Population Council conducted a participatory mapping exercise in an urban township and rural community. Groups of students from both primary and secondary schools, roughly 11 to 15 years of age, were asked to draw the area that represented their community and rate its level of safety. Their drawings were compared with Google satellite images for each locality (figure B6.6.1).

FIGURE B6.6.1   Accessible urban area, by sex and grade

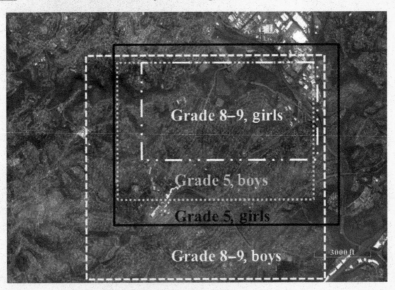

Image: © Population Council. Used with permission. Further permission required for reuse.

In urban areas, the space mapped by younger girls (6.33 square miles) was 2.5 times larger than the area mapped by older girls (2.62 square miles). In contrast, older boys mapped an area twice as large as younger boys, 7.81 square miles compared to 3.79 miles. The results show that at age 11, girls' physical space was larger than that of boys of the same age but then fell dramatically after puberty. The same was true in rural areas.

Boys reported a number of spaces as "very" or "extremely" safe, including primary and secondary schools, but girls did not use these categories to describe any space. In fact, urban secondary schools were ranked as very unsafe by adolescent girls. Libraries were rated as somewhat safe by younger and older urban girls, whereas older boys described them as extremely safe. Older girls in particular reported most spaces in their restricted navigable areas as unsafe.

The findings suggest that participatory mapping tools are a useful instrument for assessing perceptions of violence and creating targeted programs for adolescents. For example, local libraries and youth centers can be transformed into safe spaces for girls by designating girls- or boys-only spaces at different times and by providing social support networks for boys and girls to negotiate insecurity and dangers in their immediate environments.

Source: Hallman et al. 2013.

Box 6.7 Working with civil society to prevent gender-based violence in Haiti

In the aftermath of the 2010 earthquake in Haiti, as people crowded into camps, women and children became increasingly vulnerable to violence and assault. To help address this risk, the World Bank Group supported the Commission of Women Victims for Victims (KOFAVIV), a grassroots Haitian organization comprising female survivors of sexual gender-based violence, and its international partner organization, MADRE, to address and prevent violence in five of Haiti's internally displaced persons camps. The project worked with KOFAVIV's community outreach workers and peer counselors—often rape survivors themselves living in the camps—and provided health and safety kits to vulnerable women and girls. This support was coupled with media outreach campaigns to promote awareness and prevention of violence as well as technical assistance to KOFAVIV from MADRE to improve project coordination, financial management, communications, long-term planning, and monitoring and evaluation. The initiative enhanced women's civic participation by building coalitions and networks with the government, international institutions, the media, and other women's rights nongovernmental organizations in Haiti.

KOFAVIV also became a lead convener in working with civil society groups, police, hospitals, and the government to address gender-based violence in Haiti. The capacity at KOFAVIV increased as more empowered community agents became involved in the initiative.

Source: World Bank 2013b.

World Bank 2006). Such mechanisms are typically designed with the aim of improving service delivery and government performance, which can align with the interests of women's groups and thus be an important channel through which collective action operates.

Varying means exist for engaging in and supporting social accountability mechanisms. Channels of direct influence include gender audits, which focus on systems and processes within institutions, and public interest legislation such as right-to-information acts. Some initiatives, such as the municipal government of Recife, Brazil's partnership with the Women's Coordinating Group (Coordenadoria da Mulher), have emphasized women's direct participation in budgeting (BRIDGE 2002).

Other social accountability initiatives that tackle gender issues include specific components enabling women's voices to be heard in ways that challenge social norms. For example, in the Indian state of Odisha in 2006, the White Ribbon Alliance for Safe Motherhood embarked on a program to address high maternal mortality and maternal health programs using three tools: maternal death audits via verbal autopsies; health facility checklists; and public hearings and rallies (Papp, Gogoi, and Campbell 2013). Public hearings provide new ways for women to collectively voice their concerns and demands in a safe space. Their demands were reinforced and legitimized by local officials and the media, contributing to leaders' enhanced receptivity to women's needs. This new understanding opened opportunities for improved service delivery. The program results reflected a general recognition among informants that "subtle mindsets—among both marginalized women as well as leaders and service providers—play as much of a role in the success or failure of social accountability as any manifest factors and structural barriers" and that accountability tools are needed to challenge "the ingrained socio-cultural norms that perpetuate health disparities in the first place" (Papp, Gogoi, and Campbell 2013; see also Windau-Melmer 2013).

Finding opportunities to expand women's political participation

Although women's political participation remains low overall, the good news is that attitudes toward female leaders are changing and a body of experience is accumulating. Promising approaches to increase women's participation include the following.

1. Use quotas. Quota systems can help overcome barriers and change attitudes around women's political participation. Quotas work if women have a prominent place on party lists and the lists are enforced, preferably with sanctions for noncompliance. Women will benefit from a quota only if they are placed in winnable positions on a party list, rather than being at the bottom with little chance of success (Dahlerup 2009). Quotas are unlikely to be a panacea, however: social hierarchies, resistance from incumbents, and entrenched gender norms can limit their effectiveness. Whether quotas work depends on the context, and care must be taken so that thresholds do not become a ceiling rather than a minimum for women's participation (United Nations Focal Point for Electoral Assistance 2013).

There is now strong evidence about the effectiveness of quotas and inclusion mandates at the national level and in collective action groups and participatory projects and programs. Less is known globally about their effectiveness in local-level political institutions, and more trials and impact evaluation across a larger number of countries and regions are needed.

2. Level the playing field. Greater access to financial resources and leadership training opportunities are needed. Promising approaches are under way in a number of countries:

- In Mexico, a federal law requires that parties spend 2 percent of their funding on women's leadership initiatives, and strong lobbying by a coalition of women's groups ensured strong enforcement mechanisms. (Ballington et al. 2012).

- In Burkina Faso, the quota law is tied to federal campaign funding and offers extra funding incentives to parties that fill the 30 percent benchmark (Ballington et al. 2012).

- In Croatia, the Gender Equality Act requires that special measures be taken to promote gender balance in all branches of government and that registered political parties adopt action plans to achieve gender balance. The Social Democratic Party established a women's wing that provided training on leadership and political communications. This training helped develop a network of experienced women politicians, and following the 2007 elections, women made up 32 percent of the party's parliamentary group and held influential positions within parliament (Ballington et al. 2012).

The Women in Public Service Project, launched in 2011 by the U.S. State Department and the Woodrow Wilson Center, partners with academic institutions around the world to empower the next generation of female leaders through training and mentoring. The aim is reach a minimum of 50 percent representation of women in public service by 2050.

3. Promote civil society activism. Strategies to increase women's participation in politics and public life, led by civil society groups or individuals, can be an important source of support for women candidates. For example, the Elect Haitian Women campaign on television and radio was run by a local women's group throughout the country to encourage voters to support women candidates (Markham 2013). In the United States, EMILY's List recruits and trains women candidates, introduces them to key donors and the media, and helps them raise funds for their campaigns.[3]

4. Increase women's participation throughout the electoral process. Electoral commissions and other bodies that conduct elections can be important entry points for increasing women's participation in national and local politics. This includes ensuring that women have the documentation needed to register to vote and that electoral processes are inclusive. Examples include the following:

■ The Democracy Monitoring Group in Uganda developed women's participation checklists and reporting templates for its observers, conducted focus groups, analyzed voter register data, and produced a comprehensive gender analysis for the 2011 elections (Markham 2013).

■ In parts of the Middle East and North Africa, young men and women are brought together as activists and party members to become accustomed to working side by side as equals. In the Republic of Yemen, youth councils have taught young women and men critical conflict prevention and mitigation skills, encouraging them to work together effectively to resolve community disputes and advocate for local youth issues (Markham 2013).

5. Consider proportional representation. Proportional representation systems outperform other systems in getting women into parliament and are more effective at implementing quotas (Krook 2006; Matland 2005; Norris 1985). In 2012, women accounted for 25 percent of members of parliament in proportional representation systems, in contrast to 14 percent in first-past-the-post systems and 18 percent in mixed proportional representation and first-past-the-post systems (IPU 2013).

* * *

Women's voices can be transformative, working to highlight and combat discrimination, focusing attention on policies that can reduce gender inequality, and directing resources to programs that can enhance opportunities for women, girls, and their families. Making real advances in women's political participation requires interventions and support on several fronts to foster positive changes in norms and practice. Collective action is an important vehicle for women's voice, and autonomous women's movements play a critical role in driving positive changes that can shift social norms over the longer term. In many parts of the world, attitudes are changing, leading to increased recognition of women's leadership abilities at the national and local levels.

Notes

1. It is worth mentioning that the Harass-Maps in Cairo and Mumbai have not lived up to their full potential yet, with 97 reports recorded in Mumbai since October 2012 and a little more than 1,200 reports in all of Egypt since 2010. See http://harassmap.org/en/what-we-do/the-map/ and https://akshara.crowdmap.com/for more information.

2. Latest data are in UN Women (2010).

3. For more information about EMILY's List, see the organization's website at http://www.emilyslist.org/.

References

Agarwal, Bina. 2001. "Participatory Exclusions, Community Forestry, and Gender: An Analysis for South Asia and a Conceptual Framework." *World Development* 29 (10): 1623–48.

Anderlini, Sanam Naraghi, John Tirman, Cerue Garlo, Shyamala Gomez, Suraiya Kamaruzzaman, Turid Smith Polfus, Elena Rey, and Lina Zedriga. 2010. "What the Women Say: Participation and UNSCR 1325." International Civil Society Action Network and Center for International Studies, Cambridge, MA.

Atkeson, Lonna Rae. 2003. "Not All Cues Are Created Equal: The Conditional Impact of Female Candidates on Political Engagement." *Journal of Politics* 65 (4): 1041–61.

Azarbaijani-Moghaddam, Sippi. 2010. *A Study of Gender Equity through the National Solidarity Programme's Community Development Councils: "If Anyone Listens, I Have a Lot of Plans."* Kabul: Danish Committee for Aid to Afghan Refugees.

Ballington, Julie, and Azza Karam, eds. 2005. *Women in Parliament: Beyond Numbers.* Stockholm: International Institute for Democracy and Electoral Assistance.

Ballington, Julie, Randi Davis, Mireya Reith, Lincoln Mitchell, Carole Njoki, Alyson Kozma, and Elizabeth Powley. 2012. *Empowering Women for Stronger Political Parties: A Guidebook to Promote Women's Political Participation.* New York: United Nations Development Programme and National Democratic Institute for International Affairs.

Ban, Radu, and Vijayendra Rao. 2009. "Is Deliberation Equitable: Evidence from Transcripts of Village Meetings in India." Policy Research Working Paper 4928, World Bank, Washington, DC.

Beaman, Lori, Esther Duflo, Rohini Pande, and Petia Topalova. 2012. "Female Leadership Raises Aspirations and Educational Attainment for Girls: A Policy Experiment in India." *Science* 335 (6068): 582–86.

Beath, Andrew, Fontini Christia, and Ruben Enikolpov. 2013. *Randomized Impact Evaluation of Afghanistan's National Solidarity Programme: Final Report.* Washington, DC: World Bank.

Beath, Andrew, Fontini Christia, Ruben Enikolopov, and Shahim Ahmad Kabuli. 2010. "Randomized Impact Evaluation of Phase-II of Afghanistan's National Solidarity Programme (NSP): Estimates of Interim Program Impact from First Follow-Up Survey." World Bank, Washington, DC.

Beyond Access. 2012. "Empowering Women and Girls through ICT at Libraries." Issue Brief, October, http://www.intgovforum.org/cms/wks2013/workshop_background_paper/268_1367875859.pdf.

Blattman, Christopher, Eric Green, Jeannie Annan, and Julian Jamison. 2013. "Building Women's Economic and Social Empowerment through Enterprise: An Experimental Assessment of the Women's Income

Generating Support (WINGS) Program in Uganda." Logica Study 1, World Bank, Washington, DC.

Breznau, Nate, Valerie A. Lykes, Jonathan Kelley, and M. D. R. Evans. 2011. "A Clash of Civilizations? Preferences for Religious Political Leaders in 86 Nations World Values." *Journal for the Scientific Study of Religion* 50 (4): 671–91.

BRIDGE. 2002. "Budgets and Gender." Gender and Development In Brief 12, Institute of Development Studies, Brighton, U.K.

Broadband Commission Working Group on Broadband and Gender. 2013. "Doubling Digital Opportunities: Enhancing the Inclusion of Women and Girls in the Information Society." International Telecommunications Union and United Nations Educational Scientific and Cultural Organization, Geneva.

Caivano, Joan M., and Thayer Hardwick. 2008. "Latin American Women in Movement: Changing Politics, Changing Minds." In *Civil Society and Social Movements: Building Sustainable Democracies in Latin America*, edited by Arthur Domike, 265–300. Washington, DC: Inter-American Development Bank, 2008.

Cecchini, Simone, and Chris D. Scott. 2003. "Can Information and Communications Technology Applications Contribute to Poverty Reduction? Lessons from Rural India." *Information Technology for Development* 10: 73–84.

Chattopadhyay, Raghabendra, and Esther Duflo. 2004. "Women as Policy Makers: Evidence from a Randomized Policy Experiment in India." *Econometrica* 72 (5): 1409–33.

Chen, Li-Ju. 2008. "Female Policy Maker and Educational Expenditure: Cross-Country Evidence." Research Paper in Economics 1, Department of Economics, Stockholm University, Stockholm.

Dahlerup, Drude. 2009. "About Quotas." Quota Project, International Institute for Democracy and Electoral Assistance and Stockholm University, Stockholm.

Dimond, Jill P., Michaelanne Dye, Daphne LaRose, and Amy S. Bruckman. 2013. "Hollaback! The Role of Collective Storytelling Online in a Social Movement Organization." In *Proceedings of the 2013 Conference on Computer Supported Cooperative Work*, 477–90. New York: ACM.

Drèze, Jean, and Amartya Sen. 2002. *India: Development and Participation.* New York: Oxford University Press.

Duflo, Esther, and Petia Topalova. 2004. "Unappreciated Service: Performance, Perceptions, and Women Leaders in India." Working Paper, Department of Economics, Massachusetts Institute of Technology, Cambridge, MA.

Evans, Alison, and Divya Nambiar. 2013. "Collective Action and Women's Agency: A Background Paper." Women's Voice, Agency, and Participation Research Paper 4, World Bank, Washington, DC.

Fleishman, Jeffrey. 2009. "In Egypt, a Village Boasts the Nation's First Female Mayor." *Los Angeles Times*, March 8. http://articles.latimes.com/2009/mar/08/world/fg-egypt-mayor8.

Fox, Richard L., and Jennifer L. Lawless. 2011. "Gendered Perceptions and Political Candidacies: A Central Barrier to Women's Equality in Electoral Politics." *American Journal of Political Science* 55 (1): 55–73.

George, Asha. 2003. "Accountability in Health Services Transforming Relationships and Contexts." Working Paper 13 (1), Harvard Center for Population and Development Studies, Cambridge, MA.

Gomez, Ricardo, ed. 2012. *Libraries, Telecenters, Cybercafés, and Public Access to*

ICT: International Comparisons. Hershey, PA: IGI Global.

GSMA and Cherie Blair Foundation for Women. 2010. "Women and Mobile: A Global Opportunity." GSMA, London.

Gugerty, Mary Kay, and Michael Kremer. 2008. "Outside Funding and the Dynamics of Participation in Community Associations." *American Journal of Political Science* 52 (3): 585–602.

Hallman, Kelly K., Nora J. Kenworthy, Judith Diers, Nick Swan, and Bashi Devnarain. 2013. "The Contracting World of Girls at Puberty: Violence and Gender-Divergent Access to the Public Sphere among Adolescents in South Africa." Poverty, Gender, and Youth Working Paper 25, Population Council, New York. http://popcouncil .org/pdfs/wp/pgy/025.pdf.

Hallward-Driemeier, Mary, and Tazeen Hasan. 2013. *Empowering Women: Legal Rights and Economic Opportunities in Africa.* Washington, DC: World Bank.

Hallward-Driemeier, Mary, Tazeen Hasan, and Anca Bogdana Rusu. 2013. "Women's Legal Rights over 50 Years: Progress, Stagnation, or Regression?" Policy Research Working Paper 6616, World Bank, Washington, DC.

Hasan, Tazeen, and Ziona Tanzer. 2013. "Women's Movements, Plural Legal Systems, and the Botswana Constitution: How Reform Happens." Policy Research Working Paper 6690, World Bank, Washington, DC.

Hausmann, Richard, Laura D. Tyson, and Saadia Zahidi. 2012. *The Global Gender Gap Report 2012.* Geneva: World Economic Forum.

Horowitz, Juliana Menasce. 2007. "How the World Rates Women as Leaders." Pew Research Center, Washington, DC.

Intel and Dalberg Global Development Advisors. 2012. *Women and the Web.* Washington, DC: Intel.

IPU (Inter-Parliamentary Union). 2008. *Equality in Politics: A Survey of Men and Women in Parliaments.* Geneva: IPU.

———. 2013. "Increased Women's Political Participation Still Dependent on Quotas, 2012 Elections Show." Press release, IPU, Geneva, March 5. http://www.ipu.org /press-e/pressrelease20130305.htm.

———. 2014a. "Women in National Parliaments." IPU, Geneva. http://www.ipu.org /wmn-e/world.htm.

———. 2014b. "Women Speakers of National Parliaments." IPU, Geneva. http://www.ipu .org/wmn-e/speakers.htm.

ITU (International Telecommunication Union). 2013. "The World in 2013: ICT Facts and Figures." ITU, Geneva.

Iyer, Lakshmi, Anandi Mani, Prachi Mishra, and Petia Topalova. 2012. "The Power of Political Voice: Women's Political Representation and Crime in India." *American Economic Journal: Applied Economics* 4 (4): 165–93.

Jones, Mark P. 2005. "Legislator Gender and Legislator Policy Priorities in the Argentine Chamber of Deputies and the United States House of Representatives." *Policy Studies Journal* 25 (4): 613–29.

Kabeer, Naila. 2013. *Paid Work, Women's Empowerment, and Inclusive Growth: Transforming the Structures of Constraint.* New York: UN Women.

Kandpal, Eeshani, and Kathy Baylis. 2013. "Expanding Horizons: Can Women's Support Groups Diversify Peer Networks in Rural India?" *American Journal of Agricultural Economics* 95 (2): 360–67.

Kar, Mehrangiz. 2008. "Discrimination against Women under Iranian Law." Mehrangiz Kar blog, December 10. http://www.mehrangizkar.net/english /archives/000416.php.

Kielburger, Craig, and Mark Kielburger. 2013. "Can Online Petitions Change the World?" *Huffington Post*, October 22.

Kombo, Brenda, Rainatou Sow, and Faiza Jama Mohamed, eds. 2013. *Journey to Equality: 10 Years of the Protocol on the Rights of Women in Africa*. New York: Equality Now.

Krook, Mona Lena. 2006. "Reforming Representation: The Diffusion of Candidate Gender Quotas Worldwide." *Politics and Gender* 2 (3): 303–27.

Let Girls Lead. 2014. "Ending Child Marriage in Malawi: Girls Empowerment Network and Let Girls Lead." http://www.letgirlslead .org/assets/pdfs/GENET-Case-Study -FINAL-1-20-14.pdf

Mahmud, Simeen. 2002. "Making Rights Real in Bangladesh through Collective Citizen Action." *IDS Bulletin* 33 (2): 31–39.

Mansuri, Ghazala, and Vijayendra Rao. 2013. *Localizing Development: Does Participation Work?* Washington, DC: World Bank.

Markham, Susan. 2013. "Women as Agents of Change: Having Voice in Society and Influencing Policy." Women's Voice, Agency, and Participation Research Paper 5, World Bank, Washington, DC.

Matland, Richard E. 2005. "Enhancing Women's Political Participation: Legislative Recruitment and Electoral Systems." In *Women in Parliament: Beyond Numbers*, edited by Julie Ballington and Azza Karam, 93–111. Stockholm: International Institute for Democracy and Electoral Assistance.

Meier zu Selhausen, Felix. 2012. "Does Agency Matter and Do Microfinance Self-Help Groups Empower Women? A Case Study of a Joint-Microfinance and Coffee Cooperative from the Mountains of the Moon in Uganda." Presented at the conference on Design and Dynamics of Institutions for Collective Action, Utrecht University, Utrecht, Netherlands, November 29–December 1.

Motevalli, Golnar. 2013. "Afghanistan's First Female Mayor Proves Critics Wrong." *Guardian*, February 24. http://www .guardian.co.uk/world/2013/feb/24 /afghanistan-first-female-mayor.

Nique, Michael, and Firas Arab. 2013. "Sustainable Energy and Water Access through M2M Connectivity." GSMA, London.

Norris, Pippa. 1985. "Women's Legislative Participation in Western Europe." *Western European Politics* 8 (4): 90–101.

OECD (Organisation for Economic Co-operation and Development). 2012. "Social Institutions and Gender Index, 2012." OECD, Paris. http://www.oecd.org/dev/poverty /theoecdsocialinstitutionsandgender index.htm.

Oxfam. 2013. "Women's Collective Action in the Honey Sector in Ethiopia: Involving Marginalized Women in Collective Action—Making a Difference through NGO Interventions." Oxfam, London.

Papp, Susan A., Aparajita Gogoi, and Catherine Campbell. 2013. "Can Social Accountability Improve Maternal Health in India?" London School of Economics and Political Science, November 6. http:// blogs.lse.ac.uk/indiaatlse/2013/11/06 /can-social-accountability-initiatives -improve-maternal-health-in-india/.

Postmes, Tom, and Suzanne Brunsting. 2002. "Collective Action in the Age of the Internet: Mass Communication and Online Mobilization." *Social Science Computer Review* 20 (3): 290–301.

Sathe, Dhanmanjiri, Stephan Klasen, Jan Priebe, and Mithila Biniwale. 2013. "Can the Female Sarpanch Deliver: Evidence from Maharashtra." *Economic and Political Weekly* 48 (11): 50–57.

Sen, Amartya K. 1999a. "Democracy as a Universal Value." *Journal of Democracy* 10 (3): 3–17.

———. 1999b. *Development as Freedom*. Oxford, U.K.: Oxford University Press.

Schwindt-Bayer, Leslie A. 2006. "Female Legislators and the Promotion of Women, Children, and Family Policies in Latin America." Background paper for *The State of the World's Children 2007*, United Nations Children's Fund, New York.

Schwindt-Bayer, Leslie A., and William Mishler. 2005. "An Integrated Model of Women's Representation." *Journal of Politics* 67 (2): 407–28.

South Asian Regional Secretariat of Women Parliamentarians. 2013. "Report on the First Meeting of the Network of South Asian Women Parliamentarians." Colombo, February 25–27, 2013.

UNICEF (United Nations Children's Fund). 2011. "Jordan: MENA Gender Equality Profile—Status of Girls and Women in the Middle East and North Africa." UNICEF, New York.

United Nations Focal Point for Electoral Assistance. 2013. "Promoting Women's Electoral and Political Participation through UN Electoral Assistance." Policy Directive, United Nations, New York, December 24.

UNSD (United Nations Statistics Division). 2010. *World's Women 2010: Trends and Statistics*. New York: United Nations.

UN Women (United Nations Entity for Gender Equality and the Empowerment of Women). 2005. "Women and Elections: Guide to Promoting the Participation of Women in Elections." United Nations, New York.

———. 2010. "Gender Justice: Key to Achieving the Millennium Development Goals." United Nations, New York.

———. 2011. *Progress of the World's Women: In Pursuit of Justice, 2011–2012*. New York: UN Women.

———. 2014. "Women in Politics," United Nations, New York.

USAID (U.S. Agency for International Development). 2013. "Connecting to Opportunity: A Survey of Afghan Women's Access to Mobile Technology." USAID, Washington, DC.

Wakunuma, Kutoma J. 2012. "Implicating Mobile Phones in Violence against Women: What's Gender Got to Do with It?" GenderIT. org, Melville, South Africa. http://www.genderit.org/resources/implicating-mobile-phones-violence-against-women-what-s-gender-got-do-it.

Weldon, Laura S., and Mala Htun. 2013. "Feminist Mobilization and Progressive Policy Change: Why Governments Take Action to Combat Violence against Women." *Gender and Development* 21 (2): 231–47.

Windau-Melmer, Tamara. 2013. "A Guide for Advocating for Respectful Maternity Care." Futures Group, Health Policy Project, Washington, DC.

World Bank. 2006. "Social Accountability: What Does It Mean for the World Bank?" In *Social Accountability Sourcebook*. Washington, DC: World Bank.

———. 2011. *World Development Report 2012: Gender Equality and Development*. Washington, DC: World Bank.

———. 2013a. *Inclusion Matters: The Foundation for Shared Prosperity*. Washington, DC: World Bank.

———. 2013b. "Women and Girls in Haiti's Reconstruction: Addressing and Preventing Gender-Based Violence." World Bank, Washington, DC.

———. 2013c. *World Development Indicators 2013*. Washington, DC: World Bank.

World Bank and IFC (International Finance Corporation). 2013. *Women, Business, and the*

Law 2014: Removing Restrictions to Enhance Gender Equality. London: Bloomsbury.

York, Jillian. 2009. "Morocco: Celebrating the First Female Mayor of Marrakesh." Global Voices, Amsterdam. http://globalvoicesonline.org/2009/06/29/morocco-celebrating-the-first-female-mayor-of-marrakesh/.

Chapter 7 Key messages

> The expansion of women's agency demands more high-quality data, as well as meaningful new indices and measurements.

> Quantitative data need to be complemented by qualitative information to accurately capture levels of agency and changes over time.

> Existing data gaps present a significant challenge, which can be overcome through urgent, concerted local, national, and international effort.

> The internationally agreed minimum set of 52 gender indicators and the statistical indicators and guidelines for measuring violence against women provide a sound basis for improving the availability of data and evidence on women's agency.

> Recent promising programs to produce more national-level data on women's agency include Data2X, the Evidence on Data and Gender Equality initiative, and the Living Standards Measurement Study–Integrated Surveys on Agriculture.

> Several promising new initiatives are combining data in composite indices to measure multiple agency deprivations across different domains.

> At the operational level, project and program indicators need to establish baselines and more systematically track agency in key domains.

> Investments in rigorous evaluations of what works are needed, particularly around collective voice, normative change, and the design of multisectoral programs.

CHAPTER 7

Closing Gaps in Data and Evidence

Monitoring change and assessing progress

"Data not only measures progress, it inspires it."

—Hillary Rodham Clinton (2012)

We wrap up by focusing explicitly on data and evidence. Progress in promoting women's voice and agency needs to be captured and monitored. Overcoming lack of data is clearly a challenge, but it is not an excuse for inaction. To measure progress and compare at the national level and across countries, more and better data must be produced for some areas, and new measures are needed for others. Efforts must also focus on increasing data quality, raising standards of data collection, and promoting a common understanding of agency measures and their definitions. Policy research

efforts are needed to broaden the evidence base through rigorous testing of interventions that explicitly aim to enhance women's agency.

As chapter 1 highlighted, agency is a complex construct that is inherently difficult to measure. Much of the evidence used in this book reflects what people *say* about what they think and do in different domains of their lives—their expressions of agency. While all data derived from self-reporting are subject to a degree of bias, the advantage of using reported behaviors rather than personal perceptions is the greater degree of objectivity and comparability across samples and contexts.

This report has shown that both qualitative and quantitative data can provide insights into agency and agency constraints and deprivations at the country level. Qualitative approaches can be designed and implemented across countries—as used by the

World Bank's *On Norms and Agency* (Muñoz Boudet, Petesch, and Turk 2013) and *Voices of the Poor* (Narayan et al. 1999, 2000; Narayan and Petesch 2002) studies, for example—or developed and applied to a particular country, as in Niger (World Bank 2014b). The focus of this chapter is more on the quantitative indicators used to track progress and hold decision makers to account. Often, however, combining qualitative and quantitative methods will provide the best way to measure agency and to provide the benchmarks that can be used to track progress in increasing agency, as, for example, in the Pathways to Empowerment Project (Kabeer 2011).

We first take stock of current efforts to measure women's agency. The chapter then highlights key gaps that must be addressed to ensure a robust evidence base to inform policy making and finally outlines key priorities for future investment to address these gaps.

Country-level data

A range of data exists at the country level that casts light on voice and agency. This section begins by giving an overview of internationally agreed gender indicators and commonly available sources before highlighting gaps and then turning to some new and composite measures that can be used to provide a fuller picture.

Internationally agreed gender indicators

The 2013 United Nations Statistics Division (UNSD) guidance on gender indicators gives important new impetus, founded on broad-based government agreement. The minimum set of 52 agreed gender indicators

cover economic participation, education, health, human rights, and political participation. These quantitative measures are complemented by 11 qualitative indicators covering national norms and laws on gender equality that are aimed at monitoring how effectively national legislation ensures gender equality.[1] Specific standardized measures of violence against women, including physical and sexual violence as well as child marriage and female genital mutilation/cutting, and guidelines for producing statistics on these and other measures of violence against women have been developed (UNDESA 2013). A selection of the indicators most relevant to measuring the agency deprivations covered in this report, including the violence indicators, can be found in box 7.1.

Collecting data on violence brings unique methodological challenges to ensuring consistency, accuracy, and quality while also adhering to established ethical standards. Following an earlier request from the United Nations General Assembly, in 2009 the United Nations Statistics Commission adopted a proposed core list of violence against women (VAW) indicators and requested that UNSD and other stakeholders draw on and further elaborate existing methodological guidelines. In 2013, the United Nations published *Guidelines for Producing Statistics on Violence against Women*, which includes four core topics (physical, sexual, psychological, and economic violence) and three optional topics (female genital mutilation/cutting, attitudes toward VAW, and reporting to authorities or help seeking). This guidance includes the nine internationally agreed core indicators on VAW (see box 7.2).

The World Bank Gender Data Portal (http://data.worldbank.org/topic/gender) includes comparable data for 144 developing and 31 developed countries.[2] This website draws on sources that provide systematically and consistently compiled data, and it reveals that many of these internationally agreed and recommended indicators are not currently collected and reported by countries. Whereas most of the countries (136) in this sample collect sex-disaggregated data on access to credit, none has data on the share of women who own land.[3] Only 22 developing countries collect disaggregated data on Internet use, and none collects data on the female share

---

Box 7.1 Selected internationally agreed indicators on agency

Economic structures, participation in productive activities, and access to resources includes:
> Proportion of population with access to credit, by sex

> Proportion of adult population owning land, by sex

> Proportion of individuals using the Internet, by sex

> Proportion of individuals using mobile or cellular telephones, by sex

> Proportion of households with access to mass media (radio, television, Internet), by sex of household head

Education includes:
> Adjusted net enrollment in primary education, by sex

> Gross enrollment ratio in secondary education, by sex

> Gross enrollment ratio in tertiary education, by sex

> Share of female science, engineering, manufacturing, and construction graduates at tertiary level

> Educational attainment (primary, secondary, postsecondary, and tertiary) of the population age 25 years and older, by sex

Health and related services includes:
> Contraceptive prevalence among women who are married or in a union, ages 15 to 49

Human rights of women and girls includes:
> Proportion of women ages 15 to 49 subjected to physical and/or sexual violence in the past 12 months by an intimate partner

> Proportion of women ages 15 to 49 subjected to physical and/or sexual violence in the past 12 months by persons other than an intimate partner

> Prevalence of female genital mutilation or cutting (for relevant countries only)

> Percentage of women ages 20 to 24 who were married or in a union before age 18

> Adolescent birth rate

Public life and decision making includes:
> Women's share of government ministerial positions

> Proportion of seats held by women in national parliament

> Women's share of managerial positions

> Share of female police officers

> Share of female judges

Source: United Nations Department of Economic and Social Affairs, Statistics Division, http://genderstats.org/.

Box 7.2 Internationally agreed indicators for measuring violence against women

1. Total and age-specific rate of women subjected to physical violence in the past 12 months, by severity of violence, relationship to the perpetrator, and frequency

2. Total and age-specific rate of women subjected to physical violence during their lifetime, by severity of violence, relationship to the perpetrator, and frequency

3. Total and age-specific rate of women subjected to sexual violence in the past 12 months, by severity of violence, relationship to the perpetrator, and frequency

4. Total and age-specific rate of women subjected to sexual violence during their lifetime, by severity of violence, relationship to the perpetrator, and frequency

5. Total and age-specific rate of ever-partnered women subjected to sexual or physical violence by a current or former intimate partner in the past 12 months, by frequency

6. Total and age-specific rate of ever-partnered women subjected to sexual or physical violence by a current or former intimate partner during their lifetime, by frequency

7. Total and age-specific rate of ever-partnered women subjected to psychological violence in the past 12 months by an intimate partner

8. Total and age-specific rate of ever-partnered women subjected to economic violence in the past 12 months by an intimate partner

9. Total and age-specific rate of women subjected to female genital mutilation

Source: UNDESA 2013.

of mobile phone or mass media users. Conversely, collection of health data is comparatively extensive—95 developing countries report on contraceptive prevalence.

To date there is also very low uptake of the recommended indicators of women's and girls' human rights. No countries systematically collect data on the prevalence of physical and sexual violence, and only 19 developing countries report on female genital mutilation and cutting. Data collection on child marriage is also limited, although nearly all countries report on adolescent

fertility (only six developing countries do not). In the domain of women's voice, coverage is mixed. Nearly all countries report on women's share of ministerial positions (171 out of 175) and seats held in parliament (170 out of 175). Yet fewer than half (70 out of 175) report on women's representation in managerial positions. Data on the proportion of judges and police officers who are female are missing from the World Bank Group's World Development Indicators database. The good news, however, is that international efforts are under way to support countries' efforts to collect a wider range of key gender-relevant data in the future, including those outlined in this chapter.

Available data and indicators

We do not have a direct measure of agency, but rather a valuable set of proxy indicators that measure reported experiences, attitudes, and behaviors. Standardized measures can be used to establish levels and patterns of women's agency at the country level and to compare outcomes across countries. Numerous surveys have incorporated relevant questions into their standard modules, particularly in the domains of intimate partner violence, sexual and reproductive health, asset ownership, and economic activity. While these indicators typically capture only proxy measures rather than a direct measure of agency, these surveys offer a validated set of measures that have been instrumental in providing a clearer picture of women's status across the globe. Table 7.1 presents a selection of key primary and secondary data sources, including those used for this report, and examples of the agency-related measures they contain.

Together these represent a wealth of publicly available data sources. However, gaps remain, and the need for more and better data is critical, as we discuss next.

Initiatives to close data and evidence gaps

More investment is needed to produce national-level data that can measure levels, patterns, and changes in women's agency. Among the key gaps are measures of agency that capture aspirations and self-efficacy, measures of control over household spending and investment decisions, measures of

mobility, and measures of participation in politics at the local level. The World Bank Group, together with governments and a number of partner organizations, is working to close these data gaps.

Data2X, a partnership of the United Nations Foundation, the William and Flora Hewlett Foundation, and the U.S. government, is producing a Gender Data Blueprint to prioritize gender data gaps.[4] To date, the partnership has identified 26 gaps across five domains, on the basis of the need, coverage, and policy relevance. Primary data gaps identified include violence against women, sexual and reproductive health, access to land, and voice (Buvinic, Furst-Nichols, and Koowal 2013).

Drawing on this initial work by Data2X, table 7.2 highlights the gaps and opportunities for improved data collection across various expressions of women's agency.

Efforts are already under way to fill some of the identified gaps. More than 70 countries have conducted studies specifically to measure the prevalence and nature of various forms of violence against women, at least 40 of these at the national level. Some focused on intimate partner violence while others encompassed a wide range of physical and sexual violence and threats of violence perpetrated by partners, other family members, other known men, and strangers. A number of cross-country efforts have also been carried out, including the landmark World Health Organization multicountry study on women's health and domestic violence against women (García-Moreno et al. 2005). Of note also are the Demographic and Health Surveys implemented by ICF International in partnership with national governments

TABLE 7.1   Selected data sources and examples of measures of women's agency

Data source	Country coverage	Frequency	Measures of agency, examples
Demographic and Health Surveys	90+	Typically every five years	Unmet need for contraceptives Experience of physical and sexual violence
Gallup World Poll	160	Varies by country (every one to two years)	Support for women's work and rights Support for women in leadership positions
World Values Survey	75	Typically every five years	Perceptions about severity of discrimination Justifications for wife beating
Regional Barometer Surveys	88	Every two to three years	Support for women in leadership positions Support for women's rights
Women, Business, and the Law	143	Every two years	Legislation to addresses domestic violence Equal weight of woman's testimony in court
Inter-Parliamentary Union	186	Updated regularly	Women in elected and ministerial positions Portfolios held by women ministers
WHO Multi-country Study of Violence Against Women	10	One time	Experience of physical and sexual intimate partner violence Help seeking for experiences of intimate partner violence Women's belief in right to refuse sex
WomanStats Database	175	Updated regularly	Women's property rights Presence of laws against domestic violence
Multiple Indicator Cluster Surveys	90	Typically every five years	Unmet need for contraceptives Justifications for wife beating Female genital mutilation prevalence
OECD Social Institution and Gender Index	102	Every two to three years	Child marriage Women's legal rights to land and other property
Reproductive Health Survey	33	Country dependent	Unmet need for contraceptives Fertility preferences
Gender and Land Rights Database	80	Updated regularly	Land owned by women Women's property rights
50 Years of Women's Legal Rights Database	100	Annually (1960–2010)	Equal property rights (married and unmarried) Equal rights to get a job or pursue a profession
IFC Enterprise Surveys	135	Varies by country	Female participation in firm ownership Female managers
LSMS–ISA	7	Varies by country	Female access to credit Household decision-making power distribution

Note: IFC = International Finance Corporation; LSMS–ISA = Living Standards Measurement Study–Integrated Surveys on Agriculture; OECD = Organisation for Economic Co-operation and Development; WHO = World Health Organization.

| TABLE 7.2 | Analysis of current data gaps and possible ways forward |

Expression of agency	Gap	Possible way forward
Freedom from violence	Current prevalence estimates are underestimates and are not collected through standardized methods.	Create a global initiative to operationalize the UNSD guidelines to collect survey data systematically at the country level and the IAEG-GS-endorsed minimum standard indicators. Expand the number of countries collecting the minimum indicators (through stand-alone surveys such as the WHO study or integrated modules as in the DHS). Invest in panel data to track progress in reducing violence and measuring related consequences. Integrate violence modules or dedicated surveys in core postconflict programming and research.
Sexual and reproductive health and rights	Indicators are limited to maternal and reproductive health services. Reliable data on many critical aspects of health are not available because of weak statistical and civil registration systems.	Expand existing surveys (DHS, RHS) to cover services other than reproductive and MCH services (for example, STI/HIV screening and prevention, treatment of obstetric fistula), and more systematically gather and automate health service provider data. Expand coverage of existing survey instruments to include SRH indicators for adolescents, complemented by data from mobile phones and other new technology. Collect data on factors that shape demand: accessibility, affordability, and appropriateness of services.
Access to land	Asset ownership is typically collected at household (not individual) level. Where data do exist (such as the LSMS), they may not be consistent across countries.	Include measures of ownership at the individual level that also consider how assets are actually controlled or shared within the household. Track both official and customary property laws.
Voice	Comparable sex-disaggregated data on women's representation at the subnational level and voter registration and turnout are not widely available.	Expand data capabilities to get accurate information on women's representation at subnational levels and in political party leadership. Advocate to election management bodies for data on voter registration and turnout to be disaggregated by sex.

Note: DHS = Demographic and Health Surveys; IAEG-GS = Inter-agency and Expert Group on Gender Statistics; LSMS = Living Standards Measurement Study; MCH = maternal and child health; RHS = Reproductive Health Survey; SRH = sexual and reproductive health; STI/HIV = sexually transmitted infection/human immunodeficiency virus; UNSD = United Nations Statistics Division; WHO = World Health Organization.

and with funding from the U.S. Agency for International Development (USAID), the International VAW Survey coordinated by the European Institute for Crime Prevention and Control, and the study on violence against women conducted by the European Union Agency for Fundamental Rights (2014). However, a gap still remains in the collection of internationally comparable data using standardized measurements. To help close this gap, the World Bank Group is exploring partnerships with the United Nations Entity for Gender Equality and the Empowerment of Women (UN Women) and other agencies to pilot the nine internationally agreed core VAW indicators in several countries using the stand-alone survey promoted by the UNSD guidelines.

The Evidence on Data and Gender Equality (EDGE) Initiative aims to accelerate efforts to collect comparable gender indicators on health, education, employment, entrepreneurship, and asset ownership. This three-year project—a collaboration between UN Women and UNSD with the Organisation for Economic Co-operation and Development (OECD) and the World Bank Group—is building on the work of the Interagency and Expert Group on Gender Statistics to develop methodological guidelines to measure asset ownership and entrepreneurship from a gender perspective. Improving questionnaires and surveys can help countries to collate data at an individual level. For example, determining which household members are going to be the subject of the survey can produce more nuanced data on control over assets. To fill the gaps, EDGE will pilot survey modules as part of existing household questionnaires (Doss 2013). EDGE is also working on the standardization

of surveys, with some regional and country specificity (UNSD and UN Women 2013).

The Living Standards Measurement Study–Integrated Surveys on Agriculture (LSMS–ISA), a collaboration of the World Bank Group and the Bill & Melinda Gates Foundation, is improving the type and quality of household data collected by statistical offices and is currently being implemented in seven Sub-Saharan African countries.[5] Several existing survey instruments could be improved by adding questions to yield richer sex-disaggregated data. Beyond asking if anyone in the household owns any agricultural land, which is common in surveys, the next question could ask who the owners are. The names of all persons on the ownership document could be listed. Questions on the respondent's right to sell, rent, or bequeath land and that person's decision-making power over its use provide data on the level of individual control (Doss et al. 2013).

Innovative ways of collecting and using sex-disaggregated data can help to illuminate key challenges and priority areas for action. Across seven countries in Europe and Central Asia, for example, the World Bank Group is working with the Food and Agriculture Organization of the United Nations to implement the Voluntary Guidelines on the Responsible Governance of Tenure of Land, Fisheries, and Forests in the Context of National Food Security through gender action plans (FAO 2013). These efforts include collecting sex-disaggregated data by recording an applicant's gender at the time of submission, as in Albania and Kosovo; as part of other information collected by the land agencies, such as personal identifier, tax number, and social security number; and by linking the property register with other government registers containing gender information, such as the civil or population register. Innovative uses include linking sex-disaggregated land data to spatial data to promote more targeted policy making and implementation (World Bank 2014a).

UN Women has partnered with United Cities and Local Governments to launch data gathering in the area of women's representation at subnational levels and in political party leadership (Buvinic, Furst-Nichols, and Koowal 2013). This effort will provide more accurate information on women's political participation and the barriers women face to exercising agency in this domain.

Continual improvement in the capacity of statistical agencies in developing countries is essential to ensure sustainability and scaling up of data collection. The World Bank Group has a number of financial instruments that offer potential support for improved measures of voice and agency. In particular, the Trust Fund for Statistical Capacity Building, which primarily supports targeted capacity improvements at the national level for low-income countries, will devote more focus and attention to filling critical gaps in gender statistics.

Additionally, new indicators on agency are needed. Selecting such indicators will require consultation with a broad range of experts, stakeholders, and national statistical offices and agreement between governments and the relevant intergovernmental agencies to select, test, and evaluate options and methodologies. The development and testing process can begin at the project or service-provider level.

For example, work for this report suggests new areas to consider for better measuring freedom from violence. Those areas include (a) measures of violence against children and adolescents; (b) consistent and culturally appropriate measures of attitudes toward violence, including masculinity and justifications for different forms of violence; (c) measures that capture access to justice and protective services for survivors of violence; and (d) measures of access to and quality of social services such as alternative accommodation and livelihood support.

Greater understanding of agency over sexual and reproductive health decisions could be gained from knowing more about sexual autonomy, including experiences of forced or unwanted sex and pregnancy intentions, such as whether respondents believe they have a right to determine the timing and number of pregnancies they have and what the reasons are for unintended and mistimed pregnancies. Control of land and housing could be better measured with more data on women's registration of usufruct or ownership rights to land and on women's use of land administration services. Specific measures are also needed that can track implementation of laws to make it possible for women to register land and property in their own names or jointly. Tracking women's appointments to high-level positions in national organizations and leadership positions in the public and private sectors would help researchers to better document changes in women's voice and influence in specific national contexts.

Policy research efforts are needed to deepen the evidence base through rigorous

Box 7.3 Measuring and expanding agency in Latin America and the Caribbean

In Latin America and the Caribbean, as in other regions, lack of rigorous measures for agency and low awareness of the importance of agency impede progress. To fill this gap, the World Bank Group's Umbrella Facility for Gender Equality (UFGE) supports initiatives aimed at expanding data, indicators, and evidence on agency and its effects on other dimensions of gender equality and road testing evidence on how to expand agency. In all projects supported by the Latin American and Caribbean UFGE, agency either is one of the outcomes or plays an instrumental role in achieving other project objectives. Some examples follow:

> In Ecuador, the Text Me Maybe pilot intervention aims to increase the evidence-base on the role of agency in policy interventions that address teen pregnancy prevalence and risk factors and road test the effectiveness of text message reminders in changing behaviors.

> In St. Lucia, UFGE funds support efforts to reduce women's vulnerability in natural disasters by enhancing their agency, especially for female heads of households, through climate adaptation activities.

> In northeast Brazil, a pilot intervention to enhance women's agency in agricultural production integrates tools to measure their empowerment relative to productivity, income generation, access to markets, and gender roles and decision-making power within the household, producer groups, and the broader community.

The Latin American and Caribbean UFGE also supports capacity building for project teams in conceptualizing and measuring agency, including through a recent workshop to review existing measures of various dimensions of agency and resources for addressing empirical challenges. The first results from this work will be available in September 2014.

For more information about the UFGE, see http://www.worldbank.org/en/topic/gender/publication /umbrella-facility-for-gender-equality.

testing of interventions that explicitly aim to enhance women's agency. Such efforts are under way, for example, through the Social Observatory in India, which documents innovations and promising practices (World Bank n.d.), and through work supported by the World Bank Group's Umbrella Facility for Gender Equality in Latin America and the Caribbean (box 7.3).

Composite indices

We do not have a single measure that fully captures what is meant by agency and the expansion of choice. Choice is quite different from income poverty, for example, where information about the amount of money that an individual or family has is compared to some threshold. Indeed, as figure 1.3 in chapter 1 showed, the ability to make choices often varies across the different expressions of agency. Combining data in an index allows different and sometimes overlapping deprivations to be brought together to produce a composite and standardized value. However, selecting the most appropriate items to capture these synergies in a single measure without losing the meaning of the underlying measures is a significant challenge.

Several recent initiatives seek to meet these challenges. The Women's Empowerment in Agriculture Index (WEAI), which was piloted in Bangladesh, Guatemala, and Uganda, measures women's empowerment, agency, and the inclusion of women in the agriculture sector.[6] It comprises two subindices. The first measures five domains of empowerment—namely, agricultural production, resources, incomes, leadership, and time. The second, the Gender Parity Index, measures the relative inequality between the primary adult male and female in each household. The results can be used to increase understanding of the connections between women's empowerment, agricultural growth, and food security. This initiative is being rolled out in 19 countries (Feed the Future 2012).

The Relative Autonomy Index is a new approach, which was developed by the Oxford Poverty and Human Development Initiative to measure women's own sense of agency.[7] Box 7.4 outlines the approach and shows some early findings from Chad, where the index is being tested.

Another important contribution is the Social Institutions and Gender Index (SIGI) database, developed by the OECD. The SIGI focuses on the underlying social institutions that influence gender roles and that can limit or enable individual or collective agency. The SIGI is also a composite index, composed of five equally weighted subindices that measure discriminatory family code, restricted physical integrity, son bias, restricted resources and entitlements, and restricted civil liberties (OECD Development Centre 2012).

These types of composite measures can offer important contributions to understanding the status of, nature of, and constraints on women's agency at the national level. The next section explores recent efforts to measure progress in women's agency at the program and project levels and presents suggestions for innovations on these measures.

Program- and project-level indicators and emerging good practice

At the operational level, indicators are needed to establish baselines and track progress. Many governments and international development agencies have developed frameworks and guidelines to monitor gender results in project activities. The voice and agency front is one in which experience and measurement guidance are now beginning to emerge. For example, USAID has issued a checklist, "Assessing Achievement of Gender Objectives," which includes women's self-efficacy, attitudes toward gender-based violence and women's access to opportunities, and laws promoting gender equality (USAID 2012). The United Kingdom's Department for International Development has published guidance notes on the design and measurement of results of programs to address deprivations of agency, including violence against women (DFID 2012).

The World Bank Group monitors key gender indicators as part of its corporate

Box 7.4 Using new measures of women's autonomy in Chad: The Relative Autonomy Index

"We know about malnutrition, but if the meat doesn't go mostly to the man, there is trouble in the house."

—A woman from Loumia, Chad (Kristof 2013)

The Oxford Poverty and Human Development Initiative (OPHI) is testing the Relative Autonomy Index (RAI) with men and women and between different women in the same household in Chad, which has some of the largest gendered economic and health inequalities in the world. OPHI, in collaboration with United Nations Children's Fund–Chad and the Indic Society for Education and Development, used the RAI within a nationally representative survey that addressed topics such as consumption, work, living standards, education, and subjective well-being, with a focus on health behaviors and outcomes.

To measure autonomy, people were asked whether their actions were coerced to some extent or done to please others and whether their actions embodied their own values. Their degree of autonomy was analyzed for actions in eight domains—including doing domestic work, doing market work, making major household purchases, participating in groups, and feeding young children.

The most striking finding is that women are less autonomously motivated than men *across every single domain*. Women ages 15 to 26 had the lowest autonomy, in sharp contrast to men of the same age. Uneducated men had greater autonomy than uneducated women in all domains (except group membership), but men and women who participated in a group had higher autonomy in all other domains without exception. However, results show that autonomy is not necessarily associated with more life satisfaction or happiness. Levels of education and household income—commonly used indicators of agency—are not strongly associated with autonomy levels either. Given these additional insights, the results suggest that the RAI could be used to enhance or replace other indirect measures of agency.

These early findings also suggest the RAI yields new information that can contribute to understanding the links between women's autonomy, agency, and development outcomes. Further analysis will explore the relationship between the individual's autonomy and specific behavior such as hand washing, exclusive breast-feeding, and child marriage. In Chad, early marriage is widely accepted—and 1 in 10 girls has had a child before age 15. Measuring autonomy in these ways, therefore, could help to identify high-impact pathways that empower multiple generations within the same household.

Sources: Alkire, Pratley, and Vaz, forthcoming; Cruz 2013; Ford 2013.

scorecard and is increasingly monitoring gender results in project activities, including useful proxy measures of agency. This section briefly reviews recent World Bank Group experience and highlights areas for improvement.

With the World Bank Group Corporate Scorecard and the International Development Association (IDA) Results Measurement System (RMS), the World Bank Group monitors key gender indicators and outcomes in areas where policies and operations of client countries are being supported. For example, the IDA's 17 RMS (covering fiscal years 2015 to 2017) includes the number of women receiving prenatal care as a key health sector indicator in relevant client countries. Since 2009, standardized Core Sector Indicators (CSIs) gather data on a uniform set of indicators at the project level to enable results to be reported at the corporate level. Among the more than 140 CSIs used across the World Bank, Group about 30 are gender specific, tracking female beneficiaries of projects. Gender-specific results track agriculture,

conflict prevention, civic engagement, social inclusion, and access to finance and health, among others (see examples in table 7.3). However, because CSIs are not yet widely incorporated across World Bank Group projects,[8] additional efforts are needed to increase their uptake and expand their scope for measuring agency.

More generally, World Bank Group projects include specific results indicators. Selected efforts to capture agency in such projects are illustrated in box 7.5.

TABLE 7.3 Selected World Bank Group Gender Core Sector Indicators related to agency

Agency dimension	Gender Core Sector Indicators
Freedom from gender-based violence	Beneficiaries who experience a feeling of greater security attributable to the project in the project areas—female (number)
Control over reproductive health and rights	People with access to a basic package of health, nutrition, or reproductive health services—(number)
Ownership and control over land	Land parcels with use or ownership rights of females, recorded as a result of the project—(number)
Voice and influence	Representatives in community-based decision making and management structures that are from the vulnerable or marginalized beneficiary population—female (number)
Voice and influence	Vulnerable and marginalized people who participate in nonproject consultations and decision-making forums—female (number)
Voice and influence	Targeted clients who are members of an association—female (number)
Voice and influence (IFC indicator)	Women's employment figures and corporate board positions awarded to women—(percentage)
Voice and influence (IFC indicator)	Small and micro enterprise capital given to women entrepreneurs—(percentage)
All dimensions depending on the project	Direct project beneficiaries—(number), of which (percentage) are female

Note: IFC = International Finance Corporation.

Box 7.5 Examples of World Bank Group project indicators related to women's agency

Gender-based violence (GBV)

> The 2008 Protection from Gender-Based Violence in Côte d'Ivoire Project measured the percentage of the surveyed population that listened to the project's radio shows about GBV at least two times and the number of women experiencing physical intimate partner violence.

> The 2012 Breaking the Cycle of Violence Project in Honduras included measures of the number of youth whose awareness of GBV increased over the course of the project.

Sexual and reproductive health and rights

> The 2010 Nepal Second Health Nutrition and Population and HIV/AIDS Project included the following agency-related indicators: the current use of modern contraceptives among women ages 15 to 49 and the percentage of married women ages 15 to 49 with unmet needs for family planning.

> The 2014 Tajikistan Health Services Improvement Project included contraceptive prevalence rate as a results indicator, measured as the share of women in project districts ages 15 to 49 using modern methods of family planning.

Control over land and housing

> The 2010 Kosovo Real Estate Cadastre and Registration Project incorporated an indicator on the percentage of women with registered use or ownership rights (both joint and individual).

> The 2007 Vietnam Poverty Reduction and Support Operation Credit measured asset ownership among women.

Voice and influence

> The 2010 Afghanistan Third Emergency National Solidarity Project included targets for the proportion of female representatives in community development councils taking active part in making decisions for community development.

> The 2010 Bangladesh Empowerment and Livelihood Improvement "Nuton Jibon" Project monitored the percentage of village-level executive committees (*gram samitis*) in which the chronically poor held decision-making positions and the percentage of such decision makers who were women.

* * *

Capturing and monitoring efforts to promote women's voice and agency require high-quality data, but gaps remain significant. Progress requires greater investment and concerted effort from governments, international agencies, and local and national implementing partners. As highlighted in this chapter, several initiatives are already under way to develop and standardize indicators that better measure agency and allow for more direct comparison across countries. Welcome research efforts are also under way to design and test new measures of agency and deepen the evidence base for policy through rigorous testing of interventions that explicitly aim to enhance women's agency, but more are needed. Together these efforts will contribute to closing important data and knowledge gaps. They will also contribute to the post-2015 agenda by increasing demand for sound measures of progress in women's agency and gender equality worldwide.

Notes

1. The full listing of indicators can be found at http://genderstats.org/.

2. Analysis is based on data available on the World Bank Gender Data Portal and includes gender data sets from the United Nations compiled by its regional commissions and sectoral agencies, as well as surveys and reports conducted or funded by the World Bank Group, such as *World Development Report 2012: Gender Equality and Development* (World Bank 2011). Other in-country sources may also be available. Users are advised to check data sources.

3. For data availability of the core list of gender indicators by International Development Association, International Bank for Reconstruction and Development, and Organisation for Economic Co-operation and Development countries, see http://datatopics.worldbank.org /gender/monitoring-progress.

4. For more information about Data2X, see the description on the UN Foundation's website at http://www.unfoundation.org /what-we-do/issues/women-and-population /data2x.html.

5. The countries are Ethiopia, Malawi, Mali, Niger, Nigeria, Tanzania, and Uganda.

6. WEAI was developed by the U.S. Agency for International Development, International Food Policy Research Institute, and Oxford Poverty and Human Development Initiative. WEAI is available at http://www.ifpri .org/publication/womens-empowerment -agriculture-index.

7. The Relative Autonomy Index (RAI) was first designed by Richard Ryan and Ed Deci.

8. For example, a recent analysis of the portfolio in the World Bank Sustainable Development Network shows that CSI uptake is found in less than half (46 percent) of projects.

References

Alkire, Sabina, Pierre Pratley, and Ana Vaz. Forthcoming. "Women's Autonomy in Chad: Measurement and Distinctiveness." Women's Voice, Agency, and Participation Research Paper Series, World Bank, Washington, DC.

Buvinic, Mayra, Rebecca Furst-Nichols, and Gayatri Koowal. 2013. "Data 2X Mapping Gender Data Gaps." UN Foundation, New York. https://app.box.com/s/amtbqh6a 99ywzyjxub9c.

Clinton, Hillary Rodham. 2012. Remarks at "Evidence and Impact: Closing the Gender Data Gap." Event hosted by the U.S. Department of State and Gallup, Washington, DC, July 19.

Cruz, Johnny. 2013. "WV in Chad: NYT's Nicholas Kristof, Babies, and Changing Lives." *World Vision Magazine*, July 19. http://worldvisionmagazine.org/story /wv-chad-nyts-nicholas-kristof-babies -and-changing-lives.

DFID (U.K. Department for International Development). 2012. "A Theory of Change for Tackling Violence against Women and Girls." CHASE Guidance Note 1, Conflict, Humanitarian, and Security Department, DFID, London. http://www.gadnetwork .org.uk/storage/VAWG_guidance1_toc1 .pdf.

Doss, Cheryl. 2013. "Technical Report: Measuring Individual Level Asset Ownership and Control." EDGE Initiative, Groningen, Netherlands.

Doss, Cheryl, Carmen Diana Deere, Abena D. Oduro, and Hema Swaminathan. 2013. "Collecting Sex-Disaggregated Asset Data." Gender Asset Gap Project Policy Brief 4, Centre for Public Policy, Indian Institute of Management, Bangalore.

European Union Agency for Fundamental Rights. 2014. *Violence against Women: An EU-Wide Survey*. Vienna, Austria: European Union Agency for Fundamental Rights.

FAO (Food and Agriculture Organization of the United Nations). 2013. *Governing Land for Women and Men: A Technical Guide to Support the Achievement of Responsible Gender-Equitable Governance Land Tenure*. Rome: FAO. http://www.fao.org/fileadmin /user_upload/landright/docs/Technical _Guide.pdf.

Feed the Future. 2012. *Women's Empowerment in Agriculture Index*. Washington, DC: International Food Policy Research Institute. http://www.ifpri.org/publication /womens-empowerment-agriculture-index.

Ford, Liz. 2013. "Child Marriage Could Trigger Surge in Africa's Under-15s Pregnancy Rate: UN." *Guardian*, October 30. http://www.theguardian.com/global -development/2013/oct/30/child -marriage-africa-teenage-pregnancy-un.

García-Moreno, Claudia, Henrica A. F. M. Jansen, Mary Carroll Ellsberg, Lori Heise, and Charlotte Watts. 2005. *WHO Multi-country Study on Women's Health and Domestic Violence against Women*. Geneva: World Health Organization.

Kabeer, Naila. 2011. "Contextualising the Economic Pathways of Women's Empowerment: Findings from a Multi-country Research Program." Pathways Policy Paper, Pathways of Women's Empowerment RPC, Brighton, U.K.

Kristof, Nicholas D. 2013. "Women as a Force for Change." *New York Times*, July 31. http://www.nytimes.com/2013/08/01 /opinion/kristof-women-as-a-force-for -change.html.

Muñoz Boudet, Ana Maria, Patti Petesch, and Carolyn Turk. 2013. *On Norms and Agency: Conversations about Gender Equality with Women and Men in 20 Countries*. Washington, DC: World Bank.

Narayan, Deepa, Robert Chambers, Meera K. Shah, and Patti Petesch. 2000. *Voices of the Poor: Crying Out for Change*. Washington, DC: World Bank.

Narayan, Deepa, Raj Patel, Kai Schafft, Anne Rademacher, and Sarah Koch-Schulte. 1999. *Can Anyone Hear Us? Voices from 47 Countries*. Washington, DC: World Bank.

Narayan, Deepa, and Patti Petesch, eds. 2002. *Voices of the Poor: From Many Lands*. Washington, DC: World Bank.

OECD (Organisation for Economic Co-operation and Development) Development Centre. 2012. "2012 SIGI: Social Institutions and Gender Index—Understanding the Drivers of Gender Inequality." OECD Development Centre, Paris.

http://www.genderindex.org/sites/default/files/2012SIGIsummaryresults.pdf.

UNDESA (United Nations Department of Economic and Social Affairs). 2013. *Guidelines for Producing Statistics on Violence against Women.* New York: United Nations. http://unstats.un.org/unsd/gender/docs/Guidelines_Statistics_VAW.pdf.

UNSD (United Nations Statistical Division) and UN Women (United Nations Entity for Gender Equality and the Empowerment of Women). 2013. "Evidence and Data for Gender Equality (EDGE) Project: Report of the Follow-up Meeting on Measuring Asset Ownership from a Gender Perspective." United Nations Statistical Division and UN Women, New York.

USAID (U.S. Agency for International Development). 2012. "Gender Equality and Female Empowerment: Policy." USAID, Washington, DC.

World Bank. 2011. *World Development Report 2012: Gender Equality and Development.* Washington, DC: World Bank.

———. 2014a. "Land and Gender: Improving Data Availability and Use in the Western Balkans." 2014. Background paper for the Annual World Bank Conference on Land and Poverty, Washington DC, March 25.

———. 2014b. "Voices of Men and Women regarding Social Norms in Niger." Poverty Reduction and Economic Management Africa Region Report 83296-NE, World Bank, Washington, DC.

———. n.d. "Social Observatory Rural Livelihoods Project in India." World Bank, Washington, DC. http://www.worldbank.org/content/dam/Worldbank/document/SAR/SO.pdf.

Appendix: Background Papers

Alkire, Sabina, Pierre Pratley, and Ana Vaz. Forthcoming. "Women's Autonomy in Chad: Measurement and Distinctiveness." Women's Voice, Agency, and Participation Research Paper Series, World Bank, Washington, DC.

Arango, Diana J., Matthew Morton, Floriza Gennari, Sveinung Kiplesund, and Mary Ellsberg. Forthcoming. "Interventions to Prevent and Reduce Violence against Women and Girls: A Systematic Review of Reviews." Women's Voice, Agency and Participation Research Series, World Bank, Washington, DC.

de Silva de Alwis, Rangita. 2014. "Women's Voice and Agency: The Role of Legal Institutions and Women's Movements." Women's Voice, Agency, and Participation Research Paper 7, World Bank, Washington, DC.

Duvvury, Nata, Aoife Callan, Patrick Carney, and Srinivas Raghavendra. 2013. "Intimate Partner Violence: Economic Costs and Implications for Growth and Development." 2013. Women's Voice, Agency, and Participation Research Paper 3, World Bank, Washington, DC.

Evans, Alison, and Divya Nambiar. 2013. "Collective Action and Women's Agency: A Background Paper." Women's Voice, Agency, and Participation Research Paper 4, World Bank, Washington, DC.

Fleming, Paul J., Gary Barker, Jennifer McCleary-Sills, and Matthew Morton. 2013. "Engaging Men and Boys in Advancing Women's Agency: Where We Stand and New Directions." Women's Voice, Agency, and Participation Research Paper 1, World Bank, Washington, DC.

Grépin, Karen A., and Jeni Klugman. 2013. "Closing the Deadly Gap between What We Know and What We Do." World Bank, Washington, DC.

Levtov, Ruti. 2014. "Addressing Gender Inequalities in Curriculum and Education: Review of Literature and Promising Practices to Inform Education Reform Initiatives in Thailand." Women's Voice, Agency, and Participation Research Paper Series, World Bank, Washington, DC.

Markham, Susan. 2013. "Women as Agents of Change: Having Voice in Society and Influencing Policy." Women's Voice, Agency, and Participation Research Paper 5, World Bank, Washington, DC.

Namubiru-Mwaura, Evelyn. 2014. "Land Tenure and Gender: Approaches and Challenges for Strengthening Rural Women's Land Rights." Women's Voice, Agency, and Participation Research Paper 6, World Bank, Washington, DC.

Rakodi, Carole. 2014. "Expanding Women's Access to Land and Housing in Urban Areas." Women's Voice, Agency, and Participation Research Paper 8, World Bank, Washington, DC.

Vyas, Seema. 2013. "Estimating the Association between Women's Earnings and Partner Violence: Evidence from the 2008–2009 Tanzania National Panel Survey." Women's Voice, Agency, and Participation Research Paper 2, World Bank, Washington, DC.

World Bank. 2014. "Voices of Men and Women regarding Social Norms in Niger." Poverty Reduction and Economic Management Africa Region Report 83296-NE, World Bank, Washington, DC.

World Bank and TrustLaw Connect. 2013. "Women and Land Rights: Legal Barriers Impede Women's Access to Resources." World Bank and TrustLaw Connect, Washington, DC. http://www.trust.org/publication/?id=1440891e-13ac-434a-bc73-9264e9aabbbf.

Index

Boxes, figures, maps, notes, and tables are indicated by b, f, m, n, and t following the page number.